Japan's First Modern Novel
UKIGUMO of Futabatei Shimei

Studies of the East Asian Institute
Columbia University

JAPAN'S FIRST MODERN NOVEL

UKIGUMO of Futabatei Shimei

Translation and Critical Commentary
by Marleigh Grayer Ryan

Columbia University Press
New York and London   1967

UNESCO COLLECTION OF REPRESENTATIVE WORKS
JAPANESE SERIES

The translation in this volume has been accepted
in the Japanese Translation Series of the
United Nations Educational, Scientific,
and Cultural Organization.
(UNESCO)

To Edward

The East Asian Institute of Columbia University was established in 1949 to prepare graduate students for careers dealing with East Asia, and to aid research and publication on East Asia during the modern period. The faculty of the Institute are grateful to the Ford Foundation and the Rockefeller Foundation for their financial assistance.

The Studies of the East Asian Institute were inaugurated in 1962 to bring to a wider public the results of significant new research on modern and contemporary East Asia.

Acknowledgments

I WOULD LIKE to express my gratitude to Professor Donald Keene for first suggesting the topic of this book to me and for the countless hours of help he gave me in preparing this manuscript. More important than any specific assistance rendered in connection with this book is the inspiration which Professor Keene's extraordinary accomplishments in Japanese literature lend to all of us undertaking work in this field.

I also want to thank Professors Ivan Morris and Herschel Webb for their patience and kindness in reading the translation and commentary through many drafts and for the valuable suggestions they offered. I am also grateful for the help I received from Professors C. T. Hsia, John Rosenberg, and Richard Gregg.

The initial research for this book was carried out under a grant from the Ford Foundation which enabled me to study in Japan with Professor Atsushi Hamada of Kyōto University, who was extremely generous with his time and for whose kindness I shall always be indebted. Professor Hisao Kanaseki of Kōbe University and Professor Manji Kobayashi of Dōshisha University have given me invaluable assistance in the preparation of the translations in this text.

I further wish to express my gratitude for the help given by Miss Miwa Kai and the staff of the East Asian Library of Columbia University and by my most sympathetic editor, Miss Phyllis Holbrook.

It is not possible for me to adequately express my deep appreciation for the patience and kindness shown me throughout these many years of study by my husband, Edward, to whom this book is dedicated.

M<small>ARLEIGH</small> R<small>YAN</small>

Columbia University

Contents

Introduction

LATE IN the spring of 1886, a young man named Hasegawa Tatsunosuke, known to the Japanese literary world by his penname Futabatei Shimei,[1] began to write his first novel. After he had struggled with it for many months, the first part was published in June 1887. The rest of the novel, which he called *Ukigumo* [drifting clouds], appeared over the next two years. During the same years, Futabatei published two translations of stories by Ivan Turgenev and several translations of Russian literary criticism. By August 1889, when the last chapter of *Ukigumo* appeared, Futabatei had established himself as one of the leading writers in Japan. He had written a perceptive, realistic novel and made considerable progress toward perfecting a new colloquial narrative style. His vivid and accurate translations of fiction taught a whole generation of young Japanese writers the power of Western literature. His novel established the value of psychological realism and the merit of a simple but carefully constructed plot.

From 1881 to January 1886, Futabatei had studied Russian at the government-sponsored school of foreign languages,

---

1. Hasegawa Tatsunosuke did not adopt his penname until 1887, but it is the custom in Japan to call him by his penname whenever referring to him. I have adopted this practice throughout this work.

the Tōkyō Gaikokugo Gakkō. There he learned to read, write, and speak Russian extremely well. Among the teachers were Russian-born émigrés and Japanese who had lived in Russia. From them and from his own reading Futabatei developed a great interest in literature and aesthetics; before leaving school he decided to make a career of writing.

Within a few days after he left school, Futabatei called on Tsubouchi Shōyō, a well-established novelist, translator, and critic. Tsubouchi took a great interest in the young man and helped him with his writing. They soon became close friends, and Futabatei turned to Tsubouchi continuously throughout the years 1886 to 1889 for advice in the techniques of writing. It was through Tsubouchi's intervention that Futabatei was able to get his first work into print. Tsubouchi also arranged for the publication of *Ukigumo*.

In 1885 Tsubouchi had completed a study of the novel form entitled *Shōsetsu shinzui* [the essence of novel]. This essay was a plea for the revitalization of Japanese fiction. The introduction of Western literature in the years preceding and following the Meiji Restoration of 1868 had not contributed substantially to the development of Japanese fiction. Novels in the first two decades of the Meiji period continued to be written in the tradition of the early part of the nineteenth century: plots were loose and disconnected, and characterization weak. Western literature might have helped writers to see greater possibilities in fiction, but of the many translations published, few attempted to present all the material of the original. Generally only the skeleton of the plot survived in the Japanese version. This practice tended to strengthen the Japanese writer's inclination to concentrate on plot and did little to transmit the conception of strong characterization which was already so highly developed in Western literature. Tsubouchi argued for more accurate translations and for the acceptance of the theories of Western realism.

Tsubouchi could not write a satisfactory realistic novel himself, but by helping Futabatei with *Ukigumo* he was able to participate in the creation of Japan's first modern novel. *Ukigumo* is a realistic novel in colloquial Japanese specifically designed to reveal the psychology of its characters. In place of the episodic tale of fantastic adventures so popular with nineteenth-century Japanese readers, Futabatei presented a story with the simplest possible plot. The whole novel hinges on the fact that the hero, Utsumi Bunzō, has lost his post in the lowest ranks of the government bureaucracy. As a consequence, he finds that his marriage to his cousin, Osei, which had been virtually assured, has now become impossible. Osei's affections soon turn to Bunzō's former colleague, the up-and-coming Honda Noboru. Futabatei tells his entire story within the confines of this plot. There are only four main characters—Bunzō, Noboru, Osei, and Osei's mother, Omasa—and a few minor characters. It was Futabatei's intention to picture the nature of his society through these characters; to demonstrate by means of the words and actions of his characters the effect of Meiji life on Japanese society.

Futabatei was a stubborn, difficult man. Whenever he believed in anything, he would defend his views with any weapon that came to hand. As a boy, he was frequently in trouble with his elders. He consistently refused to accept the advice of his family or his teachers and clung to his own opinions no matter what the cost. From boyhood on, he was extremely idealistic and could never learn to compromise with the realities of life. He maintained this approach even after reaching maturity and, as a consequence, soon found it difficult to make his way as a professional writer. He achieved his first success with *Ukigumo* and his translations of Russian fiction. By 1889 Futabatei was a novelist of considerable reputation and could easily have continued writing for a living if he had been willing to accept commissions for new works or to make the effort to produce articles with popular appeal. He refused to take this course. He abhorred the idea of writing for money and was now ashamed that he had begun his career in 1886 with such a plan in mind. Furthermore, he was unhappy with *Ukigumo;* it had not satisfied the ideal of perfection he had envisaged when he started it. In no mood to start another novel, he chose to turn his back on the literary world. In August of 1889 Futabatei accepted a post in the office of *Kampō,* the official gazette of the Japanese government. This did not put an end to his study and writing, but it effectively removed him from the center of the literary scene; it was not until 1897, when he resumed publishing translations of Russian fiction, that he became known to the public again.

The story of Futabatei's life from 1886 to 1889, the years during which he was writing *Ukigumo,* represents an important part of Japanese literary history. His first attempts at translating, the success of his novel and Turgenev translations, the suffering he endured in trying to make peace with his principles, and his ultimate inability to compromise his ideals, all form part of that story. *Ukigumo* introduced an entirely new conception into Japanese literature. Through it Japan learned that the life of an ordinary man could provide material for a novel which would be as interesting as the tale of the bravest warrior. It is the product of the dreams and aspirations of one of Japan's most intelligent writers, a man so sensitive to his own shortcomings that he was unable to continue his literary career in spite of his considerable success. Although he was one of the most famous writers of his day, Futabatei Shimei chose to adopt a new profession in 1889, but not before he had created the model for modern Japanese realism upon which subsequent writers have built a new literature.

COMMENTARY

Chapter 1

Futabatei's Early Life and Education

FUTABATEI SHIMEI was born in Edo (modern Tokyo) in the residence of the Owari han situated in Ichigaya. In a short series of autobiographical notes in his journals, he gives his birth date as April 4, 1864, and, although other records list various different dates, his own statement is now generally accepted.[1] His father, Hasegawa Yoshikazu, the son of Mizuno Shigesaburō, had been adopted into the Hasegawa family in 1853 when the head of the Hasegawa family died without an heir. Futabatei's mother, Shizu, was the eldest daughter of Gotō Uemon. The Hasegawa, Mizuno, and Gotō were all samurai families of Owari han. Records for 1868 indicate that the Gotō and Hasegawa families each had a fixed annual income of 7 koku 6 to of rice;[2] samurai with stipends of 10 koku or less were on the lowest level of

1. Futabatei, *Ochiba no hakiyose: futakagome*, XI, 41. His *koseki* [family records] and other documents give his birth date as November 29, 1862. A chronology compiled just after his death lists it instead as March 10, 1864. There is general agreement that he was forty-five when he died on May 10, 1909, and some date in 1864 is thus indicated for his birth. Nakamura, *Futabatei Shimei den* pp. 22–23. Tsubouchi quotes the journal entry giving the April 4, 1864, date in his biography, "Futabatei no koto," *Kaki no heta*, p. 7. Uchida Roan does the same in "Futabatei no isshō," *Kinō kyō*, p. 340.

2. Nakamura, *Futabatei Shimei den*, p. 22. One koku equals 4.96 bushels. There are ten to in 1 koku.

their social class. Shizu was twenty-two and Yoshikazu was twenty-six when their son was born.[3]

Owari was one of the wealthiest and most culturally sophisticated han in Tokugawa Japan.[4] Its first daimyo was the ninth son of Tokugawa Ieyasu, founder of the line of shoguns which headed the government of Japan from 1603 to 1868. Owari, in common with all other han, was required to maintain a fully staffed residence in Edo, where its daimyo spent every other year, returning in between to the han castle in the city of Nagoya. Although the Hasegawa family was not of high rank, Yoshikazu was appointed to a relatively good post in the Edo residence in 1862, reputedly because the daimyo was attracted by his intelligence and good looks.[5] Yoshikazu was in charge of the household accounts of the Ichigaya residence, which implies that he had the confidence of the administrative heads of the han. Throughout his career as a public servant, Yoshikazu maintained an excellent record. He was promoted several times between 1868 and his retirement in 1885.

In January of 1868 the emperor declared an end to the administration of the Tokugawa shoguns and the era known as Meiji began. It was a time of the greatest political uncertainty. There had been organized armed resistance to the change in government in the southern part of Japan, and although the Edo forces of the last shogun surrendered without fighting in April of 1868, there were instances of civil disturbances in the city throughout that year. The transfer of authority from the shogun to the new authorities required

3. According to the Gotō koseki, Shizu was born on September 15, 1841. The Hasegawa koseki lists Yoshikazu's birth date as March 10, 1838. Nakamura, *Futabatei Shimei den*, p. 22.

4. Owari was one of the *shimpan*, han of members of the Tokugawa family or outsiders treated as members of the family. The three highest ranking shimpan were known as the *Sanke* [*three houses*]. These were Owari, Kii, and Mito, and their first daimyo were Ieyasu's ninth, tenth, and eleventh sons respectively. Owari was the wealthiest of the three and the fourth wealthiest han in the country. A table showing the wealthiest han is given in Craig, p. 11.

5. Nakamura, "Shōgai to sakuhin," *Futabatei annai*, p. 6.

several months of negotiations during which an aura of lawlessness prevailed that often frightened the residents of Edo. Looking back on this period in later life, Futabatei recalled:

The members of the families living in the residence lay down every night with a bundle of clothes beside their pillows. We had decided to run away if we were attacked since there were very few men in the residence at the time [the summer of 1868] and it would have been impossible for us to resist an enemy. There had been several cases of people being ambushed on the streets and of wanton attacks by stray samurai.

In the course of his work, Yoshikazu frequently left the confines of the residence and went into the city. His son realized how dangerous this was:

If my father went out and did not come home after nightfall, I would get very frightened. I felt very uneasy as I waited for him to come home safely. I would go outside to look for him. Beneath the darkening sky, among the rows of pine trees growing inside the walls of the residence, I would search the path he took home—walking back and forth, waiting for him. Sorrow filled my heart, and looking up at the darkening sky, I would feel chilled and lonely.[6]

Futabatei lived with his mother, father, and grandmother in the residence. His journal for 1889 includes notes which were to serve as material for a future autobiography. When he was born, he relates that

my father was not yet thirty and my mother was also still quite young. Neither of them was especially given to doting on me, but my grandmother was terribly affectionate and made a great fuss over me. She could not bear it if my father scolded me and so I grew up a very spoiled child. I number among the things I feared most as a child first my father and then a painted image of Shōki[7] which was in the house.

6. Futabatei, "Shuyo sakan," *Zenshū*, X, 28. Written in 1908.
7. Shōki (Chung K'uei) was a retainer of the T'ang emperor Hsuan Tsung (r. 713–756) who committed suicide when he failed in the civil service examinations. The emperor posthumously appointed him to court rank and gave him a fine burial. In Japan he has been the subject of two

One of my aunts tells me that I was timid of strangers and rather shy as a child. On the other hand, she says that I would talk to people who came often and I knew quite well in an adult manner beyond my years.

When I was about four my father began making models of characters for me to copy. However, I liked drawing pictures better than practicing calligraphy. I enjoyed sketching figures and so on in the evening. I not only enjoyed drawing for myself but took special delight in picture scrolls and such, and I used to spend hours with them. Besides drawing, I was most fond of hearing old stories. Every night I would coax my grandmother to tell me *Shitakiri suzume*[8] or some other fairy tale.[9]

Feeling that Tokyo was not a proper place for the boy to start his education in those uncertain times, Yoshikazu sent his family home to Nagoya late in 1868[10] while he remained in Tokyo. Just at that time he received a promotion which increased his income by 2 koku annually. In January of 1871, Yoshikazu was given a new rank in the Nagoya han administration, and in October he was promoted again. Then prefectural subdivisions replaced the han system. The two Owari han, Nagoya and Inuyama, were joined to form Nagoya prefecture in December 1871. Yoshikazu was appointed to the prefectural administration in March of 1872. Nagoya prefecture was renamed Aichi prefecture in May 1872, and in November Yoshikazu was given a rank in the Aichi prefectural government.[11] With each change in administration, Yoshikazu gradually bettered his position.

Nō plays, *Shōki* and *Kōtei*, in which he appears as a protective deity. Shōki dolls and banners picturing him are prominent during the Boys' Festival. He is shown as a strong, fierce, and manly figure.

8. "Shitakiri suzume" ("The Tongue-Cut Sparrow") is one of the most widely known fairy tales of Japan and demonstrates the evil consequences of greed. In Seki, ed., *Folktales of Japan*, trans. Robert J. Adams, pp. 114–118.

9. Futabatei, *Ochiba no hakiyose: futakagome*, p. 41.

10. Or early 1869. They left Tokyo in the twelfth month of Meiji 1, which coincided with the period from December 14, 1868, to January 12, 1869.

11. Nakamura, *Futabatei Shimei den*, pp. 25–26, and "Shōgai to sakuhin," pp. 6–7.

In Nagoya, Futabatei's formal education began. He had his first lessons in the Chinese classics with his mother's brother, Gotō Aritsune, who lodged with them. He also attended a private school run by a Confucianist named Nomura Shūsoku.[12] In September of 1871, the boy was enrolled in a school for Western studies which the han had established a year earlier to counterbalance the Chinese and Japanese studies taught at Nagoya's famous traditional school, Meirindō. The school was called Tsūshō Yōgakkō and had both Japanese and foreign instructors. Two of the subjects taught there were English and French. Futabatei studied French with two teachers, one a Japanese named Hayashi Masajūrō and the other a Frenchman, P. Mourier. Mourier was a student of the classics of Japan, particularly the *Kojiki* and *Nihon shoki,* spoke Japanese quite well, and was the author of a Japanese grammar.[13] Futabatei left the school in July of 1872 and returned to Tokyo with his mother and grandmother in November of the same year.

Reflecting on his life in Nagoya, he wrote:

I liked going to school, not because I found my studies interesting, but rather because I enjoyed playing with my friends. I made friends with all the children in the neighborhood. Among them were two older boys. Perhaps everyone has had this experience—but when the two of them were friendly with each other, we all joined ranks under them and played together, but if they had a falling out, the rest of us took sides with one or the other. I was a terrible coward and at such times I usually attached my-

12. No record of this school appears in the extensive survey of government and private schools published by the Ministry of Education in 1892. Over nine hundred private schools are listed for Aichi prefecture, including a great many which specialized in Chinese studies. Nomura's school may be listed under some other teacher's name, but it is impossible to tell without further information. *Nihon kyōiku shi shiryō,* comp. Mombu Daijin Kambō Hōkoku Ka, VIII, 401–60. My information comes from Nakamura's biography; he learned of the teacher's name through a personal acquaintance. *Futabatei Shimei den,* pp. 28–29.

13. Nakamura, *Futabatei Shimei den,* p. 41. Mourier lived in Japan from 1871 to 1873. *Meiji bunka kankai Ōbei jimmei roku,* ed. Shigehisa Tokutarō and Amano Keitarō, p. 562.

self to the more frightening of the two and flattered and cajoled him.

Although I was so cowardly with others, I was quite a bully with members of my own family and I was very naughty. I was so difficult that I had my mother dress me every morning. Often once would not be enough. If something displeased me, I would have her change my clothes two or three times. I must have annoyed her very much. When I think of it now, I feel that my personality at that time was wretched.[14]

Ryūko, Futabatei's second wife, relates a family legend about him when he was young:

He learned to write when he was about four. He used to go through three notebooks a day. . . . He would sit writing and refuse to go out to play. His mother said, "Writing characters and drawing pictures can be done after dark, when the lamps are lit. You should go outside and play during the day." Even if he did go out to play, he would wait impatiently for the evening to come. When he saw that the lamps were being brought out at his friends' houses, he would leave hurriedly after announcing that it was time to go home and start writing. As soon as he reached his room, he would set to writing with great enthusiasm.[15]

A childhood friend, Nakamura Tatsutarō (1860–1942), later recalled details of the 500-mile trip from Nagoya to Tokyo when the family was on the way to rejoin Yoshikazu. Nakamura, who was four years Futabatei's senior, traveled with Futabatei, his grandmother, and the daughter of another family.

In those days we had no rickshaws and the train only ran between Tokyo and Yokohama. Although he was still just a child, Tatsunosuke showed the greatest strength and endurance. He

14. Futabatei, *Ochiba no hakiyose: futakagome*, p. 42. Of this entry, Tsubouchi says: "In this one passage dating from 1889 or 1890, we can see to what extent Futabatei was already engaging in self-criticism and analysis. He must have been the very first to have this kind of approach." "Futabatei no koto," p. 9.

15. Hasegawa Ryūko, "Arishi hi o shinobu," *Futabatei Shimei kenkyū,* I, No. 1 (October 1937), 5. An interview dating from 1923.

and I walked all the way wearing straw sandals and *hakama*,[16] our hair tied back in a bushy knot. The only time we got into a palanquin was when we were crossing Hakone mountain.[17]

The family's return coincided with Yoshikazu's appointment to the Aichi prefectural government. In August of 1873 he was promoted again. In December he received an appointment to the Shimane prefectural administration, but he remained in the Tokyo office of the prefecture until May of 1875, when he and his family moved to the Shimane prefectural capital, Matsue. Yoshikazu was made an official in the prefectural accounting office and was promoted again shortly after taking up his position. It is assumed that Futabatei was attending a school in Tokyo in the period from November 1872 to May 1875, but no records have been found to confirm this.[18]

In Matsue, Futabatei was enrolled in two schools. One was a private middle school called the Matsue Hensoku Chūgakkō.[19] At the school the boys were given general instruction in the natural sciences including world geography and physics, the geography of Japan, and the history of Japan. English was the core of the curriculum, however, and it was here that Futabatei began the study of the English language which he was to continue throughout his life.[20] The private school was known as Sōchōsha. It was directed

16. Loose, flowing trousers. The boys were wearing *Yoshitsune bakama*, a type of hakama which had been particularly popular in the 1860s. They were of the pattern and design reputedly worn by the famous hero Minamoto Yoshitsune.

17. "Chikuba no tomo tarishi Hasegawa kun," *Futabatei annai*, p. 115. Written in 1909. Nakamura became one of Japan's leading architects, was the author of several standard works on modern architectural methods, and was awarded a doctorate in engineering in May 1899.

18. Nakamura, *Futabatei Shimei den*, p. 33.

19. *Hensoku*, literally irregular, was the term applied in this period to private middle schools, in contrast to the *seisoku*, or regular, publicly maintained schools. *Meiji bunka shi*, comp. Kaikoku hyakunen kinen bunka jigyō kai, III, 63.

20. Nakamura, *Futabatei Shimei den*, pp. 33–34, 42.

by a highly energetic Confucianist named Uchimura Rokō (1821–1901), who was also a teacher at the middle school. Uchimura was the son of a tradesman and had been admitted to study in the shogunal Confucian school, generally reserved for samurai, by virtue of his outstanding intelligence. He had taught in Edo and Osaka for some time before returning to Matsue, in 1864, where he was in charge of the Confucian training in the han's official school and was also politically influential in the han government. Uchimura was awarded many honors and his opinions on education continued to be highly respected after the Restoration.[21]

At Sōchōsha, Futabatei studied the Chinese classics and Chinese and Japanese history. The study of Chinese philosophy in Nagoya, Matsue, and later in Tokyo provided him with the base on which he built his adult philosophy. Reflecting on the beliefs he held in his early twenties, he wrote:

I had as my ideal in those days the word "honesty." I wanted to live a life free of shame before Heaven or man. This concept of honesty had been nurtured in me by Russian literature, but an even greater influence was the Confucian education I had received. . . . [In my childhood] I was greatly affected by both nationalism and Confucianism. The Confucian concept of living according to one's ideals was strongly implanted in my mind. It may not have been more than a superficial understanding of the concept, but I was very earnest in my pursuit of it. To cite an example, when I listened to my teacher's lectures, I simply had to bow. In doing so I was not paying my respect to the teacher's merits so much as to the "Way." This was the kind of religious or philosophic inclination I knew from early in my life. The oriental Confucian influence and the Russian literary or Western philosophic influence became bound up together. To these were added an interest in socialism. From these various influences my moral philosophy was formed—my honesty which permitted me to stand before Heaven and man alike with no sense of shame.[22]

21. *Nihon kyōiku shi shiryō,* II, 465–66, and Nakamura, *Futabatei Shimei den,* pp. 34–35.
22. Futabatei, "Yo ga hansei no zange," *Zenshū,* X, 38. Originally published in 1908.

The nationalistic impulse he mentions here received strong impetus during his years in Matsue. For Futabatei, nationalism and military preparedness or military expansion were closely linked. He had been attracted by the military even as a child. He later recalled, half seriously, that when he had seen the smart uniforms of a troop of samurai stationed at the Ichigaya residence, he had first developed "an interest in the problems of country and in the problems of government." In Nagoya he had often stopped to watch schoolboys marching in drill formation, one of the new military arts recently added to the han school curriculum.[23] In Matsue he became an adherent of Japanese expansion into Korea and determined to become a military officer. He later told Uchida Roan that as a boy it was his "life's ambition to be a general." His mother's older brother, Gotō Aritsune, was called to serve in the Imperial Army in the Satsuma Rebellion of 1877 and fought against the rebel forces.

To Futabatei, who favored Saigō, it was incomprehensible that his uncle should have become a soldier in the Imperial Army. He accosted his uncle several times and argued the point with him. It seems that Futabatei's ideas on the solution of problems in the Far East stemmed from Saigō's position on the subjugation of Korea.[24]

Saigō Takamori (1828–77), a samurai of Satsuma han in Kyushu, had been one of the most influential figures in bringing about the overthrow of the Tokugawa shogunal government. Following the Restoration, Saigō served as a member of the oligarchy which directed the course of government. In 1873, because of the Korean issue, he resigned from his position in the council of state. Japan had been unsuccessful in her attempts in 1872 to force Korea to open diplomatic relations; the envoys had been insulted and Japanese nationals mistreated. Saigō and several other members of the council of state favored an aggressive policy toward

23. Futabatei, "Shuyo sakan," p. 27.
24. Uchida, "Futabatei no isshō," pp. 343–44.

Korea.[25] In 1873, during the absence from Japan of the more "conservative" oligarchs, the council voted to send Saigō to Korea to persuade her to capitulate and to threaten the use of force if necessary. When the other members of the council, who were traveling in Europe at the time, returned to Japan, they succeeded in reversing the council's decision. Saigō and his adherents resigned. He returned to Satsuma, founded military schools which produced a crop of fanatically loyal samurai followers, and in 1877 led an open rebellion against the central government. After seven months of fighting, Saigō and his men were defeated by the Imperial Army and Saigō was killed.

Although personal loyalty to Saigō accounted for most of the fervor shown by his followers, various other issues, many highly emotional, were involved in the rebellion and in the attitude people showed toward it. Saigō, an outspoken defender of the privileges of the samurai class, argued for a more generous settlement of samurai pensions than the one the central government had made. He had seen Korea as a natural place for Japanese expansion. Korea, he argued, would be an excellent place for former samurai to find economic opportunity. He failed to see that an expedition to Korea might seriously weaken the Japanese economy and endanger her defenses. The possibility that Japan might be defeated in the venture or that Russia might object to Japanese expansion on the mainland did not seem to deter him.

Another problem facing the new Meiji administration was the settlement of the boundaries between Russia and Japan, and this question, too, occupied Futabatei's attention. Both nations claimed the Kurile Islands and Sakhalin. In 1853 Russian Admiral Putiatin attempted unsuccessfully to force Japan to sign a treaty which would clarify possession of the two areas. Temporary settlement was reached by the Treaty

25. Saigō offered to go to Korea as an envoy, confident that he would be killed and thereby give Japan reason for declaring war. Three of Saigō's letters concerning this plan are translated in Tsunoda, De Bary, and Keene, pp. 655–57.

of Shimoda, 1855, which provided that the Kurile Islands south of Urup would be ceded to Japan; Urup and those north to Russia; and Sakhalin was to be under joint Russo-Japanese control. After 1868 one faction in the government urged Japan's expansion northward and felt that Japan should obtain control of all the Kuriles and of Sakhalin by purchase or force. Meanwhile the government had embarked on a policy of colonization of Hokkaido. Other members of the government, fearful that Russia might attack Hokkaido if Japan pursued an aggressive policy, opposed the expansionist faction and pressed for conciliation. In 1875, after a long series of negotiations, Japan gave up its claim to Sakhalin and Russia ceded all the Kuriles to Japan.[26]

The settlement was not popular. Many felt that Japan's position had been weakened and that she should never have conceded Sakhalin. The issue aroused Futabatei's youthful national pride:

In our relations with Russia, the matter of the exchange of Sakhalin and the Kuriles came into the open and caused a great commotion among the public. Subsequently publications like *Naigai kōsai shinshi*[27] stirred up a lot of hostile feeling. Public opinion was seething. Feelings which I had held from early childhood—the feelings of a dedicated man of the Restoration—rose up within me. The public indignation over the treaty and my own feelings merged. The result—I decided that the greatest threat to Japan's future lay in Russia.[28]

In February of 1879 Futabatei withdrew from the schools

26. Borton, pp. 86–101; 158–59.
27. Futabatei seems to have made an error here. *Naigai kōsai shinshi* [new journal of domestic and foreign relations], which began publication in 1879, four years after the treaty, took no stand on the Kurile and Sakhalin exchange. Furthermore, it did not make any point of fearing Russia's aggression in the Far East. Nakamura, *Futabatei Shimei den*, p. 43. Futabatei has probably confused it with another journal or simply named it at random in an attempt to suggest titles of periodicals influential at the time. The style and tone of this article indicate that it was one of those written by another writer from Futabatei's words; this may account for the confusion in the name of the journal.
28. Futabatei, "Yo ga hansei no zange," p. 35.

in Matsue he had been attending. On the thirtieth of March he and his grandmother returned to Tokyo, leaving Yoshikazu and Shizu in Matsue, and went to live with relatives. Yoshikazu continued to better his position. He had been promoted twice more in 1877 and was promoted four times between 1879 and 1882. In June of 1884 he was appointed to a high ranking post in Fukushima prefecture. He retired from the government in April of 1885 and, in the following month, went to live in Tokyo. Exact details concerning the family's income during his tenure of office are lacking, but it must have been more than adequate, for when Futabatei entered Tōkyō Gaikokugo Gakkō in 1881, he was considered comparatively wealthy by his classmates.[29]

In 1879, when Futabatei went to Tokyo, he became friendly with another boy from Nagoya, Nagami Matsutarō. Both wanted to enter military service, and this common bond formed the basis of their friendship. They tried for admission to the newly founded officers' training school, Rikugun Shikan Gakkō. The school had opened in June of that year amidst great splendor. Imperial princes and ambassadors of foreign nations gathered on the purple-draped platform at the inauguration ceremonies. "The strength and weakness of the Army rests on the spirit of its officers," declared the Imperial proclamation commemorating the opening, "and for this reason we have founded this school. . . . Our hope for the future progress of the Army lies in this school."[30]

Nagami was accepted and eventually came to be considered one of the most talented men on the general staff. Futabatei, however, was not admitted because he was too nearsighted to pass the physical examination. He took the test again in 1879 and 1880 but failed each time.[31]

29. Nakamura, *Futabatei Shimei den,* p. 26.

30. *Shimbun shūsei Meiji hennen shi,* comp. Shimbun Shūsei Meiji Hennen Shi Hensan Kai, III, 403. A reprint of an article from the *Tōkyō Akebono* of June 4, 1878.

31. Uchida, "Futabatei no isshō," pp. 345–46; Nakamura, "Futabatei Shimei den," pp. 381–82.

In Uchida Roan's opinion, Futabatei's desire to enter the school stemmed from a relatively mature evaluation of the contemporary political situation:

Observing the situation in the Orient, Futabatei conceived a great ambition. In expectation of a future crisis in the Far East, he decided that he would become an actor in the drama. His ambition to become an officer was not, by that date, simply a childish desire to wear a uniform, whatever it may have been in earlier years. Consequently as soon as his military ambitions were thwarted, he turned his thoughts to the foreign service and entered the foreign language school's Russian department.[32]

While awaiting admission to the Army officers' school, Futabatei attended several small private schools. From early May through late October 1878, he studied algebra with the mathematician Morikawa Kingo. From the first of February through the thirtieth of October 1879, he attended two schools: Seibikō, an academy for Chinese studies, and Seigijuku, where he studied mathematics with Kagami Kōshō.[33] In February of 1880, he turned to Morikawa again for instruction in mathematics for two months. During that time he attended lectures at the Tōkyō Shūshin Gakusha, where the moralist and philosopher Nishimura Shigeki (1828–1902) taught ethics.[34]

32. "Futabatei no isshō," p. 346.
33. Kagami also taught for the Army. He was a member of the first Japanese learned society in the natural sciences, the Tōkyō Sūgaku Kai, Tokyo Society of Mathematicians. The society, founded in 1877, had practitioners of both traditional Oriental mathematics and Western style mathematics among its members. *Meiji bunka shi*, V, 61–62.
34. Nishimura founded Shūshin Gakusha, Society for Ethics, in 1876. He felt that a new moral philosophic base was needed to match the new civilization being built in Meiji Japan and that until then no one had tried to construct one. The government's efforts and the endeavors of the leading figures in private life were devoted to material betterment. It fell to those like himself to work for the spiritual betterment of contemporary Japanese life. "From ancient times," he said, "the moral teachings of our country have all followed Confucianism. Today, however, Western learning is entering our country and there are many points which Confucianism does not cover. Present day intellectuals despise the circuitous ways of the Confucianists and not a few would be rid of Confucianism entirely. Al-

Seibikō was considered one of the "more important" private schools in Tokyo by contemporaries. The director, Takatani Ryūshū (1818–85), who published a history of Japan entitled the *Nihon zenshi* in 1879,[35] had founded Seibikō in 1873.

The school had a reputation for political radicalism. In May 1878 a student named Sugimura Bun'ichi was party to the assassination of the Home Minister, Ōkubo Toshimichi (1830–78). Ōkubo, like Saigō Takamori, came from Satsuma han and had also been a leader of the Restoration. Ōkubo's assassins claimed that they were avenging the death of Saigō in the Satsuma Rebellion, which Ōkubo had been instrumental in suppressing. On the afternoon of the day of the assassination, a statement of the assassins' motives for committing the crime was delivered to the offices of various newspapers. The six former samurai involved in the plot asked that the statement be made public.[36] Sugimura's fellow students made copies of the statement and kept them at school. When the police came to search the school, the students hid them in the ceiling on the second floor. In writing about Futabatei in later years, one of the students, the journalist Tsuchiya Dalmu, listed him among those involved in the incident. This is not possible, since Futabatei did not enter the school until the following February, but it seems likely that, given his earlier partiality to Saigō's cause, he did ex-

though we must not discard it entirely, we cannot teach the people by Confucianism alone. If we are to guide the people in our own time, we must blend and combine Western and Eastern thought, and construct a single new moral philosophy suited to this age." Quoted in *Meiji bunka shi,* III, 541.

35. Uchida, "Futabatei no isshō," p. 345; Kuroita, p. 216.

36. The thirteen-page document listed crimes the assassins felt Ōkubo had committed against Japan. They included neglecting Japan's development in his concern with foreign relations, ruling in self-interest, and suppressing the rights of the people, restricting freedom of speech, and the like. The newspapers printed only part of the statement. *Shimbun shūsei Meiji hennen shi,* IV, 391. Reprinted from the *Chōya shimbun,* May 15, 1878.

press his approval of the assassination, thereby causing Tsuchiya to associate him with the incident.[37]

Additional political flavor was given to the school by the presence of Nakae Chōmin (1847–1901), who lectured at Seibikō occasionally, although by then he had already opened his famed French academy. Nakae had spent three years in France, studying French philosophy and history, and returned to Japan to advocate principles of liberalism and democracy.

Among Futabatei's friends at the school was Nishi Genshirō (1860–1923), who later entered the foreign service, studied in China, and served in various posts overseas.[38] Nishi and Futabatei joined in a cause which precipitated their departure from Seibikō. In June and July of 1879 ex-president Ulysses Grant visited Japan. The head of the Tokyo Municipal Assembly, Fukuchi Gen'ichirō (1841–1906), addressed Grant, welcoming him in the name of the people of the city.[39] Numa Morikazu (1843–90), an outspoken advocate of people's rights and member of the assembly, claimed that Fukuchi was not entitled to speak in the name of the people since he was an appointed and not an elected official. When their quarrel ended in Numa's assaulting Fukuchi, the newspapers covered the episode in full. Takatani, the head of Seibikō, composed a defense of Fukuchi's cause in Chinese and sent it off to the newspapers. It was

37. Tsuchiya, "Sanjūnen mae no Hasegawa kun," p. 116. Written in 1909.
38. Uchida, "Futabatei no isshō," pp. 345–47. Nishi also entered the Tōkyō Gaikokugo Gakkō but stayed only briefly. With the help of the Russian language teacher, Furukawa Tsuneichirō, he took an examination for the Foreign Service and was almost immediately sent to China. He subsequently graduated from Brussels University, served in many European and Asian legations, and was ambassador to Siam and Rumania.
39. In his speech Fukuchi said that all the people of the city were happy that Grant had arrived safely and saw in his visit the beginning of new and friendly ties with Japan's distant neighbor to the East. For the text of the speech see *Shimbun shūsei Meiji hennen shi*, IV, 74, a reprint of an article from the *Tōkyō Nichi Nichi* dated July 4, 1879. Fukuchi was editor of the *Nichi Nichi* at that time.

printed in the *Chōya shimbun*. When Futabatei and Nishi saw their teacher's letter in the paper, they went to his office and began to argue with him about his position. He scolded them for daring to approach him in such a tone, and the boys left the school.[40] As so often in his life, Futabatei here demonstrated how intractable he could be when he felt a principle had been violated. The incident assumes added significance when seen in the context of Futabatei's later political liberalism, a position by no means incompatible with his desire to be a military officer or his defense of Saigo Takamori.

Futabatei's literary tastes while at Seibikō reflected his political inclinations. He is remembered as having been especially fond of the poem "Chēng ch'i ko" (in Japanese, "Seiki no uta"—Song of Righteousness) by the Chinese patriot Wen T'ien-Hsiang (1236–83). Wen T'ien Hsiang, a minister of the last Sung Emperor, on pain of execution, refused to switch his allegiance to the Mongols. He died courageously after making his famous statement, "I cannot serve two masters." His poem itself is not an extreme statement of nationalism but acquired this meaning through association with his act of sacrifice. Several poems with the same title were written in Chinese by nineteenth-century Japanese patriots like the Mito Confucianist, Fujita Tōko, and the fervent Restorationist Yoshida Shōin, all strongly linked to nationalism and Restorationism in Japan.[41] Futabatei also enjoyed the Chinese poems of Kumoi Tatsuo (1844–70), a former samurai who had led 3,000 men in a revolt against the Meiji government in 1870. On holidays Futabatei would make copies of these poems and recite them for his fellow students.[42]

40. Tsuchiya, pp. 116–17.
41. Giles, *A History of Chinese Literature*, p. 248; *Chūgoku gakugei dai jiten*, pp. 666–67. The poem is translated by George Margoulies in *Le Kou-Wen Chinois*, pp. 312–15. An English translation appears in Giles, *Gems of Chinese Literature*, pp. 201–2.
42. Kumoi was a retainer of Yonezawa han. He was opposed to the dissolution of the Tokugawa shogunate and based his appeal to his followers

Even after entering the foreign language school in May 1881, Futabatei maintained his interest in Chinese. His classmate, Kuwabara Kenzō, recalled:

We were in the same class, but since I was two years his junior, Hasegawa was like an older brother to me. He had a great talent for absorbing languages and was clearly superior to the other students. In class he was always the leader. Furthermore, he was exceptionally well grounded in Chinese studies, an advantage which showed in various ways. It was entirely owing to his influence that we came to take an interest in Chinese studies.[43]

Futabatei experimented with writing in Chinese for many years after he ended his formal study of the language; his journals for 1888 and 1889 contain several attempts at narrative prose and fiction in Chinese.

His interest in Russia grew, as we have seen, out of his evaluation of the contemporary international problems facing Japan. To him Russia was the greatest threat to Japan's future. "We would have to protect ourselves in some way. The Russian language would be the most essential weapon for our defense. This chain of reasoning led me to enter the Russian department of the foreign language school." In time, Futabatei's interest in the Russian language would evolve into a passion for Russian literature. The transformation came about almost by accident:

The value of the study of literature revealed itself spontaneously from my researches in the Russian language. Perhaps this statement will be clearer if I explain that at the time the language school had the same curriculum as a Russian middle school. Physics, chemistry, mathematics, and other subjects were all taught in Russian, and we were also instructed in rhetoric and Russian literature. In the class on literary history we had to read representative works by representative Russian authors. In the process, without my being at all aware of what was happening, I fell under the influence of Russian literature. Of course

on the evils of changing the old feudal system, Harootunian, pp. 73–75; Tsuchiya, p. 116.

43. Kuwabara, p. 122.

my background in part explains this. I had from childhood a kind of artistic predilection; it was stimulated by Russian literature and emerged and developed naturally. An interest in literature moved along side by side with my excessive chauvinism. At first neither was stronger than the other but soon my nationalistic fervor was quieted and my passion for literature alone burned on.

What Futabatei found so exciting in this new foreign literature was the novelists' perception and treatment of society.

I did not love literature in the ordinary, literary sense. Instead I became fascinated with the observation, analysis, and predictions of social phenomena or problems which the Russian writers treated—things which had never occurred to me to consider in my earlier preoccupation with the problems of the nation as a whole.[44]

In the course of his career at Gaigo Gakkō, Futabatei abandoned his plans to join the Foreign Service or indeed to enter the government at all, passed through a period of being greatly taken with Socialism, and soon decided on a literary career. In all of these phases, the teachers at the school played no inconsiderable part, but the ultimate decision to become a writer grew as much from Futabatei's natural sensitivity to literature as from the stimulation he received from the encouragement of others.

Gaigo Gakkō

The foreign language school, Tōkyō Gaikokugo Gakkō (known as Gaigo Gakkō), opened in 1873. Although there had been some preliminary attempts at Russian language studies even earlier, as well as a few tentative experiments in teaching Russian by government and private institutions, Gaigo Gakkō was the first school to offer a systematic program in Russian studies. As early as 1808, the shogunal government, realizing the potential political threat of Russia,

44. Futabatei, "Yo ga hansei no zange," pp. 35–36.

directed several scholars to learn Russian.[45] Japanese fishermen repatriated from Siberia, where they had been shipwrecked, and Russian sailors captured by the Japanese furnished the first linguistic information to Japanese officials, who set to work compiling maps and dictionaries. After the first Russian consular mission was established in Japan in 1859, more sophisticated language studies were undertaken by both Russians and Japanese, as a result of which better dictionaries and a few grammars were written. Russian was officially taught in the shogunal Bansho Shirabe Dokoro [office for the study of barbarian writings] for the first time in 1862. In 1863 instruction in Russian was offered at a government school in Nagasaki.

After the Restoration a concerted effort was made to enroll talented students from all over Japan in foreign-language training programs. Bansho Shirabe Dokoro was revived for the purpose of teaching English and French, and a new government language school called Gogaku Dokoro was founded to teach German, Russian, and Chinese. In 1873 the two were merged to form the Tōkyō Gaikokugo Gakkō. Within a year the English department was made into a separate school, and by 1881, when Futabatei entered the school, French, German, Chinese, Korean, and Russian were the languages taught.

Gaigo Gakkō was closed in 1885 and its various departments incorporated into other institutions. By then 4,634 students had attended the school, although only 63 had

45. Berton, Langer, and Swearingen, p. 6. The first official Russian mission to Japan in 1792 had even earlier stimulated the writing of various studies about Russia by Japanese scholars. The mission, headed by Adam Laxman, landed in Ezo (modern Hokkaido) and brought back Japanese castaways, including a ship's captain named Kōdayū who had spent several years in the Aleutians, Kamchatka, and Irkutsk, and ten months in St. Petersburg. Laxman was not successful in establishing trading relations with Japan, but Kōdayū brought back maps and books from Russia which, together with his own statements regarding conditions in Russia, provided material for several treatises. He also instructed Japanese scholars in the Russian language. *Ibid.*, pp. 3–5. For further information on Kōdayū, see Keene, *The Japanese Discovery of Europe*, pp. 59–68.

actually been graduated. Of the 567 who studied in the Russian department, 20 received degrees. Government scholarships were offered to all students in the Chinese, Korean, and Russian departments; twenty-five to thirty a year went to students of Russian.[46]

A certain difference was noticeable between the students entering the French and German departments and those studying Russian, Chinese, and Korean. English, German, and French were associated with all that was modern and progressive, and proficiency in these languages was thought to provide a key to Westernization. The French and German divisions, therefore, tended to attract students who wished to use the languages as part of their preparation for higher education in the humanities or natural sciences, and this accounts, to a large degree, for the number who left before graduation. After only a year or two, many transferred to other schools. Students of Russian, Chinese, and Korean were less academically inclined. Many expected to use the foreign language in business or government service, planning to work as interpreters or translators or to take positions in foreign countries. For some, at least, the chief attraction in the school lay in the grants offered by the government. In the hopes of receiving an education without having to pay for it, many young men who would not otherwise have chosen to specialize in languages applied to Gaigo Gakkō.[47]

Both Russians and Japanese taught in the Russian department from its inception. The first Russian teacher was the geographer and linguist Leon Mechnikov (1838–88). He had become interested in Japan as the result of a chance meeting in Switzerland with Ōyama Iwao, from whom he

---

46. Berton, Langer, and Swearingen, pp. 8–16. After 1865 Russian was also taught at several private schools, the most noteworthy being that directed by Father Nikolai, a priest of the Russian orthodox church who had been chaplain to the Russian consulate. He founded his school in Tokyo in 1872.

47. Nakamura, "Gaikokugo Gakkō to Futabatei," *Tembō*, No. 5 (May 1946), pp. 75–77.

learned enough Japanese to amaze his hosts in Japan.[48] Mechnikov was a political radical. He had been fired from various Russian government positions because of subversive activities, he had fought under Garibaldi in Italy, and he remained throughout his life an outspoken critic of absolutism and tyranny.[49]

The outstanding Japanese teachers at the school included Ichikawa Bunkichi and Furukawa Tsuneichirō. Ichikawa (1848–1927) had been sent to Russia to study by the shogunal government in 1865. He remained in St. Petersburg until 1873—although the other Japanese students had returned home at the time of the Restoration—and knew the novelist Ivan Goncharov and many members of Russian high society. When he did return to Japan, he was appointed to Gaigo Gakkō, but he remained at this job for only one year, and in 1874 he went back to St. Petersburg.[50] After five years in Russia, Ichikawa returned to Japan, and devoted himself once more to teaching at the school until it closed in 1885. Although only thirty-seven at the time, he was reputed to be something of a misanthrope and apparently refused to accept public office. He entered on a secluded life which continued, despite his many contacts with high political figures and his linguistic ability, until his death in 1927.[51]

Furukawa Tsuneichirō (d. 1900) also learned Russian abroad. After serving as secretary to Ōkubo Toshimichi, he

48. Ōyama (1842–1916) went to Europe for the second time in 1871 to inspect military installations and study tactics and weapons. He remained there until 1874. After returning to Japan, he became one of the leading exponents of modern military methods.

49. Berton, Langer, and Swearingen, p. 15. Leon was a brother of Nobel Prize winning biologist Ilya Mechnikov. Leon was in Japan from 1873 to 1874. *Meiji bunka kankel Ōbei jimmei roku,* p. 562.

50. He traveled as a secretary to the mission headed by Enomoto Takeaki (1836–1908). The purpose of the mission was to settle the question of Japan's rights in the Kuriles and Sakhalin.

51. Nakamura, *Futabatei Shimei den,* p. 52. Ichikawa, however, taught Russian again in 1892 at the Rogaku Kan, a school for Russian studies. *Shimbun shūsei Meiji hennen shi,* VIII, 184.

was stationed in the Japanese consulate in Vladivostok and began his study of Russian. His Russian was considered to have been superior even to Ichikawa's, and he gave generously of his time to assist the boys of the language school. After the school closed, he worked in the office of the government publication, *Kampō;* it was he who helped Futabatei find employment there in 1889. That year, when a new government-sponsored foreign language school, also called the Tōkyō Gaikokugo Gakkō, was established, Furukawa was put in charge of the Russian department. He subsequently recommended that Futabatei be appointed to the teaching staff. When he died, Futabatei quietly and unobtrusively helped pay the necessary expenses and assisted his family in various ways.

Largely as a result of the scholarships offered by the government, the original Tōkyō Gaikokugo Gakkō had many more applicants for entrance to the Russian department than it wished to accept. A preliminary entrance examination in general subjects was given to each candidate, followed by a test in Russian. Of the 250 applicants in 1881, 48 passed the preliminary examination and were permitted to begin studying Russian. After three or four weeks they were tested again, this time on their ability to pronounce Russian; of the 48, only 25 were allowed to go on. A boy had to be at least thirteen to enter the school, but most were older. The average age of Futabatei's classmates in the first year was between fourteen and fifteen, but he was already seventeen. As a consequence of being older than the others and the best student in the school, he led in all academic and social matters. The other boys and the teachers respected his ability; his fellow students seem almost to have idolized him. He organized groups like the extracurricular Russian-speaking society which met weekly for language practice.[52]

All the boys with scholarships had to live in the dormitory, sleeping 8 to a room and 4 to a bed. Among Futabatei's

52. Nakamura, *Futabatei Shimei den,* pp. 45, 52–53, 220; Kuwabara, p. 122.

closest friends at school were Ōtaguro Jūgorō (1866–1945), who later became a wealthy industrialist, and Okano Hiroki. The three boys, classmates who shared the same room in the dormitory, remained loyal friends for life, helping each other whenever necessary. Ōtaguro described how intensely Futabatei pursued his studies:

He studied very seriously. His ability to read and the sharpness of his powers of comprehension were truly amazing. He was always reading. Even when he went to bed, he kept a book next to his pillow and if he woke up during the night he would at once begin to read. Not surprisingly, he did very well in class. He was so bright that not only his classmates but even students in other classes respected him. The teachers addressed him by the Russian equivalent of Mister, although they never referred to any of the rest of us that way.

All classes at the school were conducted throughout in Russian and students were also required to write compositions in Russian.

Sometimes we would grind out pages of work in a great hurry just before the papers were due, dashing them off without much concern for what we said. This was never true of Hasegawa. He would rewrite his papers any number of times, polishing the style, as if each were the first he ever submitted to the teacher. There would not be a single mistake in syntax or grammar. When I saw what he had drafted and realized how much better what he had written was than my composition, I would ask him if he hadn't worked hard enough already. He would answer, "No, it still won't do."

Because of his extraordinary ability, Futabatei set the standard for the others. On Saturday of each week the students were examined individually on their work.

There would often be sentences whose meaning I could not understand and I would have to admit defeat, but that was never the case with Hasegawa. He would walk out of the examination room perfectly calmly. "How did it go?" I would ask. "Oh, it was nothing," he would reply. "But what did that phrase mean at such and such a place?" "Well, this is the way I interpreted it," he would say, analyzing it to the last detail. That is how we came to consider him the standard against which to judge our own work: if he ever said he did not understand something, we could be quite sure that we would never have understood it ourselves.[53]

When the boys reached the advanced classes, they no longer studied from the ordinary Russian high school texts used in the early grades. Instead, they were taught the masterpieces of Russian literature directly from the novels themselves. Generally, however, only one copy of each novel was available in the school, and the teachers, not being able to ask the students to read ahead and then lecture to them about the work, read the novels aloud in class. The students, we are told, were "as enchanted as if they had been listening to a Japanese novel." [54]

The instructor most skilled in the art of reading aloud to students was a Russian who went by the name of Nicholas Gray. Gray arrived in Japan with his wife in June of 1884.[55] He had left Russia out of dissatisfaction with the political situation, traveled to America and became a citizen, and eventually moved on to Japan to teach at Gaigo Gakkō. He was, by common agreement, an extremely dynamic and conscientious teacher, and he exerted a strong influence on all his students. Ōtaguro describes Gray's talent for reading: "It was wonderful to hear him read a novel. His voice, his expression, his whole way of reading were marvelously skillful." Uchida Roan further tells of reports he heard:

53. Ōtaguro, pp. 117–18. First published in 1909.
54. Ōtaguro quoted in Nakamura, "Shōgai to sakuhin," p. 10.
55. They arrived in Yokohama on June 16, 1884, aboard the British steamer *Oceanic* from San Francisco, *Japan Weekly Mail*, June 21, 1884. No record has been found of Gray's departure from Japan, but Mrs. Nicholas Gray is listed among the passengers departing from Yokohama for San Francisco on February 23, 1886, *ibid.*, February 27, 1886. Compare also *Meiji bunka kankei Ōbei jimmei roku*, p. 556. Futabatei mentions that Gray had returned to America in an entry in his journal dated June 24, 1889. *Ochiba no hakiyose: futakagome*, p. 60.

Gray seems to have been extremely enthusiastic about literature. When he lectured on Russian literature, he analyzed a work in the most minute detail. He displayed a remarkable talent for reading aloud the masterpieces of Goncharov and Dostoevsky. He brought the text to life with gestures and by modifying his voice to imitate the different characters. He waved his arms, stamped his feet, rolled his eyes, and shook his head. Gray's lectures enabled the students to rise above the limitations of language lessons and savor the wonder of literature. It would have been impossible for anyone not to learn to love literature after hearing him.[56]

In addition to hearing the novels read to them, the students were introduced to the art of literary criticism:

The teacher read the novels through to us from beginning to end. The students sat silently and listened as they were read. . . . When a novel was finally finished, we wrote criticisms of the characters of the heroes and heroines, and passed our papers in to the teacher. He would go over each paper carefully and correct it.

Here again Futabatei showed exceptional talent, for "there were hardly ever any red marks on Hasegawa's papers. When there were, they were put there merely to call his attention to some colloquial Russian usage." [57]

Uchida Roan believed that Gray changed the course of Futabatei's career and directed him toward literature.[58] This may have been an exaggeration, but there is no doubt that the young man was deeply affected by Gray's readings and lectures. Gray passed on to Futabatei a strong sense of the beauty and rhythm of the Russian language and, by extension, of the aesthetic value of composition. Hearing his teacher's voice, the young man sharpened his perception of the musical or lyrical possibilities of language. When he began to write and translate himself, he tried to create a Japa-

---

56. Ōtaguro, p. 119; Uchida, "Futabatei no isshō," p. 354.
57. Ōtaguro, p. 119.
58. Uchida, "Futabatei no isshō," p. 354.

nese style which would be as euphonious as the language of the Russian master novelists.

As so often happens with young people absorbed in a foreign language, Futabatei went through a period when he believed that Russian had certain aesthetically pleasing qualities lacking in Japanese. Looking back on his school days in later life, he wrote:

It was not that I felt that there was no rhythm in Japanese. We speak of *goro* in Japanese and *goro* is rhythm, of course, but in Japanese, I felt, the rhythm was not particularly clear or distinct. You cannot say it is not there but somehow it just is not terribly clear. This may be because the rhythm of Japanese is so subtle while the rhythm of Western languages is more obvious. However, when you read Japanese out loud the rhythm of the language does not emerge very positively and so tends to sound quite flat. It seemed to me that the difference was that in Japanese intonation and modulation are lacking. But Western writing—this seemed true of all Western writing, but particularly of Goncharov—is more exciting to read aloud than to read silently.[59]

Futabatei came to appreciate Goncharov through Gray's recitations. When Gray read aloud, he found it "almost unbearably exciting." Once, when the class was studying a Goncharov novel, Futabatei became so excited by Gray's rendition of the text that he borrowed the novel and took it to his room. Disappointed to discover that it lost much of its magic when he read it to himself, he realized that his admiration had owed much to Gray's delivery. Nevertheless, he found qualities in Goncharov's style which survived the faultiest delivery:

Style, too, can live and die, depending on how it is read aloud. But some styles have a rhythm of their own which is not dependent on the skill of the reader. Even if you read to yourself, this rhythm transmits itself to you. No matter how you try to murder it, the rhythm alone passes into the very being of the

59. Futabatei, "Yo no aidoku sho," *Zenshū*, XV, 180. An article written in 1906.

reader. There are, of course, differences in reaction depending upon whether a person has the ability to savor rhythm or not, and consequently the same text may seem interesting to one person and not to another. But the rhythm of Goncharov's style would be exciting to anyone, I imagine. If it is read very poorly, there is some danger that its power may be partly destroyed, but even so his writing is far more exciting than that of other novelists. I was not alone in this opinion. All my classmates felt that way. In point of style, I was most fond of Goncharov.[60]

While a student at Gaigo Gakkō, Futabatei frequently went with friends to hear a singer named Tsuruga Waka-tatsu.[61] The performances took place in a *yose* theater where entertainers and audience alike sat on *tatami* mats In this casual and informal atmosphere, the audience could talk, drink, eat, and smoke while the performance was in progress and, if they cared to, they could sing along with the music. Wakatatsu was one of the contemporary exponents of a style known as *shinnai bushi,* originally created by Tsuruga Shinnai (1714–74).

Shinnai bushi is a combination of song and narrative accompanied by samisen music. It opens with a musical interlude, followed by a song which sets the scene for the story. This passage leads to a straight narrative recital of the tale to musical accompaniment. At certain points in the narrative the performer shifts from declamation to song or falls silent while a musical interlude is played. The piece ends with a song summing up the tale and perhaps adding a moral message. The tales are almost invariably highly romantic love stories.[62]

Futabatei was talented at imitating the voices of narrative performers, particularly Wakatatsu, and used to delight his

60. *Ibid.,* pp. 180–81.
61. Ōtaguro, p. 120.
62. Malm, *Japanese Music,* pp. 188–91. *Shinnai bushi* is one of several styles of similarly constructed ballads; it is distinguished by the use of an extremely high pitch marking the opening of main phrases, followed by a swift lowering of the pitch in a series of descending fluttering notes, until the singer's voice is at the level normally used for recitation.

school friends with his mimicry. He also enjoyed two other types of musical narrative, the *tokiwazu*, founded by Toki-wazu Mojidayū (1709–81), and the *kiyomoto*, originated by Kiyomoto Enjudayū (1777–1825).[63] Both forms resemble shinnai bushi in construction and as frequently devolve on romantic, melodramatic plots. A doomed love affair which ends tragically in a double suicide is a frequent theme. Historical and semihistorical legends also provide many plots. The differences between the three varieties of song may be defined in terms of the pitch used by the performers, the presence or lack of specific musical embellishments, variations in the size or thickness of the samisen, and so on.

Uchida Roan comments on Futabatei's appreciation of these popular musical narratives:

Futabatei was fond of narrative music in a way which one would not have expected of such a serious man. When he was a student, his favorite was a blind shinnai singer named Wakatatsu. He would go any distance to hear Wakatatsu perform. At times, when things were quiet in the dormitory, he would sing one of Wakatatsu's pieces in his low, throaty voice, earning the applause of the other students. He himself was proud of having the kind of voice which he thought suitable for tokiwazu, and his friends greatly admired his surprisingly beautiful voice.

While listening to the performers or while singing the pieces himself, Futabatei grew more conscious of this sense of goro, or tonal balance, which he mentions in the passage quoted above. When a Japanese writer speaks of goro, he is referring to that indefinable quality in his language of what sounds right to a cultivated ear. Ōtaguro gives an example of Futabatei's sensitivity to the difficult language of a toki-wazu narrative:

He said that in a line about flowers of some sort, one of the words had been inserted by the author in a rather illogical place, and to make sense it would have to be moved to another

63. Ōtaguro, p. 120, and Kuwabara, p. 123, describe Futabatei's partiality for various types of musical narratives.

part of the sentence. But as far as the song was concerned, if that word were not where it was, the goro would be all wrong; it had to be left undisturbed.[64]

The language of shinnai bushi, tokiwazu, and kiyomoto makes them among the most difficult literary forms of Japanese.[65] In a style far closer to poetry than prose, the narrative moves rapidly along, often with only vague allusions in oblique metaphors to necessary details of the story. The piece pours forth in a flow of highly conventionalized poetic diction. The narrative portions are written in a fixed meter of lines of five and seven syllables, but the dialogue closely approximates spoken Japanese. When Futabatei started to write, his experience in studying such texts and in hearing so many of them delivered orally, coupled with his training in learning Russian by ear, was certainly instrumental in helping him to create a new colloquial written language.

Although Futabatei enjoyed Goncharov's style, his favorite author in those early years was Dostoevsky. He was especially interested in Dostoevsky's psychological approach and in what Futabatei referred to as his "religious" message. He saw *Crime and Punishment* as a novel with an important moral theme: man cannot live by reason alone; sympathy and love must guide him. "The idea behind *Crime and Punishment* is that man's great mistake—an error particularly common to the young—lies in his desire for fame. It tells us that it is wrong to make the urge for greatness the sole goal of life." To him, Raskolnikov was a "little Napoleon" who considered it shameful to be bound by the ties of conventional morality. "His basic philosophy was that a man must have the courage to live as he believed he should, even if by doing so he collided directly with the forces of the world to the detriment

64. Malm, *Japanese Music*, pp. 191–99; Uchida Roan, "Futabatei yodan," p. 501; Ōtaguro, p. 120.

65. These three varieties of recitation are also often referred to simply as *jōruri*, a word which has become the generic term for narrative samisen music. Jōruri is also used to mean the narrative of the puppet plays. The word derives from a sixteenth-century romance called *Jōruri hime monogatari* [the tale of Princess Lapis Lazuli]. Malm, *Nagauta*, pp. 4–5, 17, 32–34.

of his own well being. He is a man who would live by logic alone." Futabatei perceived that Raskolnikov's ideas contained a great untruth: "for our power to survive as men does not lie in logic; it lies in sympathy or love. I am not referring, of course, to self-love, but to the pure love of other human beings."

As he read *Crime and Punishment*, he reacted on two levels. At first, he was so deeply moved by the story that he felt as if life had assumed a new dimension, but he was unable to formulate his reaction to the novel. Then, after a short time, the lesson he describes above revealed itself to him and helped him to further his understanding of the value of fiction.

In the Bible or in the Chinese Classics, we find reference to the significance of life, but without further explanation it is difficult for us to understand what this means. A novel, I realized, can readily make us comprehend this significance without any further explanation at all. I believed firmly that the novel form, working outside the limitations of formalized religion, could accomplish more than religion. I did not come to this conclusion merely by reading Dostoevsky's novel—I had had similar thoughts before—but my conviction was greatly strengthened by *Crime and Punishment*.[66]

His experiences in Gaigo Gakkō taught him much about the possibilities of developing a written style and of creating fiction which could enlighten as well as entertain. As we have seen, he became increasingly sensitive to the beauty of language. His efforts to perfect his written Russian and his absorption with Japanese narrative forms indicate his growing concern with style and composition.

Toward the end of his school career he attempted a translation of a novel by Gogol. Unfortunately the manuscript was lost and little is known about its contents. It is evident, however, that he was already preparing for a writing career; translation was a natural point of departure. The choice was

66. Futabatei, "Yo no aidoku sho," pp. 181–82.

obvious. The Japanese public was deluged with translations from many languages, primarily English, from the 1870s on. Translations of novels, plays, critical essays, moralistic guides, political tracts, and so on appeared in great number. Some, particularly the novels and self-help handbooks, sold thousands of copies. Any young man with a knowledge of a foreign language and a facile pen in his hand stood a good chance of making a name for himself as a translator.

In Futabatei's case, however, his talent was not limited to the ability to read a foreign language, nor was his interest in literature restricted to a desire to achieve success in a career. His analysis of his youthful reactions to *Crime and Punishment* provides our first clue to his critical perception. Within months after leaving Gaigo Gakkō, he was translating and writing highly sophisticated literary essays centered on Russian critical theory. Although we do not know when he became interested in aesthetics, it is obvious that he had given much study and consideration to such theories while still in school; the works he completed shortly afterward are by their nature too complex and highly developed to have been constructed quickly.

Futabatei apparently displayed an unusual ability to study and absorb difficult ideas. Ōtaguro describes him in his school days:

He was an extremely creative person. If he learned something, he would not rest until he had made it his own. Belinsky's many essays on aesthetics were in our school library. Hasegawa read them through completely. When he had finished, we had a discussion about aesthetic theory. What he said was not merely a repetition of Belinsky's views; he had already created his own aesthetic theories from his reading.[67]

The theories of Belinsky, which will be discussed in greater detail below, were based on Hegelian philosophy and advocated a particular kind of realism. This was an entirely new conception in Japan; Futabatei was its first and most

67. Ōtaguro, p. 119.

fervent advocate. Western theories of realism were just beginning to find acceptance in the Japanese literary world in the mid-1880s. No fiction had yet been written along the lines of the Western realistic novel, if only because the old-fashioned language traditionally employed in fiction was unsuited to the medium. Realistic fiction demanded a fresh contemporary language. A half year after leaving school Futabatei began to write Japan's first modern realistic novel and composed it in colloquial language. The training he had received in Gaigo Gakkō, combined with his earnestness and inborn talent, largely accounted for his success.

Futabatei was never graduated from Gaigo Gakkō. This resulted from a series of events, over most of which he had no control. The final decision to leave school, however, rested with him. The basis of his decision was his resentment of a change forced upon the school's administration by the central government, coupled with personal antagonism for an educator named Yano Jirō (1845–1906).

In September of 1885 the Ministry of Education ordered the dissolution of Gaigo Gakkō as part of an over-all plan to reorganize the educational system in accordance with European and American models. The students were assigned to two other schools on the basis of the presumed differences in the pupils enrolled in the study of cultural and practical foreign languages. The German and French departments were transferred to the preparatory school which was intended to supply students for Tokyo Imperial University. The Russian, Chinese, and Korean departments were made part of the commercial high school, the Tōkyō Kōtō Shogyō Gakkō. Yano, the principal of the commercial high school, was one of Japan's leading exponents of democratic education. He had formerly been in the Ministry of Foreign Affairs and was a friend of Mori Arinori (1847–89), the Minister of Education. Mori had worked closely with Yano in establishing the commercial high school. Both men were ardent believers in training young people to fill specialized jobs in Japan's growing industrial economy and rapidly expanding foreign commerce.

The students in the Russian department considered it degrading to be shifted to the commercial school. Most of its students belonged to the merchant class; they lacked either the classical training of boys like Futabatei or the literary education which had been so important at Gaigo Gakkō. The friendship between Mori and Yano made it seem to Gaigo Gakkō students that the decision of the Ministry of Education had been based on personal considerations—a blatant example of the evils of a dictatorial, despotic government; they were encouraged in this attitude by Gray and other Russians on the staff.[68]

Yano made a conscious effort to help Gaigo Gakkō boys adjust to the change, and as a result many of Futabatei's friends who initially had objected strenuously became reconciled to the situation and continued their education. Futabatei was then in his last semester and was to be graduated that spring, but he decided to leave school in January of 1886. Yano called him to his office several times and tried to persuade him to stay in school, offering among other things to help with a career. Futabatei, however, considered Yano meddling and officious. More important, perhaps, having already decided on a literary career, he felt no need for a diploma or Yano's recommendation for a government or business post. Finally, Yano offered to let him graduate even without taking the final examinations, provided he did not officially withdraw from the school, but Futabatei refused. He left school on the nineteenth of January.[69]

Looking back on his actions in later life, Futabatei realized that his decision had been characteristic of his rebelliousness against authority. As part of his continuing cry for liberty, he wrote:

I wanted nothing to do with a government-sponsored school. Gaigo Gakkō had been eliminated and reduced to being the

68. Nakamura, *Futabatei Shimei den*, pp. 66–69.
69. Uchida, "Futabatei no isshō," pp. 348–51, and Kuwabara, p. 123.

foreign language section of the commercial school. Then, in a short space of time, the foreign language department disappeared and the students all became students in the commercial school. I left as quickly as possible. My parents urged me to enter the university but, just as I could not remain in a government-sponsored commercial school, so I could not enter a government university.[70]

The various changes in administration of Gaigo Gakkō occurred shortly after Futabatei's father, Yoshikazu, retired from his government post after nearly twenty years of service. He had been in charge of the accounting office in Fukushima prefecture and, upon retirement, moved to Tokyo in May 1885. He bought a large house and storehouse behind it in the Kanda section. His pension amounted to 10 yen a month. In addition, he had the income on a 2,000 yen government bond.[71]

In January of 1886 Futabatei went to live with his parents for the first time in many years. He realized at once that he would be draining their small capital if he did not support himself. Furthermore, he was desperately desirous of being independent. "I felt that receiving aid from my parents restricted my freedom," he later recalled, "and I hoped to free myself from my dependence on them and work by myself." [72]

Futabatei had already decided on the career he wanted. His earlier plans to enter the foreign service had been abandoned during his last years in Gaigo Gakkō. By 1886 he knew he wanted to be a writer and wasted no time in forming associations which would help launch his career.

70. Futabatei, "Yo ga hansei no zange," p. 37.
71. Nakamura, *Futabatei Shimei den,* p. 82. In 1885 1 koku of rice sold for 6.53 yen.
72. Futabatei, "Yo ga hansei no zange," p. 37.

Chapter 2

Tsubouchi Shōyō and Futabatei: The Emergence of the Modern Novel

F O U R D A Y S after leaving Gaigo Gakkō, Futabatei went to call on Tsubouchi Shōyō (1859–1935). By January of 1886, Tsubouchi had already gained considerable reputation as a novelist, translator, and critic. He was impressed by Futabatei's knowledge of Russian literature and by the young man's earnest desire to become a writer. He gave Futabatei the benefit of his experience and encouraged him to translate and devote himself to creative writing. Futabatei had much to say concerning artistic theory but had not yet learned how to construct a novel, nor had he discovered a literary style suitable to the type of novel he wanted to write. Tsubouchi spent many hours listening to the young man's theories and reading his manuscripts. He helped him develop his ideas and bring them to fruition. Their friendship lasted virtually unbroken throughout Futabatei's life, but it was during these early formative years that Tsubouchi exerted the greatest influence.

Although Futabatei, an ardent defender of realism, could speak fluently and convincingly of aesthetic theory, he never managed to write successful literary criticism. Tsubouchi, by contrast, was a superb critic. In 1886 he was still at the outset of his long, illustrious career, but already he had expressed the credo for modern realism in his essay entitled

Shōsetsu shinzui [the essence of the novel]. He finished it in March 1885, but publication had been delayed, and it was still appearing as a series of paperbound pamphlets in January 1886 when the two men met. Futabatei, excited by the essay, was eager to discuss it with its author.

Futabatei found in *Shōsetsu shinzui* theories similar to those he had studied while at Gaigo Gakkō, but differences too. Tsubouchi was well versed in Japanese and English literature, but he had not read Russian criticism and fiction, nor had he seriously studied the Hegelian theories which so directly influenced the critics familiar to Futabatei. Differences in literary theories stimulated hours of discussion. Tsubouchi was greatly impressed by Futabatei's views, though he later admitted he had never succeeded in understanding the theories very well. He encouraged Futabatei to translate Russian criticism for the Japanese public.

Tsubouchi despised the type of literature being written in his country. Some fiction he found cheap and tawdry; the balance he considered simply dull. Contemporary novels tended to be loosely constructed and episodic. Many were written in the belief that the function of the novel was to offer a moral guide for men's lives. Writers twisted their plots unconvincingly in order to make their works prove that virtue would always be rewarded and vice punished. Fantastic tales of adventures in exotic foreign lands enjoyed a great vogue, though scant attention was paid to accuracy of detail. A more serious problem lay in the fact that writers, concerned almost entirely with plot, devoted little attention to characterization. In *Shōsetsu shinzui*, Tsubouchi describes the faults in contemporary Japanese fiction and suggests methods for improving it. He urges tightly constructed plots with logical development and characterization based on a penetrating analysis of man's nature. Tsubouchi also reviews the problems involved in fashioning a modern literary style. Aware that the traditional styles were inappropriate to realistic fiction, he offers tentative suggestions for a new style.

Although Tsubouchi was not the only writer arguing for reform of contemporary fiction, he was one of the most influential. He had first expressed his dissatisfaction with current literature even earlier, but *Shōsetsu shinzui* surpasses in scope and dimension his other essays. It established him as the leading advocate of reform; from that time on, writers often turned to him for advice and guidance in their efforts to construct a modern literature. Futabatei was most directly affected by Tsubouchi's theories, but many other writers who did not even know Tsubouchi personally followed his advice and thought of him as their teacher.

Soon after meeting Tsubouchi, Futabatei began under the older man's guidance to translate Russian fiction, and late in the spring of 1886 started his first novel, *Ukigumo*. By the time it appeared in June 1887, the literary world was ready to accept a novel written in conformity with Tsubouchi's theories. The excellent critical reception given *Ukigumo* is ample evidence of the far-reaching influence of Tsubouchi's essay and the leadership he offered the literary world. His intellectual accomplishment in a sense epitomizes the greatness of his period. In a few short years Japanese novelists went from writing superficial, vacuous, titillating, episodic tales to creating serious, carefully constructed, realistic novels. More than anyone else, Tsubouchi was responsible for this development, and in his most talented pupil, Futabatei, his theories found their most effective exponent.

Shōsetsu shinzui reflects an idealistic attitude toward the novel unprecedented in Japanese literary theory. It places the novel on the same level of artistic expression as poetry, music, and the fine arts. For the first time, fiction was described as a legitimate pursuit for intellectuals. But when Tsubouchi tried to write an artistic novel, he failed. He himself was unable to avoid the contrived coincidences and convoluted plots he so abhorred in the writings of others. Eventually his critical perception forced him to see his own failings, and in 1889 he stopped writing fiction. From then on Tsubouchi directed his energies into teaching literature, writing criticism, and translating the complete works of Shakespeare. His dynamic leadership inspired whole generations of writers and actors, just as it had created a fine novelist in Futabatei. Tsubouchi's early career provides a capsulized survey of the kind of literature being written in Japan in the 1880s. Through it, we can see the failings of a generation educated too hastily on Western theory. We can also sense, however, the potential greatness in Japanese literature. It is all too easy to hold up for ridicule the plots of novels written by mediocre writers in the 1880s or to cite passages from inept translations of Western fiction made by men of inferior ability. Yet the mistakes made by one of the most brilliant minds Japan has ever produced permit us to make a more legitimate evaluation of the literature of the period and thereby to understand better the extent of Futabatei's contribution.

Shōsetsu shinzui, the first major work of modern literary criticism in Japan, was started in 1881 while Tsubouchi was still a student at Tokyo University. He had been an enthusiastic reader of Japanese literature from early boyhood, borrowing books from the famous Daisō lending library in Nagoya, where he grew up, to satisfy his appetite for Tokugawa period novels and plays. The youngest son of a large samurai family, Tsubouchi had been trained in the Chinese classics both at home and in private school. His family hoped he, like his father before him, would take a government post, and every effort was made to ensure his receiving the best possible modern education. Tsubouchi began to study English in 1872 and in 1874 entered the new Aichi Eigo Gakkō, the prefectural English school.[1]

1. The Daisō library was an old establishment in Nagoya. Beginning as a sake and apothecary store, it had become a lending library in the 1770s. Literary figures frequently stopped there. In the Tokugawa era writers as famous as Takizawa Bakin and Jippensha Ikku visited the Daisō on their way to and from Edo. Books from the library have gone into the Tokyo

In 1876 he and seven other boys from Aichi were chosen by the prefecture to go to Tokyo for further study. Tsubouchi was accepted at Kansei Gakkō, the foremost school in the country and forerunner of Tokyo University. When he reached the final stage of his training at the university, he became seriously interested in Western fiction for the first time. He had several Western teachers, including Ernest Fenollosa, at Tokyo University but he seems to have had difficulty in understanding their lectures and did not benefit greatly from classwork. His interest in fiction was stimulated by the enthusiasms of his classmates rather than by what he learned at school. His closest friend was a Tokyo-born literature student, Takada Sanae (1860–1938). Takada roused Tsubouchi's interest in English and French novels and encouraged him to read books not included in the classroom assignments. Tsubouchi joined the group of young men from the university who spent their days talking of Western literature and liberal theories in restaurants or bars.[2]

In April of 1880 Tsubouchi published a translation of Scott's *The Bride of Lammermoor* (1819), written in the metered poetic Japanese narrative style popular in the early nineteenth century. The translation was entitled *Shumpū jōwa* [spring breeze love story] following the contemporary custom of giving romantic and vaguely erotic titles to novels and translations. The publishers hoped that the translation

University Library, the National Diet Library, and Waseda University Library. Kawatake and Yanagida, pp. 49–50.

Tsubouchi was born in the village of Ōta, about thirty miles from Nagoya, where his father held a responsible position in the local division of the Owari han administration. The family left Ōta in 1869, when his father resigned his position. *Ibid.*, pp. 59–70.

2. *Ibid.*, pp. 87–93. While still a student Takada became acquainted with the leaders of the Kaishin-tō, one of the new political parties. After graduating in 1882, he taught in the Tōkyō Semmon Gakkō, and in 1890 he was elected to the first Diet. He served six consecutive terms in the lower house and in 1915 was elected to the House of Peers. From 1901 on he held various government posts and was appointed Minister of Education in 1915. He became president of Waseda University in 1931.

would appeal to the general public; this is apparent from the title itself, from Tsubouchi's introduction, which stresses the similarity between *Lammermoor* and Japanese love stories, and from the illustrations which depict the characters as Japanese clothed in traditional Japanese garments.[3] In order to get it published it was arranged that Tachibana Kenzō, a teacher at the Tokyo English language school, should be named as the translator instead of Tsubouchi. Although only the first part of the projected complete translation was ever published, *Shumpū jōwa* assumed an important place in the history of modern literature because it first introduced Scott to the Japanese public.[4]

Tsubouchi demonstrated in this first published translation the concern for accuracy and stylistic beauty which was to characterize his later masterpieces. However, he was not beyond excising the original text when the material proved inappropriate for his audience or converting Scott's imagery into expressions corresponding more closely to the language of traditional Japanese literature. Thus the first chapter of *The Bride of Lammermoor*, which reveals how the author came upon the ancient story, is completely omitted. Again, although Tsubouchi retains the opening of Chapter V, describing the feelings of Ashton and Lucy as they leave the cottage of the blind prophetess, Alice, he fails to include

3. Tsubouchi recalled that "after Oda Junichirō's free, *kambun-chō* translation of *Ernest Maltravers* appeared with such success under the erotic title *A Spring Tale of Flowers and Willows*, publishers decided that every translation of a Western novel had to be given a title like 'Spring,' 'Flowers,' or 'Romance.'" *Senshū, Bessatsu*, II, ii, 1–9. For a discussion of this point see Homma, *Tsubouchi Shōyō*, pp. 83–90.

4. Tsubouchi had not intended to publish the translation, but Takada showed it to his friend Ogawa Tameichirō, who in turn sent it to a publisher. Ogawa, an official in the Bureau of Statistics, was well versed in Chinese and Japanese literature. He made some minor corrections in the translation and wrote an introduction to the book. He also arranged to have it printed under Tachibana's name since he felt that an unknown student like Tsubouchi could not attract an audience. Tsubouchi and Takada knew Tachibana because he had taught Takada English and his younger brother was their classmate. *Senshū, Bessatsu* II, iii, and Kawatake and Yanagida, pp. 98–99.

the history of the wild cattle the characters encounter on their path. Tsubouchi translated Scott's "had, by her frequent rambles, learned to know each lane, alley, dingle, or bushy dell" [5] as

. . . koko kashiko to shōyō shi,
Sansui no ki o saguritareba,
Keikyoku no ato o uzumetaru nobe no komichi,
Matsukaze no hibiki ni wasuru tagitsuse wa iu mo sara nari,
Kaigan arasoitachi,
Rōboku ōutsu taru yūkoku no sumizumi made,
Nabete eshirazaru wa nakarikeri. . . .[6]

[Wandering here and there
exploring the wonders of mountain and river,
of paths through fields filled with brambles,
or the waterfall echoing in the wind through the pines,
every corner of the warring cliffs and ravines thick with ancient trees—
there was none unknown to her. . . .]

Tsubouchi's inclination to embellish descriptions of nature is even more pronounced in other passages too long to be included here.

Tsubouchi faithfully renders information regarding the complicated and completely alien political background of *The Bride of Lammermoor*. Furthermore, unlike many of his contemporaries, he does not leave out passages relating to the personality of the characters; their heroism, warmth, and pride are fully revealed. *Shumpū jōwa* can be considered a reasonable, intelligent translation of Scott's novel. However, it is still far from the precise style of translation which Futabatei introduced a few years later.

In 1881, Tsubouchi experienced two major setbacks at the university. During the school year he received a very low grade on an examination given by the English literature in-

---

5. Sir Walter Scott, *The Bride of Lammermoor* (London, 1926), p. 49.
6. *Shumpū jōwa, Senshū, Bessatsu* II, 39.

structor, William Houghton. That year Houghton, who offered the university's first lectures on *Hamlet,* asked on the examination for a discussion of Gertrude's character. Tsubouchi apparently did not understand what was meant by the question and wrote a moral criticism of her actions rather than the description his teacher wanted. The poor mark made him acutely aware of his inadequate understanding of Western literature and led him to undertake a comparative study of fiction and plays in the East and West. *Shōsetsu shinzui* eventually resulted from these studies.[7]

Tsubouchi also failed his final examination in Fenollosa's course in political science and was forced to repeat the year. This had a further sobering influence on him; he abandoned his earlier carefree habits and began to study seriously for his various classes. His scholarship was withdrawn as a result of his failure, and he left the dormitory where he had been living since entering school. In the fall of 1881 he began to teach English at a small private school, Shimbun Gakusha.[8] He taught only part time while attending the university but gradually increased his hours as he felt a greater need for money. To supplement his income, he started a small school in his lodging house, where he tutored as many as fifteen boys at a time in English. In May 1882 he started to accept boarding students. He soon had so many students living with him, he was forced to move several times to larger quarters.[9]

Tsubouchi was graduated from Tokyo University and re-

7. William A. Houghton (1852–1917) was an American scholar who was resident in Japan from 1877 to 1882. *Meiji bunka kankei Ōbei jimmei roku,* p. 558. Kawatake and Yanagida, pp. 103–4.

8. Takada was one of the founders of the school, which opened in January 1881 as a training place for boys preparing for the university and various professional schools. It offered English, mathematics, and Chinese studies. The enrollment increased from an initial 7 students to between 100 and 150. Kawatake and Yanagida, pp. 106–7.

9. *Ibid.,* pp. 107–9; 114–15. Tsubouchi found his students through various personal contacts. Those who boarded with him were almost all relatives of friends or of former students. Tsubouchi taught his boarders and visiting students in the evening after returning from Shimbun Gakusha. He is remembered as having been a particularly colorful and dynamic speaker.

ceived his bachelor's degree in July 1883.[10] Instead of finding employment with the government or in a government-sponsored school, as was the custom for Tokyo University graduates, he continued to divide his time between writing and teaching. In the fall of 1883 he became a teacher in Tōkyō Semmon Gakkō, a private school with which Takada and several other former classmates were associated. Takada himself had found a post for Tsubouchi at the school.

Semmon Gakkō, later renamed Waseda University, was founded in 1882 by Ōkuma Shigenobu (1838–1922) and other leaders of the Kaishin-tō, a moderate liberal political party working for the establishment of a constitutional government. When Tsubouchi joined the staff, the school had only a political science and a law department; only in later years was he able to lecture on literature and the theater. At first he taught chiefly Western history and constitutional theory, but in 1886 he began to teach psychology and sociology as well.[11] Tsubouchi remained at Waseda until 1915; he helped found its Faculty of Letters in 1890, edited its famous literary journal, *Waseda Bungaku,* and was recognized throughout the years as its most famous lecturer on English literature.

Tsubouchi did not join the Kaishin-tō or the collateral political groups formed by Takada and his other friends, but he was obviously in sympathy with the Kaishin-tō's views. Late in 1882, while still at the university, he published a thinly disguised political allegory in the *Tōkyō eiri shimbun,* an illustrated newspaper edited by Maeda Kenjirō, a friend of Takada's and a member of the Kaishin-tō. The allegory was entitled *Seiji tō kōshaku,* literally "Lectures of the Pure Administration Tea Shop." Seiji is the name of the man who

10. There were 107 men graduated from Tokyo University in 1883, bringing to 648 the number who had graduated since the first class of 1876. *Tōkyō Teikoku Daigaku gojūnen shi,* facing p. 1256.

11. Kawatake and Yanagida, pp. 118–19; 197–200. It appears that Tsubouchi's lectures consisted largely of explanations of the English textbooks used for these subjects. The students read such standard high school texts as Swinton's *Outlines of the World's History* and the *Union Readers.* In time, Tsubouchi wrote several textbooks for use in these courses.

owns the shop. The word *seiji tō,* meaning "pure administration hot water," is also a pun on another word, *seiji-tō,* meaning "political parties." Tsubouchi wrote the piece to explain the nature of constitutional government and the parliamentary system. To make the lesson as palatable as possible, it is presented as a simple, amusing narrative told by the old man who owns the tea shop to one of his guests. In writing the allegory, Tsubouchi imitated the jesting, pun-laden colloquial style made popular by the Tokugawa writer Shikitei Samba (1776–1822) and still practiced in Tsubouchi's time by Kanagaki Robun (1829–94).[12]

This was the first of several political allegories Tsubouchi published in the *Eiri shimbun* promoting the view that political parties and the active participation of an enlightened public were necessary to good government. Between October 1882 and January 1883, he wrote seven allegories in the same vein for the *Naigai seito jijō,* the official organ of the Kaishin-tō. These were more openly propagandistic in tone. They attacked the officials in control of the government, accusing them, among other things, of using public funds to perpetuate their power. That same spring another group of Tsubouchi's allegorical pieces appeared in the *Nagoya shimbun.*[13]

In January 1884 a translation of Scott's narrative poem *The Lady of the Lake* (1810) was published under the title *Shunsō kiwa* [romance of the spring window]. Although the translation was originally made by Tsubouchi and Takada, the book appeared under the name of Hattori Seiichi, a Kaishin-to member and former teacher of Takada's, and a well-known editor and writer of the time.[14] Tsubouchi was

12. Kawatake and Yanagida, pp. 119–20. For an example of Kanagaki's style see Keene, *Modern Japanese Literature,* pp. 31–33.

13. Kawatake and Yanagida, pp. 120–22.

14. Hattori Seiichi (1842–1908) was from a rich samurai family. Beginning in 1874, he published and edited a number of newspapers and magazines. His publications often contained articles attacking the ruling oligarchy, many written by himself. As a result, they were suppressed by the government one after the other.

responsible for about two-thirds of the original translation and Takada for the rest. The translation included two long poems in Chinese by Tsubouchi's former classmate Amano Tameyuki.[15] Tsubouchi started the translation in the summer of 1880, shortly after the *Shumpū jōwa* appeared. The manuscript seems to have been completed two years later. For their labors, Tsubouchi and Takada received only 20 yen.

The style of *Shunso kiwa* marks a complete departure from Tsubouchi's other works of the period. It is written in a tight, stiff classical prose known as *kambun-chō,* which evolved from the Japanese manner of reading Chinese texts. This style is characterized by the use of difficult Chinese words and the absence of colloquial vocabulary or grammatical forms. Tsubouchi and Takada originally chose the kambun-chō because of the great popularity it enjoyed at the time.[16]

However, *Shunsō kiwa* is a story which Tsubouchi himself describes as more often resembling a popular Chinese novel than Scott's poem. This was due, in some measure at least, to Hattori's editing. During the two years between the time Tsubouchi and Takada sold the manuscript and its date of publication, Hattori revised the text considerably, adding completely unrelated material, difficult Chinese words and phrases, and revising the sequence. The preface, almost undoubtedly written by Hattori, refers to *The Lady of the Lake* as a Western novel of political significance in the struggle for popular rights.[17]

In May 1884 Tsubouchi's translation of Shakespeare's *Julius Caesar* appeared. His power and skill as a translator

15. Amano Tameyuki (1859–1938) achieved fame as one of Japan's first professional economists. A son of a Saga han samurai family, he went to Tokyo in 1875, entered Kansei Gakkō, and was graduated from Tokyo University with Takada. He, too, helped in the original formation of Semmon Gakkō. He was elected to the first Diet in 1890 and received a doctorate in law in 1899.

16. Kawatake and Yanagida, pp. 128–29.

17. Tsubouchi's comments on *Shunsō kiwa* are quoted in the introduction to the volume of his collected works in which it appears, *Senshū, Bessatsu* II, iv–v; 6–7.

and writer are here revealed as in none of his earlier works. Unable to secure a sufficiently annotated edition of the play, he was troubled by doubts as to his competence in understanding the original and consequently spent close to three years writing and revising the translation. As he indicates in the introduction, he chose a style similar to that used in jōruri texts. Following Japanese custom, he inserted short descriptive passages, to be delivered by a narrator, in between Shakespeare's lines of dialogue wherever he considered them necessary for understanding and continuity. On the whole, however, Tsubouchi's version is a direct and faithful translation.

Tsubouchi employed in his *Julius Caesar* the rhythmical, metered style of jōruri which more closely approximates Western narrative poetry than any other Japanese verse form.[18] The translation is, however, remarkably free of the typical literary devices which Tsubouchi favored in most of his other writings of the period; puns, portmanteau words, and classical allusions are conspicuous by their absence. His avoidance of conventional elegance of expression at times resulted in disappointingly pedestrian language. Some of Shakespeare's best lines lose their original beauty because of the compressed, commonplace Japanese expressions. At other times Tsubouchi's version is very powerful: Cassius' attack on Caesar (1, 11, 90–131), for example, beats out a steady flow of venom and hate whose force rivals the original.[19]

The translation was printed under Tsubouchi's own name.[20] The publisher went to considerable lengths to produce a book of high quality, but because of its high price, it sold few copies. Critical reaction, however, was favorable,

18. For a discussion of the language of jōruri as used by the master of the form, Chikamatsu Monzaemon (1653–1725), see Keene, *Major Plays of Chikamatsu*, pp. 26–30.

19. *Jiyū no tachi nagori no kireaji, Senshū, Bessatsu* II, 313–14.

20. The translator is given as "*Bungaku shi* [bachelor of letters] Tsubouchi Yūzō." His subsequent writings were published under his own name, as in this case, or under one of his several pennames.

and it was soon hailed as the "first real translation in the Far East."[21] The publisher, taking advantage of the contemporary political climate to present Shakespeare's play as the story of the overthrow of a tyrant by the people, gave the book the title *Jiyū no tachi nagori no kireaji* [the sharp blade of freedom's sword].[22]

In July 1884, Tsubouchi completed a freely translated version of about half of Edward Bulwer-Lytton's *Rienzi* (1835). The following spring it was published under the title *Gaiseishi den* [the biography of a patriot].[23] The Japanese public was already well acquainted with Bulwer-Lytton; his *Ernest Maltravers* and its sequel, *Alice* (1837-38), had enjoyed great popularity when they appeared a few years before in free translations.[24] As was true of Tsubouchi's two translations of works by Scott, the *Gaiseishi den* differs in places from the original, but it successfully conveys the romantic excitement of the story of the daring fourteenth-century Roman revolutionary. Rienzi's ambition, his patriotic fervor, Roman life, and political ferment in his day all appealed to the imagination of Meiji readers.

Tsubouchi wrote *Gaiseishi den* in the same style he had

21. In the *Yomiuri shimbun*, June 6, 1884. Quoted in Kawatake and Yanagida, p. 131.

22. It was published by the Tōyō kan, whose chief editor was Ono Azusa (1852-86). Ono was one of the most active members of the Kaishin-tō, a close associate of Ōkuma, and a leading figure in the administration of Semmon Gakkō. Tsubouchi describes the efforts made by Ono on his behalf in "Futabatei no koto," p. 28.

23. *Rienzi* and Scott's *Ivanhoe* were Tsubouchi's favorite English historical novels at the time, and he began the translation with great enthusiasm. He was not commissioned to do the second half, however, and never finished the work. Tsubouchi's recollections are quoted in *Senshū, Bessatsu* II, 6.

24. The Japanese version of *Ernest Maltravers* and *Alice* appeared in 1878 and 1879 under the title *Karyū shunwa* [a spring tale of flowers and willows]. It was written in kambun-chō by Oda Junichirō (1851-1919). *Karyū shunwa* was one of the first books to introduce popular European fiction to Japan. Oda followed his initial success with a similarly free rendition of Bulwer-Lytton's *The Last Days of Pompeii* (1834), issued under the title *Kisō shunshi* [the history of a strange spring] in 1879-80. A good deal of Bulwer-Lytton's popularity in Japan is attributable to his being a political figure as well as a novelist. Yoshitake, pp. 54-57.

employed in *Shumpū jōwa*. As we have noted above, this literary style most closely resembles in its poetic qualities Western narrative poetry. When used in fiction, it was known as *Bakin-chō* after its most famous exponent, the early nineteenth-century novelist Takizawa Bakin (1767–1848).[25] The most striking characteristic of the style is the repetition of phrases of seven and five syllables arranged in various combinations; it is therefore also frequently referred to as *shichi-go-chō* [seven-five rhythm]. The style remained very popular throughout the nineteenth century and was still widely used in the late 1880s. It soon was to become a major source of controversy among writers and critics who associated it with many of the weaknesses they considered inherent in contemporary Japanese fiction.

The long introduction to *Gaiseishi den*, Tsubouchi's first published essay in literary criticism, anticipates some of the same themes he treats in *Shōsetsu shinzui*.[26] In the introduction Tsubouchi deals primarily with obligations of the novelist to portray the deeper emotions of man; depiction of love, hate, jealousy, fear, and the like is the proper business of the writer. He believed that a cataloguing of superficial events, no matter how exciting, would not make a true novel.

He begins his introduction by briefly tracing the long tradition of fiction in Japan from ancient times through the first half of the nineteenth century and goes on to say:

With the changes of the Restoration, popular writers disappeared and the novel consequently declined for a time. Today we are having a great revival; it is the age of the story. All around us various kinds of romances and stories are being published, all eagerly competing with each other to cater to fashion. Even in the type of magazine or newspaper which specializes in informing the public on what is new and unusual, they print stories which are simply versions of old, stale novels. Because of this

25. Bakin's life and works are described by Leon M. Zolbrod in *Takizawa Bakin: Major Edo Author.*

26. There is a good deal of similarity between this introduction and the introduction to *Shōsetsu shinzui*. See the translation by Keene in *Modern Japanese Literature*, pp. 55–58.

trend, even though the number and variety of novels and romances current in our country are greater than one can possibly
estimate, they are almost all ridiculous imitations. It is a very
rare plot indeed which is genuinely original. Most are either
copies of Bakin, or imitations of Tanehiko and Shunsui.[27] Our
present-day popular writers have made a mold called "morality"
(based on the concept of praise and blame) . . . which they
make the very basis of novels and romances. They eagerly try to
fit their plots into this mold. Because of the basically narrow
limitations of this mold, even when they are not deliberately
copying the old masters, they are actually constructing stories
with the same old plots without realizing it.[28]

The mold into which contemporary writers were forcing
their plots was the belief that the function of a novel was
to encourage virtue and chastise vice. This conception had
a long history in both China and Japan, but was most strongly
associated by Meiji critics with Bakin's novels and particularly
with his *Hakken den* [biography of eight dogs] (1814–41),
which relates the fantastic exploits of eight heroes, all of
whom have the same dog as an ancestor. Each of the eight
represents a cardinal virtue. As the praise-and-blame theory
was actually practiced, any plot, no matter how fantastic or
erotic, which demonstrated that good triumphed over evil
was acceptable. Although a great admirer of Bakin's works,
Tsubouchi strongly opposed this conception. Western novels,
he perceived, could enable Japanese to break this tradition
and introduce an entirely new spirit into their fiction. He
realized, however, that few translations made before 1885

27. Ryūtei Tanehiko (1783–1842) was a writer of popular fiction. Born in
Edo, he held a stipend from the shogunate and was better educated and
more sophisticated than many other novelists of the Tokugawa period. His
most famous work is *Nise Murasaki inaka Genji* [the false murasaki and the
country genji] (1829–42), which he left unfinished.

Tamenaga Shunsui (1790–1843) worked in a pawnshop, performed for
eighteen years in yose halls, and wrote or had his name attached to a great
quantity of a type of love story known as the *ninjōbon*. He made his reputation with *Shunshoku umegoyomi* [plum blossoms in early spring] (1832–33).
Tamenaga was especially talented at picturing the everyday life of Edo
townspeople and in depicting the romantic problems of its young people.

28. *Senshū, Bessatsu* II, 445–47.

in fact demonstrated the value of Western fiction to readers and novelists:

Quite a few translations of Western stories have been made recently but most have been by scholars working in their spare time and not by novelists; they are renditions of the plot and cannot be thought of as true novels. . . . They do not reflect the essential nature of Western novels. They are only translations of the surface matter, and I do not feel that they are adequate for an understanding of the Western novel form. Because of the inadequacy of our understanding of Western literature, out of the many new works and new publications there are perhaps not even a handful which are genuinely original. There is really not a single writer today who truly understands the meaning of a romance and can weave a tale.

Tsubouchi goes on to say that he offers this translation of *Rienzi* in the hope that it will give readers some better idea of Western fiction. People do not listen to theories, he believes, and a real example is a much more effective means of demonstrating his essential principle:

The novel is art; it is nothing other than a variety of poetry. The novel should be concerned with the emotions of men and the ways of the world. By emotions I mean passion and feeling. The seven emotions of man are joy, anger, grief, fear, love, hate, and desire. The talent of a true novelist lies in his ability to depict these emotions, to investigate them carefully—minutely, exhaustively, leaving little out—to make hypothetical, imaginary people move within the structure of his plot until we can see them as real people. Because the task of the novel is to reflect mankind, those which simply picture man's outer life should not be called novels. When they reach the point where they study the essence of mankind, then, for the first time, we will see a true novel.[29]

Between 1885 and 1890 Tsubouchi wrote and published nine original novels; of these he completed six and left three unfinished. They included domestic tragedies with complicated plots and political allegories dealing with such

29. *Ibid.*, pp. 447–50.

themes as the opening of the Diet and the revision of treaties with foreign powers.[30] Despite his great output, Tsubouchi seems to have found writing difficult; apparently he became increasingly convinced he would never be able to write the type of novel he prescribed.[31] In 1890 he abandoned writing fiction, leaving a novel entitled *Gaimu daijin* [the foreign minister] unfinished. From then on he devoted his attention to translations and to critical studies of literature and the theater. He also helped to compile several textbooks.

Tsubouchi's most famous novel is *Tōsei shosei katagi* [the character of present-day students], published in seventeen paperbound booklets between June 1885 and January 1886.[32] It is a loosely woven story of a group of university students and their various sweethearts. The novel, obviously drawn from Tsubouchi's own experiences, delighted contemporary young intellectuals by its lighthearted portrayal of the curious mixture of old-fashioned customs and new Western vogues which made up their world. It was one of the most discussed novels of its day.

Tōsei shosei katagi differed very markedly from the kind of novels Tsubouchi attacked in the introduction to *Gaiseishi den* or in *Shōsetsu shinzui*. There are no strong, death-defy-

30. *Kyō warambe* [child of the capital] (1886) satirizes the struggles of the Japanese people in their attempt to be represented in a Parliament against the opposition of the Satsuma and Chōshu han clique which dominated the ruling oligarchy. Tsubouchi describes his allegory in *Senshū, Bessatsu* I, 2.

Mirai no yume [dream of the future] (1886), which is subtitled *Naichi zakkyo* [mixed residence inside Japan] describes the Japan of the future when foreigners and Japanese live together in the same communities and when the Diet has already been opened. Tsubouchi describes it in its introduction, *Senshū, Bessatsu* I, 555. Tsubouchi lost interest in his imaginary world, however, and never finished the novel.

31. Tsubouchi's statements regarding the difficulties he experienced in writing novels in 1888 and 1889 are quoted in Kawatake and Yanagida, pp. 177–80. He was deeply troubled by the essential dishonesty that he felt existed in his writing novels for sale, and he vowed (in his diary for January 1889) never to write another for money. He was also very unhappy with his experiments in adopting various new literary styles.

32. Novels were frequently published in separate sections, an attempt (as Tsubouchi recalled) to discover whether or not they would sell. *Senshū, Bessatsu* I, 1.

ing heroes—in fact, it is somewhat difficult to decide who the hero is—and no supernatural events occur. It is one of the first Japanese novels in modern times to deal with members of the intellectual class and the first written by a man who prided himself on being something of a scholar.

This latter point caused considerable criticism when the novel was published.[33] Some readers were horrified at the idea of a university graduate writing a popular novel dealing in part with lower-class people (there are several geisha in the novel). Critics decried his use of vulgar language. In reply, Tsubouchi reminded his audience of Dickens and other great Western novelists whose faithful reproduction of the speech and mores of the common people had made them world famous. *Tōsei shosei katagi* was also attacked because it contained discussions of political matters; it was considered unsuitable to treat anything so serious as politics in a novel. It would be better, the critics maintained, if he had translated a Western political novel instead, and not attempted to mix intellectual problems in what was essentially a vulgar, popular Japanese novel. Tsubouchi obviously felt that all the events which took place in the life of an ordinary student were suitable material for his story and that the inclusion of as many aspects of the Tokyo world as possible would enhance the realistic atmosphere he was trying to produce.

Shōsetsu shinzui was published in nine paperbound booklets between September 1885 and April 1886. One part had appeared in a magazine as early as 1883, and several other sections were printed in various journals before the publication of the whole work in pamphlet form. Tsubouchi had hoped to have its printing coincide with the publication of *Tōsei shosei katagi,* but various difficulties within the publishing firm prevented this, and the novel reached the public

33. Uchida Roan recalled that his relatives were astonished to find that the author of *Tōsei shosei katagi* had a university degree. Novelists were thought of as lower class, while graduates of the university, still being so few in number, were highly respected. *Roan zuihitsu: shien no hitobito,* pp. 2–3.

several months before the essay.[34] The two works were designed to complement each other; *Tōsei shosei katagi* was to be the realistic novel which demonstrated the main points set forth in *Shōsetsu shinzui*.

Shōsetsu Shinzui

The basic theme underlying all the arguments presented in *Shōsetsu shinzui* had already been stated by Tsubouchi in the introduction to *Gaiseishi den;* the novel is a form of pure art and requires no justification other than its mere existence. Whatever the reader may learn from the novel, whatever moral or spiritual betterment may accrue from it, is incidental to its ultimate value as a work of art.

Tsubouchi begins by describing the arts:

All art does not fall into one category. We might divide the various arts into two: visual arts and abstract arts. . . . Although they are alike in being designed to delight the eye or gladden the heart, some forms of art appeal mainly to the heart and others to the ear or the eye. Material arts primarily appeal to the eye through form, but music and song appeal to the ear, and poetry, theatrical narration, and novels appeal to the heart. [p. 28]

He rejects the notion, however, that the aim of art is to elevate man's spirit through the joy it produces. It has been suggested, he says, that

after art has gladdened the heart and eye of man, he will enter a wondrous domain; this is supposed to be the aim of art. According to this argument, in entering this domain, the observer will unconsciously be affected; he will forget his miserable desires, cast off his shallow emotions, and rejoice in other, purer and nobler thoughts. This may very well happen, but it is a natural reaction and should not be called the aim of art. It is an ac-

34. Kawatake and Yanagida, pp. 136–45.

cidental result and it is difficult to speak of it as the basic aim of art. [p. 27]

After tracing some of the many forms of poetry which have evolved in the West, Tsubouchi concludes that poetry in the Western sense is much closer to the novel in Japan than it is to Japanese *waka* or *haiku*. The Japanese poetic forms he finds too restrictive for modern life, and he does not see them on the same level as Western poetry, which can tell a complete story, describe the whole range of human emotions, and picture man's physical surroundings in great detail. He reminds his reader that he was not the first in Japan to feel the inadequacy of the traditional Japanese poetic forms; since the publication of a collection of poems in the Western manner, *Shintaishi shō* [selections of new style poetry] (1882), the Japanese public had been made increasingly aware of the potentialities of Western verse form.

A novel can be called an unrhymed poem or a waka of an unrestricted number of syllables. . . . It would not only be possible to call the novel a poem and stand it on the high pedestal of art, it would be perfectly appropriate. The aim of the novel lies in man's emotions and in the world around him. Stitching with threads of originality, it skillfully weaves a fabric of all human emotions. Beautifully, it creates a fabric made of unrestricted, unlimited, hidden, wondrous, mysterious causes and an endless variety of effects. It portrays the secrets of destiny. It is the duty of the novel to make visible that which is hard to see. The perfect novel depicts what is difficult to paint in a painting; makes palpable what is difficult to express in a poem; portrays the mysterious which is impossible to project on the stage. [pp. 31–32]

Tsubouchi traces the development of fiction from its origins in mythology, through fables and allegories, and finally describes the emergence of the novel. A parallel development is shown for the theater. He observes that religion has been associated with literary forms at various stages in their development in both the East and West. In the discussion of the allegory he attempts to establish a distinction between the way praise and blame are used in allegories and in didactic novels:

The allegory has as its central theme praise and blame, and uses a story as an expedient for expressing that theme. On the other hand, the didactic novel is basically a story; the morality is only a decoration. Therefore no matter how illogical the plot of any allegory may be or how preposterous its story, we do not condemn it if it is a good allegory. But if a didactic novel has an outrageous plot as its basic story, we certainly cannot call it a well-wrought novel even if it is permeated with morality. Our didactic novelists in the East do not understand this distinction; they make punishing vice and praising virtue the focal point and basic rule of the novel, and carelessly portray essential human emotions! [pp. 45–46]

In the discussion of theatrical forms, Tsubouchi finds the novel superior to the theater by nature of its very abstractness. This is an interesting conclusion in itself, in that it demonstrates how earnestly the author was trying to prove the artistic merit of the novel. It is also of particular interest in light of Tsubouchi's subsequent lifelong devotion to the theater.

The domain of the novel is broader than that of the theater. It portrays conditions great and small throughout all times to perfection. In portraying man's life, the theater appeals to the ear or eye of the audience, and its domain is narrow. The novel, on the other hand, appeals to the reader's heart and stimulates his imagination, and its domain is very broad. In the theater, mountain, water, grass, trees, the landscape near and far, the quality of a house, and its equipment are shown on the stage. Lightning, wind, and rain are presented to the eye and ear of the audience by means of stage properties. In a novel all these things are made into beautiful words and appeal to the mind's eye. There are, of course, differences in the degree of pleasure achieved, depending on the sensitivity of the reader's imagination. Some go beyond the words themselves; some stop with what is written for them. [p. 54]

In the section entitled "Shōsetsu no shugan" [the primary

objective of the novel] Tsubouchi repeats his belief that the main goal of the novel is to portray human emotions; to picture life and customs is its second task. It is difficult enough to recount the surface events of life, but to probe deeper and uncover man's inner thoughts is far more difficult. And yet "the novel which pictures only the outer surface cannot be called a true novel. With the story which penetrates to the very core, we see a novel for the first time." [p. 60] Tsubouchi then speaks again of the tradition of didactic novels which violate this principle. He cites as an example Bakin's *Hakken den:*

The eight men in Bakin's masterpiece, *Hakken den,* are personifications of virtues—they cannot be called human beings. The author's intention from the very outset is to construct a novel transforming the abstract virtues into men, and he persistently portrays the virtues of these eight men with the greatest thoroughness. When one describes *Hakken den* from the point of view of a didactic novel, it is a tale without peer in the East or West, but if one accepts the portrayal of man's emotions as the basic rule for a novel, it is difficult to speak of it as a flawless jewel. . . . These eight creatures are Bakin's ideal men; they are not pictures of actual human beings—therein lies the flaw. [pp. 60–61]

If the aim of a novel is to picture life, what is the difference between it and a historical record?

If you look at the surface, there is not the slightest difference between a novel and a history. But the hero of a novel is not a historical person; he is only an invention devised in accordance with the author's plan. Once the author has presented him in the world of the novel, he cannot make him move as he, the author, wishes. He must think of him as a real person and portray his life as it would naturally progress. [p. 63]

Throughout *Shōsetsu shinzui* Tsubouchi either quotes directly from or makes reference to critics and novelists of both the East and West to support his thesis. In discussing the function of the novel to portray real life, Tsubouchi quotes at some length from the great classicist Motoori Norinaga

(1730–1801). Motoori states that, although *Genji monogatari* often appears to be greatly concerned with Buddhism or Confucianism, that is not its main purpose. Its essential purpose, and the essential purpose of many ancient Japanese stories, is to picture the world.

"The tale is a form which describes things existing in the world and the ways of man's emotions. When it is read, one can easily see the state of the world, and one can understand well man's doings and the manifestations of his emotions. To obtain this understanding is, I feel, the reason men read novels." [p. 69][35]

In the section "Shōsetsu no shurui" [types of novels] Tsubouchi distinguishes two main categories under which various types of novels fall: didactic and artistic. Didactic novels are subdivided into those which demonstrate the glory of virtuous behavior and promote respect for goodness and those which warn the reader of the dangers of evil by describing the wicked and immoral.

The artistic novel is of a completely different nature from the didactic novel. Its aim is solely to picture the state of the world. In constructing characters and in building the plot, it makes manifest this aim. It simply brings to life these imaginary characters in their unreal world. In doing so, it attempts to approach the truth. [p. 72]

The reader will learn from the artistic novel, not because the author has set down a lesson for him but because he will see life objectively. The realistic novel is of itself a natural criticism of the world. It offers a mirror of life in which the reader can see the wise and the foolish.

In "Shōsetsu no hieki" [the advantages of the novel] Tsu-

35. Tsubouchi quoted from Motoori's *Genji monogatari tama no ogushi, Motoori Norinaga zenshū* (rev. ed., 1927), VII, 493. The importance of Motoori's thesis in influencing Tsubouchi is demonstrated by further examples in Homma Hisao's *Tsubouchi Shōyō*, pp. 67–79. Homma does not deny the great influence of English literary theory on Tsubouchi but feels that the idea of divesting fiction of its current moral trappings and returning to stories which convey the true nature of a time and place owes a good deal to Motoori.

bouchi elaborates on his earlier idea that the novel is designed only to bring pleasure to the reader.

The novel is art; it is not something to be used for practical purposes. An attempt to make the novel the means of bestowing practical benefits would be a distortion of its purpose. Just as music or painting contain beneficial aspects, though they are not immediately apparent, so the novel too offers practical benefits which its author never planned. An artist seeks only to give his reader an awareness of beauty and gladden his heart; there is nothing else for him to desire. As I have already mentioned, those artistic products which have extraordinary beauty and have attained perfection greatly move the heart of man. They elevate his soul in mysterious ways and add to his store of knowledge, but this is a result naturally born; it is not the aim of art. To call it the direct advantage of art is a grave error. [p. 76]

Tsubouchi goes on to cite four advantages that the perceptive reader will gain from novels, reiterating that such advantages are to be considered not the primary goal of fiction but merely an auxiliary result. The novel, he says, can ennoble a man's character through the observation of the beautiful. The comprehension or absorption of a sense of pure beauty will enable a man to escape his baser emotions and learn what heights a human being is capable of. In searching for an example of fiction which is true art, Tsubouchi finds few in Japanese literature. He compares the level of Japanese fiction to the *ukiyoe*. Just as a woodblock print is not a great painting, so Japanese novels are not mature, fully realized works of art.

The second advantage to be gained from fiction is learning to evaluate good and evil. Here Tsubouchi emphasizes again that this is not the central theme of fiction, and the Eastern novelists who think it is are mistaken. A novel should never be used for teaching women and children, as was the practice in Japan. It is a sophisticated art form for adults. The author cannot be condemned for presenting reality on the grounds that he will corrupt the young and innocent; he is concerned with the truth. In this very truth there is a teaching, but its scope is broader than that of traditional morality.

Although this teaching is outside the limitations of traditional morality, it instructs us and improves our inner and outer life. Therefore we call it teaching. For example, to teach men proper manners, to sharpen their wit, to make them understand what human emotions are, to inform them of the boundlessness of desire are all varieties of teaching. When novel readers realize the existence of these teachings and grasp their truth, they will realize the true benefits of the novel for the first time and savor the fruits of joy as well. [p. 88]

The third benefit of the novel lies in telling the reader of the life and customs of people in his own or in other times. Referring to Walter Scott's explanation of the historical novel, Tsubouchi describes how a good novel can bring the past to life more vividly than a history book. Even a contemporary novel becomes, as time passes, an historical novel, and through such a work as *Genji monogatari* the reader can learn of past centuries. And finally, Tsubouchi sees the novel as a device for teaching literary style. *Genji monogatari* or the *Shui hu chuan*[36] can demonstrate to the reader the vast range of expression available to the great writer.

The first part of *Shōsetsu shinzui* approaches its conclusion with an appeal for the revitalization of Japanese fiction which conveys the evangelical qualities present throughout the book:

If the novel actually has all the advantages we have mentioned, then we would be greatly remiss in our duty if we did not gradually reform and perfect our immature Japanese novels. We should make them fully realized creations, as they are in the West, until the novel in Japan becomes one of the great arts of our nation. [p. 95]

36. A Chinese novel set in the province of Shantung in the early twelfth century. Written in purely colloquial language, the novel deals with the exploits of a band of robbers. The version now in use was edited in the early seventeenth century. It has been translated by Pearl Buck under the title *All Men Are Brothers* (1937).

The second part deals more specifically with the techniques of novel writing and less with general theory. The underlying assumption for all the techniques recommended is that the author of a novel is seeking to mirror real life and to invest his imaginary figures with a dynamism which will bring them to life in their fantasy world. The kind of novel which Tsubouchi recommends was not being written in Japan in his time, and he felt that close examination of various possible modes of expression was essential.

One of the longest sections of *Shōsetsu shinzui* is entitled "Buntai ron" [essay on style]. The problem is set forth tersely:

Words are the tools of thoughts; they are also their decoration. They cannot be neglected in composing a novel. No matter how skillful the plot, the novel will not be successful if the style is poor. If the language is not expressive, the description will not be effective. In China and in the West, the written and spoken languages are, for the most part, the same, and there is no particular necessity to choose either as a literary form. In our country, however, the situation is different. There are several literary styles. Each has its flaws and its merits, its advantages and disadvantages, and they vary according to where they are used. This is why we must select a literary style for the novel. [p. 101]

Tsubouchi distinguishes three main styles which have been used in the long history of the Japanese novel: *gabuntai* [rhetorical], *zokubuntai* [colloquial], and *gazoku setchū buntai,* which combines the first two. It is the last of these that he recommends for the modern novel.

Gabuntai, the traditional Japanese style which had its greatest exponent in Murasaki Shikibu, he finds graceful, flowing, and delicate, but too soft and feminine to serve as an instrument for the expression of modern life. It lacks, he feels, directness and vitality and is in general too reminiscent of the ancient world of the nobility. Paradoxically, it is also used as an instrument of satire, notably by Shikitei Samba in his most famous story, *Ukiyoburo* [the bath of the floating world] (1809–13). The dialogue in this satirical commentary on a day in a public bath in Edo represents an early example of the use in a work of fiction of the language actually spoken by the common Japanese people, but Tsubouchi refers here not to the dialogue but to Samba's narrative. He cites an example of Samba's deliberate use of gabuntai to heighten the sarcasm of his text, otherwise famed for its cynical view of the city people of his time. The possibility of implied sarcasm added to the general softness and lack of force inherent in gabuntai leads Tsubouchi to question its validity for modern fiction.

Tsubouchi defines zokubuntai as composition in the colloquial language. It is easy to understand, and this he sees as its greatest advantage. In the West and in China, Tsubouchi feels, such a style has been used with excellent results. The rhythm and delicacy of the words blend smoothly with the sentiments expressed and reveal the deepest feelings with surprising accuracy. In Japan, however, a great discrepancy exists between literary words and words in common use, and Tsubouchi cannot conceive of a smooth style which resorts entirely to the vocabulary of the spoken language.

Tsubouchi's doubts extended far beyond the question of the appropriate vocabulary for modern novels. Before the Meiji period and for at least a decade after it began, most intellectuals wrote either in Chinese or in kambun-chō. Children of the upper classes were trained to read the Chinese classics, Chinese history, and Chinese philosophy, and to write Chinese prose and poetry. In the schoolroom teachers lectured on the meaning of the Chinese classics. Books on Japanese history were also often written in Chinese, and Japanese philosophers frequently wrote in Chinese rather than Japanese. As a result, the vocabulary of the Chinese classics and Chinese history was a standard part of the written vocabulary of the upper classes. Literacy was very widespread in premodern Japan,[37] but children of the lower classes usually did not receive a thorough training in Chinese and their

37. The high rate of literacy in premodern Japan is discussed by Herbert Passin in *Education and Society in Japan.*

command of this vocabulary was generally inadequate to read serious works. Popular novels were composed in a vocabulary drawn largely from speech, but to intellectuals this style seemed crude and vulgar.

By the 1860s intellectuals with liberal tendencies began to feel the need for educating the entire population equally. If all the people were to participate in the government and to work for the advancement of their country, it was essential that they be informed of political, social, and economic problems. Newspapers, textbooks, and magazines which explained technical advances in the West, Western history, or the parliamentary system, for instance, had to be written in a language everyone could understand. Chinese or kambun-chō would obviously not be as effective as a style which derived from colloquial vocabulary and colloquial syntax.

Many solutions were offered, some of them too extreme to be practicable. In 1867 Maejima Hisoka (1835–1919) presented a memorial to the emperor suggesting the elimination of Chinese characters in writing Japanese and proposing instead the exclusive use of the Japanese phonetic syllabary, hiragana or kana.[38] Adherents of this proposal published a kana newspaper in 1872–73 and a few scattered articles and books in the 1870s. In 1883 a society for the advancement of this theory was formed. Another extreme view was offered by those who suggested the elimination of both characters and kana and the exclusive use of Roman letters (*rōmaji*) to write the Japanese language. Articles advocating the adoption of rōmaji, an idea which had been advanced even in the Tokugawa period, began to appear sporadically from 1874 on, and its adherents formed a society in 1885.[39] Mori

38. Quoted in *Meiji bunka zenshū*, ed. Yoshino Sakuzō, XII, 5. In addition to working for years for reform of the written language, Maejima was the founder of Japan's modern postal system and contributed to the development of the telegraph system. He was a member of the Kaishin-tō and held many public offices throughout his life. He also taught at Semmon Gakkō. He had been a student of Yoshida Shōin.

39. For a description of these movements, see *Meiji bunka zenshū*, XII, 4– 12. Documents pertaining to the "Kana Kai" and the "Rōmaji Kai" are re-

Arinori, when he was chargé d'affaires in Washington in 1873, decided that Japanese was too weak a language for a modern country and that it should be abandoned in favor of English.[40]

In contrast to these extremes, educators like Fukuzawa Yukichi (1834–1901) proposed simply that writers should maintain the existing forms but modify vocabulary and syntax to make the written language intelligible to all classes of society.[41] In textbooks and newspapers the more moderate approach prevailed, and by the late 1870s articles and books written in relatively straightforward prose closely approximat-

printed on pp. 57–128. The basic argument of both groups was that characters were too difficult to read. Books almost exclusively in kana had been written for centuries before, and popular stories were frequently written with almost no characters, but intellectuals used a vast number of characters in their writing and were unable to accept the idea that Japanese could be written without them. The main argument used against the kana and rōmaji theories was that the large number of homophones in Japanese (largely due to the loan words from Chinese) made the language incomprehensible without characters.

40. In 1872 Mori addressed a series of letters to American educators asking for their advice on ways to modernize Japan. The letters were subsequently published under the title *Education in Japan: A Series of Letters.* One of the problems he discusses in his lengthy introduction to the book is that of the written Japanese language. He describes the way Chinese is used, adding that "without the aid of the Chinese, our language has never been taught or used for any purpose of communication. This shows its poverty. The march of modern civilization in Japan has already reached the heart of the nation—the English language following it suppresses the use of both Japanese and Chinese. The commercial power of the English-speaking race which now rules the world drives our people into some knowledge of their commercial ways and habits. The absolute necessity of mastering the English language is thus forced upon us. It is a requisite of the maintenance of our independence in the community of nations. Under the circumstances, our meagre language, which can never be of any use outside of our islands, is doomed to yield to the domination of the English tongue, especially when the power of steam and electricity shall have pervaded the land. Our intelligent race, eager in the pursuit of knowledge, cannot depend upon a weak and uncertain medium of communication in its endeavor to grasp the principal truths from the precious treasury of Western science and art and religion. The laws of the state can never be preserved in the language of Japan. All reasons suggest its disuse." p. lvi.

41. Blacker, p. 8.

ing the spoken language began to appear in ever-increasing number. In most discussions of language reform or modification, there is reference to the fact that in Western countries speech and writing are one and that Japan will never be able to take its place among the advanced nations of the world until her written and spoken languages are merged.

Novelists became concerned with this problem much after educators, political figures, and journalists had begun to grapple with it. By 1882 poets had begun introducing colloquial vocabulary into their work, largely stimulated by a desire to translate and adopt poetic forms used in the West.[42] *Shintaishi shō* heralded this trend. But until about 1885 novelists remained content to use either the kambun-chō or the Bakin-chō, even when they were translating from Western literature or were writing about Western subjects.[43] From then on, however, they became deeply engrossed in the question. Tsubouchi's presentation of the problem in *Shōsetsu shinzui* and in subsequent articles was a major factor in arousing widespread interest in revision of the literary language used in novels.

Lacking a satisfactory narrative style, novelists turned naturally to the spoken language for material. Here again they were faced with problems peculiar to Japanese. To begin with, as Tsubouchi points out in his "Buntai ron," there was no universally accepted standard language. There were a great many dialects in existence; none had been fully accepted, although a variety of upper-class Tokyo speech was already coming to be considered standard. By using examples from contemporary Tokyo speech, Tsubouchi demonstrates the difficulties inherent in adopting the spoken language for narrative. Different forms of verbs, different words, and a different grammatical structure were used by the members of

42. For a discussion of the new verse forms and the language used in the new poems see Sansom, pp. 404–8; and Keene, *Modern Japanese Poetry*, pp. 10–17.

43. Tsubouchi attributed this to the overwhelming prestige of the classical literary forms. "Futabatei no koto," pp. 13–16.

the several classes of society. Furthermore, the structure of the speech varied depending upon whom the speaker was addressing. He used one kind of diction to his social superiors and another kind to his inferiors. He also used different language when speaking to a person than when speaking about him.

Tsubouchi considers the difficulties in making an arbitrary choice among all the possibilities insurmountable and rejects the colloquial language as a suitable medium for the narrative portions of a novel. He feels that the dialogue in a novel, however, should be written in a style closely resembling the speech of the class to which each character belongs. This will enhance the realism and enable the novelist to inject greater vitality into the novel. Tsubouchi reminds his reader again of the novels of Tamenaga Shunsui where the colloquial dialogue was used so successfully. At the close of his discussion of zokubuntai Tsubouchi expressed his hope that a suitable colloquial narrative style will one day be developed in Japan, for he recognizes that without it the novel will never attain the artistic level he seeks.

Tsubouchi's solution, which he admits is only a temporary measure, is to use a mixture of gabuntai and zokubuntai. Zokubuntai is to be used for dialogue, and gabuntai for the descriptive background narrative.

The final sections of *Shōsetsu shinzui* deal with plots, the historical novel, the hero, and the use of narrative. The plot of a novel, Tsubouchi demonstrates, must be well planned, consistent, and unified. He briefly explains the classical Western definition of tragedy and comedy and notes the absence of tragedy in contemporary Japanese literature. The novels of Bakin he would classify as tragicomedies. Most of the other books written in his century, he finds, are comedies whose primary aim is to appeal to the most vulgar tastes of the reader. He decries the use of obscene jokes to fill the pages of a novel when the author's imagination is inadequate to decent humor. He cites *Hizakurige* [a journey on foot]

(1802–22) as an example of a story in which the author will go to any lengths to make his reader laugh.[44]

Art, Tsubouchi believes, is not intended to cater to the tastes of one small segment of the reading public for a short span of time; it must have more universal appeal. The construction of a strong plot and the investigation of man's real condition and emotions will result in contemporary novels which are truly art. Tsubouchi finds no essential difference between the novels of Bulwer-Lytton and Japanese romances. Both are tales of love and adventure, but even in such a romantic story as *Ernest Maltravers,* Bulwer-Lytton never stoops to the vulgar and does not use obscenities. The most important rules for the composition of comedy or tragedy, he finds, are for the author to be objective; to use psychologically accurate characterizations; to resist a desire to shock, titillate, or terrify; and to build his plot rationally from beginning to end.

The discussion of the historical novel is a continuation of the preceding section. In it, Tsubouchi defines the historical novel as going beyond the limitations of straight history. The greatest difference between the two is that the historical novel, as exemplified by the works of Scott, fills out the historical record, amplifies the characterization, investigates psychological motivation, and brings vitality to the events of the past. The most obvious dangers, he finds, are discrepancies in the chronology, deviations from the actual events, and anachronisms.

Tsubouchi defines the hero and demonstrates his significance in the novel. The hero, as the central figure in the plot, must be portrayed with consistency and psychological accuracy. The writer should be objective and avoid identifying too strongly with the hero. Tsubouchi describes two types: the real, as exemplified by Genji and Tanjirō in

44. *Hizakurige* is a humorous account of a trip taken by two men from Edo to Kyoto. It was written by Jippensha Ikku (1764–1831). The loosely constructed plot tells of their various adventures at teahouses and inns along the way. It has been translated by Thomas Satchell under the title *Shank's Mare* (new ed., Tokyo, 1960).

Tamenaga Shunsui's *Umegoyomi;* and the ideal, as found in Bakin's *Hakken den.* It is easier, he realizes, to embark on the construction of a real hero than an ideal one, for the author has only to work from his own experience. The difficulties arise later. Because he is trying to reproduce human emotions as they really are, it is essential that his portrayal be total. Unlike the writer of ideal novels, the realist has no convenient moral pattern within which to construct his characterization.

The final pages of *Shōsetsu shinzui* are devoted to a brief discussion of the narrative portions of a novel. While descriptive narrative is necessary, particularly to historical novels, Tsubouchi cautions against long passages which will bore the reader. He favors Scott's method of inserting a few lines of historical description and allowing the remainder to be revealed in the course of the story. He decries the common Japanese practice of ignoring descriptive elements entirely and depending on illustrations to show how people are dressed and what the scene looks like.

In both contemporary and historical novels, the accurate description of objects is an essential part of the novelist's art. Tsubouchi also discusses the two methods of describing personality in a novel. The author may allow the events in a novel to reveal the nature and personality of the characters, or he may write his own description of their personalities. The former method was the most commonly used in Japan; the latter was practiced very successfully in the West. Here Tsubouchi cites Bulwer-Lytton's description of Nina di Raselli in *Rienzi* (Chapter XI of the original) as an example of the method of revealing personality through direct description. Tsubouchi recommends a mixture of both methods for the most thorough presentation.

In *Shōsetsu shinzui,* Tsubouchi has applied the methods of Western criticism to Japanese literature. He began to prepare his material while still a student at the university, reading various English literary journals at the library and studying the fiction of the West for purposes of comparison. The Western critical essays he read included Scott's "Essay on Romance" (1824); an article entitled "Rhetoric and Belles Lettres" which appeared in the encyclopedia *Chambers's Information for the People;*[45] and Ernest Fenollosa's "Bijutsu shinsetsu [the true meaning of art] (1882).[46] Tsubouchi did not model his essay on any specific Western work but rather used the general method of systematic analysis then prevalent in Western criticism. He also studied Japanese literary criticism and in his essay referred directly to works which would help to demonstrate that his views were not at variance with previously accepted Japanese theory. He quotes at some length, as we have seen, from Motoori Norinaga's commentary *Genji monogatari tama no ogushi* (1796). He also includes a discussion by Bakin on the requisites for the successful construction of a plot.[47] Tsubouchi does not accept the opinions of other writers, Japanese or Western, uncritically. He specifically objects, for instance, to Fenollosa's statement that the main object of art is to enable man to enter a purer, nobler state.[48] Tsubouchi considered this a natural result of the power of art, as we have seen, but he could not accept it as a goal or ultimate objective of art.

Tsubouchi was not blind to the flaws in either Western or Japanese fiction and was critical of the sort of work he himself was doing. He wrote didactic political allegories,

45. A two-volume encyclopedia edited by William and Robert Chambers and first published in 1849. Revised editions appeared in 1858 and 1859, but the article on rhetoric remained virtually unaltered in the various editions. The article was translated into Japanese and published by the Ministry of Education in 1879 under the title *Shūji oyobi kabun.* The ministry subsequently published a complete translation of *Information for the People,* including this article, in 1884–85. *Meiji bunka zenshū,* XII, 2–3; 4–38.

46. A series of lectures on fine art delivered in 1882 and later published in Japanese. The theories advanced by Fenollosa in these lectures are based on Hegelian philosophy. *Ibid.,* XII, 11; 157–73.

47. There were seven basic qualities Bakin believed every good novel should have. They are discussed by Zolbrod, p. 262. Tsubouchi quotes Bakin's views in *Shōsetsu shinzui,* pp. 138–39.

48. *Ibid.,* pp. 25–27; Fenollosa, "Bijutsu shinsetsu," p. 160.

and yet his essay argues against didactic literature. He admired Bakin more than any other Japanese novelist with the exception of Murasaki Shikibu, but he did not hesitate to state his preference for realistic fiction over the fantasies of Bakin. While he made translations of Western fiction which deviated greatly from the original text, he argued for accurate translations in his introduction to *Gaiseishi den.*

Tsubouchi wanted to see Japanese fiction purged of its weaknesses, and his comparisons with Western fiction were made to show that his nation's literature could be improved by moderate reforms. In discussing the novel, he refers to works he had translated, like *Rienzi,* or to those which had been translated by others, thereby making it possible for his readers to better understand his arguments. In citing examples from Western fiction, however, he does not advocate the total acceptance of the methods of the West accompanied by a rejection of Japanese techniques. Instead, he pleads for the development of a conscious theory of what the novel should contain and how it should be written, in contrast to the comparatively unintellectual approach employed by his contemporaries. His insistence that the praise-and-blame theory should be abandoned was offered on both philosophic and practical grounds. Philosophically, Tsubouchi did not believe that a novel should be used to teach anything, and, practically speaking, he saw that this moralistic formula was being adopted simply as a crutch and was, in fact, destroying any possibility for the construction of a successful novel. Tsubouchi suggests instead that novelists should concentrate their energies on writing stories with stronger characterization by the use of a more penetrating analysis of human nature; fully developed plots which would be within the range of possible human experience; and a contemporary literary style.

In the long history of Japanese literature, there had been no analysis of the novel form which could compare with the detailed discussion in *Shōsetsu shinzui.* Tsubouchi's methodology owes a great deal to Western models; the definition of art, the historical review of the origin and development of fiction, and the subdivision of fiction into various categories are all techniques familiar to nineteenth-century European criticism. The significance of the work lies in the application of these techniques to the problems of the Japanese novelist and in Tsubouchi's recommendations for the reform of Japanese fiction.

Tsubouchi could not write the novel he described in his essay. *Tōsei shosei katagi* was to demonstrate the value of realism, but the characterization in the novel is weak and shows little psychological penetration. The plot is rambling and undeveloped, and the characters fail to come to life. The story contains several instances of painfully contrived coincidences, and the life history of one of the leading characters, a modest, self-sacrificing geisha, is so complicated as to be singularly unsuitable to a realistic novel. In the dialogue, Tsubouchi's style is quite vivid; it is highly colloquial and authentic. The narrative portions of the novel are considerably less successful. Here the style is very uneven, and it is obvious that Tsubouchi was struggling to develop a method which would be modern but at the same time aesthetically pleasing. Many passages are in gabuntai, and in some cases the rhythm is graceful. Other passages are heavily weighted with Chinese loan words and almost approach kambun-chō. These portions seem more appropriate to expository writing in an essay than to a novel. In all, the narrative lacks the force and vitality Tsubouchi himself considered requisite to a modern novel.

In many ways, Futabatei's *Ukigumo* is the novel Tsubouchi was suggesting in *Shōsetsu shinzui*. It is a realistic contemporary story centering on the study of man's inner self. The dialogue reveals the personality of the characters and their actions in the novel are consistent with their personality. There is a bare minimum of background description, but it is adequate to give the flavor of the setting. The characters are described with the moderation Tsubouchi recommended. In place of writing protracted descriptions,

Futabatei lets the characters speak for themselves, and through their words we learn of their nature. Futabatei was not satisfied with Tsubouchi's solution for a narrative style. His dialogue is in the colloquial, as Tsubouchi prescribed, but he was not able to adopt the gabuntai for his narrative and chose instead to work toward the new style Tsubouchi had hoped for. Tsubouchi's theories were given life in Futabatei's work rather than in his own.

Futabatei and Tsubouchi

By the time he met Tsubouchi in January 1886, Futabatei had already studied the works of Belinsky and other Russian critics and had read widely in Russian fiction. He admired Turgenev, Dostoevsky, and Goncharov and fully recognized the value of realism, but he did not know how to apply his ideas to a work of fiction. His theories were still in the formative stage, and he needed someone to consult with who could help him organize his ideas. He found this person in Tsubouchi. The other students at Gaigo Gakkō were younger and less sophisticated than Futabatei. Tsubouchi was an older and far more experienced man. By 1886, he had translated Scott's *Bride of Lammermoor* and *Lady of the Lake,* Bulwer-Lytton's *Rienzi,* and Shakespeare's *Julius Caesar;* written over a dozen political allegories and two novels; and taught for five years. Because of Tsubouchi's advice and guidance, Futabatei rapidly changed from a thoughtful, intelligent schoolboy into a skillful novelist and brilliant translator. Their friendship was one of the most important elements in Futabatei's development as an artist.

In his diary for 1886 Tsubouchi kept a brief record of Futabatei's visits. The entries are terse, and yet we can gather from them something of the nature of the men's discussions. The first entry is dated January 25, 1886: "Hasegawa Tatsunosuke came. We talked of art at length." Again, on March 7, "Hasegawa came and we discussed art. The tenor of the discussion was: the aim of art is to reveal truth. In Heaven's creations there is nothing which is not beautiful. However, ugliness is the opposite of beauty. If everything that exists is beautiful, what is ugliness?" And on March 17, "Hasegawa came tonight. We discussed art and the novel at length, and also the writing style used in novels." [49]

Futabatei dominated these discussions. He was fired with enthusiasm for the Hegelian interpretation of art he had learned in Gaigo Gakkō and tried to convince Tsubouchi of its vitality. The fervor he had once exhibited for political justice had been transferred to literature, and Tsubouchi was amazed at the earnestness with which he maintained his views. Although he had been writing about literary theory for several years and had formed close associations with leading figures in the literary and intellectual world, Tsubouchi had never met anyone like Futabatei before. In his biography Tsubouchi recalled his first impressions of Futabatei. He felt that Futabatei's belief in humanism had its origins in Gray's lectures at Gaigo Gakkō:

. . . Futabatei was deeply affected by Russian literature of the 1840s which, having as its watchword service to humanity, directly or indirectly advocated freedom for the people and liberation of the serfs, and which contributed to the acceleration of those movements. However, we cannot deny that Futabatei had it in his very nature to become a leading figure in his time, for of all the students at Gaigo Gakkō, he was the only one who achieved so much. While the other students simply listened passively to Gray's lectures, Futabatei apparently engaged in independent study and read as many novels and works on literary theory as he could.

When I first met him in January of 1886, he was perhaps our leading authority on Russian literature. Among critics, he favored Belinsky, and among authors, he was fond of Pushkin, Lermontov, Gogol, Turgenev, and Goncharov. Of these, he

49. Tsubouchi quotes from his diary and explains the meaning of the entries in "Futabatei Shimei," *Senshū*, XII, 509–10. This article was originally written in 1909.

esteemed Turgenev and Goncharov most highly. . . . His very personality was markedly influenced by Russian literature.

I myself was quite inexperienced at the time. I had been made to read the standard classics at the university, but my own favorites were primarily from English nineteenth-century fiction. I was just beginning to read the great popular writers from Scott, Lytton, and Dickens to Dumas and Marryat. When I encountered Futabatei, I heard completely new literary theories and saw a completely new type of personality.

He was extraordinarily pensive (what psychoanalysts would call introverted). He was scrupulous, unsparing, and critical of everything and would never decide an issue easily. He was generally argumentative and cautious to the point of being irritating, yet there was a strange kind of charm in his stubbornness. (This charm is what they call the demoniac influence. On meeting Futabatei, everyone was affected by it.) I had never dreamed that there might be someone like him among us, and I was more amazed at his unusual personality than at his arguments.[50]

Tsubouchi was fascinated by this young man with his questioning mind and welcomed his visits. At first their discussions were mainly about literature, and particularly they talked about Tsubouchi's work. On one early visit, Futabatei brought a copy of a section of *Shōsetsu shinzui*.[51] He was determined to learn more about Tsubouchi's views than could be discovered merely by reading the essay. Tsubouchi recalls:

His attitude was humble and searching, rather than critical. "On what basis did you reach this conclusion?" "From what you say here, could you also say that—?" he asked. But as you know, what I wrote was very superficial and if you probe into my ideas a bit, they have no depth. I realized the superficiality of my own

50. "Futabatei no koto," pp. 55–56.
51. "Futabatei Shimei," p. 512. Tsubouchi here corrects a previously published statement that Futabatei had brought *Shōsetsu shinzui* on his first visit. Uchida Roan, however, repeats the error and adds that Futabatei had pasted a sheet of paper on the back of the book on which he had written various questions. "Futabatei no isshō," pp. 355–56. Uchida's version is frequently quoted in articles about Futabatei.

thoughts for the first time while I was talking to him. After that, I made an effort to listen carefully to what he said.[52]

As the years passed, their talks encompassed the whole range of intellectual problems, from literary theory to human psychology.

I called on Futabatei only once or twice at most, but he came to my house at least once every ten days until 1889 or 1890. At first our discussions dealt primarily with literature; we argued about and criticized the contents and forms of art. About the time *Ukigumo* was published, we became much closer and the tone of our talks changed. Even when we spoke of literature, our conversations centered on matters relating to human problems. We turned from the criticism of characters in novels to the criticism of real people living and dead. Our discussions of the ideal nature of writers and individuals ended in an analysis of each other's own personality.[53]

Many other young novelists visited Tsubouchi's house in those years, and Futabatei came in contact with professional writers for the first time. He heard their arguments, joined in their discussions, and learned how the literary world operated. At the time, Tsubouchi not only taught more than thirty-six hours a week but also wrote and translated a steady stream of books. Sunday was his day of rest, and on that day he opened his house to literary friends. They came early in the morning, ate and drank, and talked the day away. Among the most frequent visitors were Saitō Ryokuu (1867–1904), a rising journalist and writer of popular satirical novels, and Aeba Kōson (1855–1922), a novelist and writer for the *Yomiuri shimbun,* the newspaper in which Tsubouchi had been publishing articles. Aeba Kōson and Tsubouchi, who were to remain friends throughout their lives, became engrossed in the movement to revitalize traditional Japanese theatrical forms and were involved in various undertakings together. Aeba was quite a heavy drinker,

52. "Futabatei Shimei," p. 512.
53. Tsubouchi, "Futabatei no koto," p. 58.

and when he appeared, the Sunday gatherings were apt to be even livelier and of longer duration than usual. He and Saitō brought news and gossip of the latest happenings in literary circles, enabling Tsubouchi to keep informed despite his heavy teaching schedule.[54]

In May 1886 Futabatei introduced Tsubouchi to a friend from Gaigo Gakkō, Yazaki Shinshirō (1863–1947). It appears that Futabatei and Yazaki had been writing fiction together, though no trace of their joint work survives, and Yazaki had literary aspirations. Tsubouchi urged Yazaki to publish as soon as possible and offered to introduce him to literary circles. By October of that year Yazaki was living at Tsubouchi's house as a kind of disciple and had started publishing stories under the penname Saganoya Omuro.[55] Yazaki and Futabatei remained good friends and frequently offered each other sympathy and advice when personal or literary problems arose. Yazaki benefited from his stay in Tsubouchi's house in one important respect: he was present while Futabatei, at the time engaged in writing *Ukigumo,* discussed with Tsubouchi theories of literary style. Yazaki, having absorbed their views, was eventually to become a successful writer of colloquial novels.

Tsubouchi's assistance to Futabatei extended far beyond matters of abstract theory. He read Futabatei's manuscripts,

54. Tsubouchi, "Futabatei no koto," pp. 29–30. Aeba Kōson joined *Yomiuri shimbun* in 1874, where he remained until 1889 when he changed to the *Tōkyō Asahi shimbun.* He was well known for his serialized novels, drama reviews, and travel pieces. He was a student of Tokugawa literature, and his novels were in the tradition of earlier nineteenth-century literature. His style was light and humorous, and his plots better constructed than was usually true of newspaper stories. Several of his early stories, biographical articles, and travel pieces are collected in *Muratake* (1889–90). In 1892, with Tsubouchi's help, he began to teach in the Tōkyō Semmon Gakkō and to publish in the magazine *Waseda Bungaku.* He was an authority on Tokugawa fiction and jōruri.

55. Yazaki took his penname in imitation of Harunoya Oboro, a name Tsubouchi had used. Yazaki recalled that he had tried to become Tsubouchi's disciple, but the older man modestly refused the role, saying that he was not equal to so great a responsibility. Quoted in Kawatake and Yanagida, pp. 183–84.

suggested changes and modifications in style, introduced him to publishers, and even lent his name to *Ukigumo* when it was published. He placed Futabatei's articles and translations in magazines where he had influence and did everything possible to launch the young man's career.

Tsubouchi and Futabatei were both given to reexamining their actions and the motives behind them, sometimes inducing periods of despair. They became extremely dissatisfied with their work and abandoned projects earlier started with enthusiasm. One cannot be sure which of the two was more precariously balanced psychologically. Tsubouchi suffered a nervous collapse in 1887, largely brought about by overwork and despair over a series of deaths in his family. However, he always considered Futabatei to be more neurotic than himself and spoke of his brooding, pensive nature and his frequent bouts of melancholia. More than once Futabatei told Tsubouchi he had been contemplating suicide; such periods of depression alternated with excitement and elation over new enthusiasms or his own work.

Both men were idealistic about literature and suffered from feelings of guilt when they realized they were writing for profit. Futabatei's reaction was considerably more severe than Tsubouchi's. It caused internal conflicts that prevented him from working and was a major factor in his eventual decision to abandon all attempts to establish himself as a professional writer and to take a position with the government. He hit on his penname, Futabatei Shimei, during one such moment of terrible frustration. He realized he could not tolerate writing for money; it was totally out of keeping with his devotion to art for its own sake. The name Futabatei Shimei, though it suggests such old-fashioned literary sobriquets as Ryūtei Tanehiko or Kyokutei Bakin, is actually an approximation of the profanity, *kutabatte shimae,* meaning "go to hell." He later recalled:

My dilemma arose from a conflict between the practical and the ideal. I could not resolve it. I was pressed by the necessity of making a living. I simply had to write *Ukigumo* and earn some money. From the point of view of my ideals, I became an un-principled human being. I made money but I was completely ashamed of myself. I felt that I was a contemptible, worthless creature. At the very extreme of my suffering, a voice burst from within me—*kutabatte shimae* it called! (Futabatei Shimei) There have been various speculations made about my penname, but in reality it originated exactly as I have described it.[56]

Being younger and less sophisticated about the literary world than Tsubouchi, Futabatei reacted more emotionally to the crassness of professional writers. As a boy, Futabatei found it difficult to compromise with an uncle who fought against Saigō Takamori or a teacher who sided with the appointed head of the Tokyo Municipal Assembly or a prin-cipal who argued for merging Gaigo Gakkō with the com-mercial school. As a man he continued to be uncompromis-ing only to discover that he could not succeed as a profes-sional writer if he refused to lower in the slightest his extremely high standards. Unable as he was to adjust his standards to the realities of life and, even more significantly, to his own talents, he could not pursue his career as a writer.

Tsubouchi could not refrain from comparing himself with Futabatei. They met constantly, and Futabatei's brooding, moroseness, and enthusiastic idealism equally affected him. He began to feel that Futabatei's sensitivity to literature was greater than his own. As they worked together over Futaba-tei's translations and his novel, Tsubouchi became even more convinced that he could not match Futabatei's genius for writing. Watching the young man work, Tsubouchi began to see his own inadequacies clearly.

After talking with him just two or three times, I realized that his appreciation of Western fiction and his erudition were be-yond what I and my colleagues had achieved. As I listened to him, I became aware how superficial my ideas were and how shallow my approach was. After two years of contact with him, I realized that I did not possess the ability to write a novel. Un-fortunately, what I knew of his literary theories was confined to

56. "Yo ga hansei no zange," p. 39.

fragmentary discussions we had together and to some short translations of literary criticism which had appeared in one or two magazines. His views were virtually unknown to the public and yet his literary theories were far in advance of the time.[57]

The relationship, so beneficial to Futabatei, was, in one sense, damaging to Tsubouchi. By 1889 he realized that he could not write a realistic novel. His domestic novels written after *Tōsei shosei katagi* had begun to approach the standards he set in *Shōsetsu shinzui:* he narrowed the scope of the plot to allow for greater development of characterizations; and his style improved so much that he could handle a colloquial narrative with reasonable competence. However, Tsubouchi never succeeded in creating an impression of real life as powerful as that found in Futabatei's *Ukigumo,* and he was too perceptive a critic not to realize it. Somehow Tsubouchi the novelist could not avoid contrived coincidences and melodrama, and he continued moreover to be tempted by political allegories. The characters in his last novel, *Gaimu daijin,* include thinly disguised versions of the Foreign Minister, Ōkuma Shigenobu, and the Prime Minister, Itō Hirobumi (1841–1909).

A Modern Language for Literature

Futabatei and Tsubouchi both participated actively in the movement to modernize literary style. As soon as Futabatei started to translate and write fiction, he became aware of the necessity of choosing a style suitable to realistic fiction, and with Tsubouchi's help, he invented the style known as *gembun itchi* [unification of the written and spoken language]. The term had been used earlier in discussions of language reform and came to refer specifically to a style used in writing fiction with the publication in 1886 of an essay entitled *Gembun itchi* by Mozume Takami (1849–1928).

Although Mozume's essay was only one of several appeals

57. "Futabatei Shimei," pp. 490–91.

for the modification of the language of literature, the subsequent adoption of the term to describe the colloquial written language of the 1880s and 1890s has given it a position of importance in literary history. Mozume decried the contemporary practice of imitating the styles of the past and advocated the use of spoken language syntax and vocabulary. Although he recognized the vastness of the problem of choosing between the various levels of speech, he dismissed it by saying that writers should apply the style used in diaries or notebooks which do not attempt to reproduce actual conversations. Mozume concluded his essay by demonstrating how passages from the literature of the ninth through the fourteenth centuries could be rewritten in modern language to make them more readily comprehensible. In rewriting, Mozume found that the major differences between these early texts and modern Japanese lay in the choice of conjunctions and tense. He also found it necessary to replace particles and nouns no longer in use.[58]

Mozume, like most writers on literary reform during the early Meiji period, emphasized the need for greater ease of communication. In his opinion, simplification of the written language would lessen the burden of educators and enable practical studies to play a larger part in the school curriculum. It would also help to destroy the regional boundaries perpetuated by dialects. Tsubouchi also mentioned in the "Buntai ron" section of *Shōsetsu shinzui* that colloquial language is more readily understandable, but ease of communication was not his primary concern. Mozume, a philologist, was not faced with the problems of a novelist. Tsu-

58. Mozume, XII, 129–39. Mozume Takami was a student of the Japanese classics and published many philological studies. He served in various educational divisions of the government throughout his life. He began publishing studies of the Japanese language in 1876 and started to lecture at Tokyo University in 1883. His most famous work is the dictionary *Kotoba no hayashi* which was published in 1888. He was awarded the degree of doctor of letters in 1889.

The development of theories relating to the gembun itchi style is traced in Matsushita Teizō, "Gembun itchi ron to sono hantai ron," *Kokugo kokobun*, XXIX, No. 11 (October 1960), 39–56.

bouchi saw the dimensions of the practical problem which the invention of a new literary style involved more clearly than most early Meiji theorists, but he was unable to reach more than a tentative solution by the time he wrote *Shōsetsu shinzui*. As he worked with Futabatei, however, he began to formulate his ideas for a new style more precisely and in later years wrote several essays suggesting methods for writing a colloquial narrative style. By 1888 critics were referring to Tsubouchi as the man who "introduced the theory of the gembun itchi novel in our country." [59]

Dialogue was written in authentic colloquial speech in several Tokugawa novels, but few examples of narrative passages in a style resembling speech are to be found in the fiction of the eighteenth or early nineteenth centuries. Until 1886 the dominant style for narrative was one which is more accurately described as poetry than prose. The use of the 7-5, 8-6, or other fixed meters in jōruri and Bakin-chō creates a poetic effect similar to iambic pentameter. The attractiveness of the style made it very difficult for writers like Tsubouchi to break with it completely. They were loath to adopt what seemed to them the far more pedestrian language of prose. This poetic narrative style suffers, however, from a seemingly deliberate vagueness of expression which renders it unsuitable for precise description. It suggests rather than defines, but by its very elusiveness evokes a wealth of associations uncommon in straightforward prose. Moreover, authors characteristically directed asides to their readers in passing, generally couched in a casual, sarcastic tone. A passage from *Tōsei shosei katagi* illustrates some of the qualities of this style:

Gyōgyōshiki jinrikisha no gossai,	Fancy rickshaws crashing through
Osanago no ashimoto abunaku,	Children toddle uncertainly
Sōzōshiki tsujibasha no rappa,	The clamouring horns of hansom cabs

59. Ishibashi Shian, *"Aibiki o* yonde," *Zenshū,* II, 192. The review appeared in the September 1888 issue of the magazine *Kokumin no tomo.*

Rōjin wa tsue ya ushinawan.	An old man might lose his cane.
Harete kazedatsu hi no tsuchi-keburi ni wa,	In the dust of the clear, windy day
Kaitate no bōshi tame ni shiroku,	His newly purchased hat whitened
Anshi no gyoshameku kan'in mo,	A bureaucrat, a Yen Ying,[61]
Hana no ue ni hachiji o egaki,	Wrinkles up his nose.
Yuishi bakari no Ōshimada ni	With great pompadours just coiled about
Hokori ga kakaru o kurō ni shite,	Irritated by the swirling dust
Seishi no hisomi o manabu mo ari.	Women affecting Hsi Shih's[62] knitted brow.
Kore sujikai no natsu geshiki.	This the summer scene at the crossroads.
Ge ni ya kakute wa chiriyoke ni,	"Surely for protection from this dust
Megane no hashi mo iriyō ka,	One needs the help of glasses,"
To uchibuyakeru inaka udo no,	Mumbles an awkward country bumpkin;
Adaguchi sae mo kotowari-nari.[60]	His idle words contain some sense.

Futabatei, from his first writings, used the gembun itchi style. His earliest effort, a translation of a story by Gogol, was in the colloquial, and in the spring of 1886 he worked on a translation of Turgenev's *Fathers and Children* (1861), which Tsubouchi cited as the first gembun itchi translation of fiction.[63] Futabatei had never been trained formally in

60. *Senshū, Bessatsu*, I, 19.
61. Yen Ying (d. 493 B.C.) was an official of the Chinese state of Ch'i known for his unusual thrift and abstinence.
62. Hsi Shih, a famous Chinese beauty of the fifth century B.C., was chosen by the Prince of Yueh to be an instrument in the downfall of his rival, the Prince of Wu. After training her for three years, the Prince of Yueh sent Hsi Shih to the Prince of Wu, who succumbed to her charms, became dissolute, and was easily defeated by the Prince of Yueh. Hsi Shih had the habit of knitting her brows when distressed, and it was said that ugly women tried to imitate her but were unable to match her beauty.
63. "Futabatei no koto," p. 23.

Japanese literature. Of course, he read novels as a boy, but his schooling emphasized classical Chinese literature at first, and later Russian literature. He wrote classical Chinese and Russian well, but except for a few boyhood compositions had never seriously attempted to express himself in Bakin-chō or any of the other gabuntai forms. His knowledge of Russian fiction directed his attention to colloquial language, for Russian critics often spoke of the need to use colloquial Russian syntax in order to create realistic fiction. Futabatei later recalled:

From the time I began writing, I used gembun itchi. The only time I had employed conventional literary styles was in my teens; even then, I was actually better at Chinese than at literary Japanese. I was incapable of writing gazoku setchū buntai and, out of a desire to write in a natural, easy style, I started with gembun itchi. But pure colloquial speech somehow has no polish. There are many roughly textured words, and writing in the colloquial seems coarse and diffuse. . . . In dialogue, which is after all a reflection of human intercourse, it may be perfectly adequate, depending on the circumstances of the plot. In narrative, however, it is quite hopeless. I felt that I had to correct this deficiency in some way.[64]

Futabatei had the greatest difficulty in creating this gembun itchi style. He studied Tokugawa period novelists, Chinese fiction, and anecdotes related by contemporary yose performers to find models for his own work. When he was writing, he often turned to examples of the Japanese poetic form *renga* [linked verse] for inspiration. He also made use of jōruri techniques which he had learned through shinnai bushi, tokiwazu, and kiyomoto. Futabatei had considerable success in adopting some of the elements of traditional Chinese and Japanese prose and poetry to the needs of the modern novel, and several fine passages in *Ukigumo* reveal the influence of one of the older forms. However, he was constantly working toward eliminating these survivals in favor of a style closer to colloquial speech. The earlier sections of

64. "Bundan gosoku," *Zenshū*, IX, 191–92. An article dating from 1907.

Ukigumo make greater use of traditional forms than do the later chapters; by the time he reached the third and final part of his novel, he had developed a narrative style which is far closer to present-day colloquial Japanese than anything written by his contemporaries.

Futabatei and Tsubouchi were not, of course, the only writers experimenting with a new literary style. Many other young authors also wished to construct realistic novels dealing with contemporary life and recognized the inappropriateness of the styles left over from the Tokugawa period. In most cases, their affection for the traditional Japanese styles made it difficult for them to adopt a completely colloquial style; they generally continued to write in the older forms with only slight modifications.

One of the foremost figures of the gembun itchi movement was Yamada Bimyō (1868–1910). Yamada was experimenting with the gembun itchi style at almost exactly the same time as Futabatei, and literary historians have never settled the question of which of them first published a gembun itchi novel. Yamada was a boyhood friend of Futabatei's, but they seldom saw each other once they were grown. Although both were considering solutions to similar stylistic problems, they apparently never discussed the progress of their work.[65]

Yamada began to write stories while still in preparatory school. In 1885 he helped form the literary group known as the Ken'yūsha.[66] A portion of Yamada's first story—*Tategoto zōshi* [tale of the harp]—was published that year in the

65. Yamada, p. 167. An article written in 1909.
66. Among the founders of the Ken'yūsha were Ozaki Kōyō (1867–1903), Ishibashi Shian (1867–1927), and Maruoka Kyūka (1865–1927). The group was opposed to using fiction for promoting political ideals and argued for a return to the styles popular in the late eighteenth and early nineteenth centuries. The Ken'yūsha members considered Bakin and his contemporaries the true masters of Japanese fiction, and most of the stories and articles they produced in this period were in imitation of the earlier Japanese writers. They decried the superficial Westernization of their contemporaries and hoped to revive interest in traditional Japanese forms. Homma, I, 369–426.

group's journal, *Garakuta bunko;* it is a recounting of the adventures of King Alfred. Yamada, a great admirer of Bakin's style, wrote this story in Bakin-chō.[67]

In August 1886 he and two other members of the Ken'-yūsha cooperated in producing a collection of poems in free verse entitled *Shintaishi sen.* With the exception of a free rendition of the legend of Rip van Winkle, the poems in this collection are all original. In this respect it contrasts with the earlier collection, *Shintaishi shō,* which included more translations from English poetry than original Japanese poems. Along with several other poets of the same decade, Yamada and his colleagues were writing poetry startlingly unlike that of traditional Japanese literature. They avoided the traditional waka, haiku, and Chinese poetic forms and wrote verses of varying lengths, using vocabulary prohibited by the rigid rules of other Japanese verse forms.[68]

Yamada first attempted to use colloquial language in the narrative portions of a story in *Fūkin shirabe no hitofushi* [a song to be played on the organ]. The story was published in July 1887 in the first issue of *Iratsume,* a journal designed for the enlightened female reader. The heroine of *Fūkin shirabe no hitofushi* is a history teacher in a girls' school who is infatuated with a young singer. Although Yamada made some use of the syntax of colloquial Japanese, he continued to depend heavily on gabuntai. Scenes are described in a mixture of objective description and poetic metaphor, a characteristic device of Bakin-chō. Yamada also uses many

67. *Garakuta bunko* circulated among the Ken'yūsha members in hand-written copies from May 1885 until November 1886 when the first printed issue appeared. The printed issues also were for private circulation. *Garakuta bunko* went on sale to the public for the first time in May 1888. In March 1889 publication was taken over by the Yoshioka Shoten, which issued it under the title *Bunko* through October of the same year.

The small portion of Yamada's story appeared in the magazine in Volumes I and II; the balance of the story was found among his papers after his death. Homma, *Meiji Bungaku shi,* I, 378–86.

68. The other contributors were Ozaki Kōyō and Maruoka Kyūka. The collection is described in *Meiji bunka zenshū,* XII, 19–20, and is reprinted on pp. 321–34.

pivot words (*kakekotoba*) and puns. In his introduction to this story he calls for writers to abandon their practice of telling contemporary stories in gabuntai exclusively and to make greater use of the more natural and powerful zokubuntai.[69]

This introduction was the first of many pleas Yamada was to voice for modification of the written style. He quickly became identified among his contemporaries with the gembun itchi movement.[70] In October 1887 he published in *Iratsume* another story with colloquial elements. He continued to write for that magazine, contributing free-verse poems and translations and subsequently became the editor. Under his guidance, it turned from a woman's journal into a literary periodical of some importance. At the same time he was contributing stories and articles to *Garakuta bunko*. In 1888 Yamada became editor of *Miyako no hana,* a new literary magazine published by the Kinkōdō, the publishers of *Ukigumo.* In the following years Yamada's stories appeared in *Miyako no hana,* the magazine *Kokumin no tomo,* and other periodicals.

Many of Yamada's stories are period pieces. In these he attempts to reproduce the language of the time of the action rather than use contemporary speech for the dialogue. The dialogue of his contemporary stories is in colloquial Tokyo Japanese. In the narrative of all his fiction, both historical and contemporary, he used colloquial syntax and vocabulary. For this reason, all his stories after *Fūkin shirabe no hitofushi* are considered to be in the gembun itchi style. The amount of colloquial language and syntax Yamada used in his stories varies, however; in some cases the style is strikingly close to that of Tokugawa novels. Like many of his contemporaries, Yamada never completely abandoned writing in gabuntai.

69. Homma, *Meiji bungaku shi,* I, 447–49; 453–54.
70. For a study of Yamada's articles on gembun itchi, see Matsushita, "Yamada Bimyō no gembun itchi shisō," *Kokugo kokubun,* XXIX, No. 1 (January 1960), 16–29. Matsushita makes the point that Yamada was primarily concerned with reforming expository prose, and most of his articles in later years did not deal with creative fiction.

In trying to settle the question of whether Yamada or Futabatei first published fiction in gembun itchi, it is necessary to decide which of Yamada's stories are actually in gembun itchi. If the admixture of a limited amount of colloquial language is sufficient to describe the style as gembun itchi, *Fūkin shirabe no hitofushi* is Yamada's first gembun itchi novel. It appeared in July 1887, the same month in which Part One of *Ukigumo* was published. However, Yamada himself did not consider his novel as gembun itchi and decided the issue in favor of Futabatei. He believed that his first gembun itchi stories were those included in the collection entitled *Natsu kodachi* [a summer grove]. He completed this collection and submitted it to the Kinkōdō office before Futabatei's manuscript for Part One of *Ukigumo* arrived, but the Kinkōdō editors refused Yamada's manuscript and published *Ukigumo* instead.[71] *Natsu kodachi* was not published until August 1888.[72]

The question of who actually created gembun itchi literature seems unimportant. Most writers by 1885–86 were aware of the possibilities of a modern colloquial literary language, and in view of the progress made by the poets in modernizing their vocabulary and literary forms, it was merely a matter of time before someone wrote a colloquial work of fiction. What does warrant attention is the difference between Yamada's and Futabatei's talent as novelists. This is not only a matter of style. Yamada's plots tend to be fantastic and contrived, and his characters are often poorly developed. His handling of both narrative and dialogue is considerably inferior to Futabatei's. Yamada's efforts to mod-

71. Yamada, pp. 166–67. Ishibashi Shian asked Yamada Bimyō the same question shortly before his death. Yamada denied emphatically that he had originated the style and regretted that his contemporaries credited him with having written the first gembun itchi fiction; Futabatei, he said, was the originator. Ishibashi reported the interview to Maruoka Kyūka, whose statement is quoted in Fukuda, p. 90.

72. One of the stories from the collection, *Musashino,* was published serially in November and December 1887. In this story, the dialogue is in imitation of late sixteenth-century speech; the syntax of the narrative is largely in the colloquial.

ernize written Japanese assure him a place in literary history, but his stories have lost their appeal and are read today only by students of the period.

Ukigumo is the first modern novel with extended passages of narrative in colloquial Japanese. This was a remarkable accomplishment and endowed *Ukigumo* with a unique distinction in literary history, but Futabatei's ability to use traditional Japanese styles skillfully is of no less interest. Some critics condemn Futabatei's inability to avoid the older styles and feel that this lack of consistency spoils the over-all effectiveness of his writing. It is true that Futabatei was not especially successful in all his experiments with older forms, but *Ukigumo* contains several fine examples of traditional writing which enhance rather than detract from its value. There is no question, however, that Futabatei's forte lay in reproducing speech; he handles dialogue with an ease and surety remarkable in so inexperienced a writer. He transfers this ability to the narrative portions of the novel through the use of the interior monologue and extensive narrative passages related from his hero's point of view. This technique, which Futabatei adopted from Russian fiction, can also be viewed as a development of a practice already familiar in jōruri forms.

The novel opens with a passage reminiscent of the *tsukushi*, or catalogue, a favorite device in the puppet plays.[73] *Ukigumo* begins with a description of a crowd of office workers hurrying home at the close of the day; the variety of mustaches, beards, and clothes they sport is painted in broad, bold strokes of ironic humor. The same technique is used again in the middle of the seventh chapter, where a busy, festive group of pleasure seekers are described as they wander about looking at chrysanthemum displays.[74] In these passages the reader's attention is focused briefly on the absurd and ri-

73. For a discussion of the descriptive passages in jōruri, see Keene, trans., *The Major Plays of Chikamatsu*, p. 27.
74. The first half of chapter vii, including this passage, has been previously translated by Keene in *Modern Japanese Literature*, pp. 59-69.

diculous aspects of the human parade. The criticism of man's foolishness is explicit but lighthearted, and the style is impressionistic. Colors, textures, noises are suggested in rapid succession; no attempt is made at sustained emotion. This technique is often used in jōruri, and even when it appears in the novel, it echoes the need of the oral narrator who must hold his audience by rhythm and word.

A passage similar to another aspect of jōruri style occurs in the third chapter. The hero, Bunzō, and his cousin, Osei, are alone in her room. The conversation has moved from the casual and impersonal to talk of the two young people themselves. The rising moon lends to the enchantment of the moment; Bunzō is about to declare his love for Osei. He hesitates and the text glides briefly into a rhythmical description of the significance of the moment, delicately indicated by a series of poetic references to ancient Japanese literature. Movement is suspended; Bunzō does not speak. Then abruptly the spell is broken by the arrival of Bunzō's aunt. He has lost his opportunity.

Acting on Tsubouchi's advice, Futabatei tried to enhance the artistry of his style in some of the early sections of the novel by using more Chinese loan words than he considered natural to a colloquial style. One direct result of Tsubouchi's suggestion is the passage describing the light of the rising moon in the same love scene.[75] Here Futabatei uses many words from Chinese literary vocabulary, and although the passage has a beauty and grace of its own, it seems inappropriate to a colloquial novel. The influence of kambun-chō is also marked in several passages where few Chinese loan words are used, and in most cases it weighs down the rhythm of the prose and produces a monotony which is not present in other parts of the novel.

As he continued to work on the novel, Futabatei became convinced that it was a mistake to use Chinese literary vocabulary which had not been fully absorbed into the spoken

75. On reflection, Tsubouchi considered his advice mistaken. "Futabatei Shimei," p. 492.

Japanese language. He studied the works of Shikitei Samba to find examples of the speech of the common people and carefully weighed words and expressions to decide if they were truly colloquial.[76]

Yazaki, who was living at Tsubouchi's house and heard their discussions of stylistic questions, numbers this among the greatest problems Futabatei had in writing *Ukigumo:*

Hasegawa said that there were many dialects within Japan and that the language varied greatly from place to place, but that the spirit, indeed the heart, of Japan was Tokyo, and therefore he had to select Tokyo speech. But he felt that by that time the language of Tokyo had already been corrupted by the many people who came to the capital from other parts of the country. He decided he would have to cull the essence of the language of the Edo period and work from Edo speech. The style had to be gembun itchi. He considered it necessary to match conversation and narrative, and therefore a colloquial language was better than kambun-chō or gabuntai. From this point of view, also, Edo words were best, he believed, but he had an extremely difficult time selecting suitable ones.[77]

As a result of his study and greater experience, Futabatei succeeded in developing a colloquial narrative style while he was writing *Ukigumo*. Although he used colloquial narrative in extensive passages even in Part One of the novel, most of the narrative in this section is in one or another of the traditional styles. As he worked on subsequent chapters, he gradually shifted from book language. From about the middle of Part Two, the narrative is almost entirely in colloquial language, although isolated instances of classical syntax or usage continue to appear. By the time he reached Part Three, Futabatei was able to handle his newly invented colloquial language with ease.

Futabatei is most successful in his dialogue. The words are sharp, biting, gentle, restrained, bold, or brittle as the plot and characterization demand. Study of the authentic

76. Futabatei, "Yo ga gembun itchi no yurai," *Zenshū,* IX, 148–49.
77. Yazaki, p. 168.

dialogue so well-represented in Tokugawa literature and in contemporary yose stories probably helped him substantially in achieving so smooth a style. Exchanges are rapid and often cutting, puns and jokes are tossed lightly back and forth between the characters, and anger pours out in a venomous stream. It is difficult to imagine any more vivid portrayal of anger, for instance, than Omasa's attack on Bunzō when she learns he has been dismissed. Her first reaction to the shocking news is quiet, almost considerate. Then her fury builds to a crescendo; she blames him for not having played up to his superior, then she compares him unfavorably with his colleague, Noboru, and finally she lights upon Bunzō's most vulnerable point, his inability to support his destitute mother. Omasa's dialogue consistently reveals her coarseness and her lack of education. She is illogical, quick-tempered, and obvious; all of her personality is conveyed by her utterances. The words of the other characters are no less self-revealing.

Futabatei also employed the interior monologue. This technique was also derived from jōruri and yose storytelling. In these theatrical forms a narrator not only tells the story but reads the dialogue for the various characters. When a character is brooding or plotting to himself, the narrator, speaking for him, reveals his unspoken thoughts to the audience. In *Ukigumo,* Futabatei uses this same device to indicate the inner workings of Bunzō's mind. As Bunzō broods over why he was dismissed, for instance, we see his bitterness, his uncertainties, and his confusion in a way which could not be so clearly revealed by objective description.

As the novel progresses, however, Futabatei, abandoning the interior monologue, shifts to third-person narrative even when he relates the story exclusively from Bunzō's point of view. This technique, though quite revolutionary, is not as successful as the interior monologue. The combination of stylistic novelty and a certain awkwardness Futabatei demonstrated in the technique led critics to conclude that Futabatei identified himself too strongly with his hero. Nakamura Mitsuo, for instance, feels that Futabatei, having lost his objectivity, became so engrossed in Bunzō's character that he could not work out the final stages of the plot.[78] Nakamura furthermore suggests that the lack of clarity especially evident in Part Three of *Ukigumo* may be attributed in part to an internal conflict within Futabatei himself. This, Nakamura believes, resulted from Futabatei's admiration for the aggressive, successful Noboru and his contempt for the desultory Bunzō, with whom, however, he most strongly identified himself. This conflict, Nakamura maintains, prevented Futabatei from sustaining a fixed point of view throughout the novel and resulted in the collapse of the plot development.[79]

It is true that the final chapters of the novel are less effective than the early portions, but this seems unrelated to any conflict in Futabatei's attitude. The apparent loss of objectivity, which Nakamura criticizes, results from a change of technique. From the eighth chapter, Futabatei is experimenting with the methods Dostoevsky used so successfully in *Crime and Punishment*. Though he keeps the narrative in the third person, he pictures the whole world from Bunzō's position. At times he stops the course of the narrative to relate the same sequence of events from the point of view of Omasa or Osei, or presents scenes in which Bunzō does not participate, but by and large every event in the novel is seen through Bunzō's eyes. Bunzō, a kindly and generous man, is often confused and vacillating, and Futabatei shows him in all his dimensions. He sought, in keeping with the advice Tsubouchi offered in *Shōsetsu shinzui*, to portray the psychological as well as the surface aspects of his hero's character. Futabatei, recognizing that psychological depth made Russian fiction superior to Japanese fiction, tried to emulate the Russian novelists within a Japanese framework. He was not entirely successful, and his lack of technical skill is evident

78. Nakamura, *Futabatei Shimei den,* pp. 121, 126–31, 153.
79. "Shōgai to sakuhin," pp. 34–37.

in the confusion of expression particularly apparent in the nineteenth chapter. This resulted not from over-identification with his hero but from his attempt to employ a technique he had not fully mastered.[80]

Futabatei could not have written *Ukigumo* in any style but the colloquial. His aim was to show what inspired men's actions; their thoughts—rational and irrational—and their deeds were both part of his subject matter. The interior monologues and the whole chapters devoted to describing events from the hero's point of view were intended to show how an intelligent, sensitive, but weak man reacted to his life. Bunzō speaks for himself; the novelist rarely intrudes his opinion into the situations described. From what Bunzō says to others, what they say to or about him, and what unspoken thoughts pass through his mind, we learn of his personality, his aspirations (or lack of them), and his successive emotions. Bunzō could not have addressed himself in any other than colloquial language, nor could he have used eighteenth-century Japanese when speaking to the other characters. A man calculates the problems of life in his own mind in the language of his generation and his class. He cannot be made to adopt the speech of other ages or other levels of society. Seen in this light, Futabatei's plan demanded a modern colloquial narrative. It could just as easily have happened that after studying Russian literature at Gaigo Gakkō, he would decide to write a Russian-inspired novel in a Japanese setting and then write it in the colloquial without any knowledge of existing arguments for the reform of the written literary language. The direct line of association linking Russian fiction and *Ukigumo* needed no connection with specifically Japanese problems.

Futabatei did not, in fact, publish any articles advocating

80. One of the major flaws in Futabatei's style was his practice of inserting asides in the midst of a description of Bunzō's thoughts. This has the effect of temporarily destroying the objectivity of the passage and making the reader conscious of the author. Since this technique was widely used in Tokugawa fiction, it acts to impair the modernity of Futabatei's style. For a discussion of this point see Kamei, pp. 23–39.

language reform. He was not involved in the discussions which appeared with increasing frequency in the literary journals, for he was too concerned with inventing a style to stop and discuss it. At times, during the years 1888 and 1889, he became sufficiently interested in the problem to jot down in his journal articles which stated unequivocally but with little originality or felicity his belief in the necessity to write narrative in the gembun itchi style. He apparently planned to take issue on specific points with critics publishing controversial opinions in the magazines of the day, and his draft essays therefore have little value as independent statements of his views. *Ukigumo* is Futabatei's most positive declaration on the value of gembun itchi; through it, he made himself one of the most famous writers of his day.

FROM JANUARY 1886 through August 1889, Futabatei devoted himself to translation, creative writing, and study. He translated a number of essays from Russian literary and aesthetic criticism and three stories by Turgenev. His first Turgenev translation, of *Fathers and Children,* was never published and the manuscript was lost; the other two appeared in magazines in 1888. They produced a great impact on the literature of the period, for they were accurate translations cast in the gembun itchi style. For years after their publication, young writers were deeply moved by the beauty and vividness of the style and found inspiration for their own work in these stories. Futabatei's translations of Russian criticism were less popular among the intellectuals of the day. They remain, however, of considerable importance in an analysis of Futabatei's approach to literature and provide a key to the understanding of his only literary essay of the period, "Shōsetsu sōron" [elements of the novel], published in April 1886.

Futabatei's most important product of this period was *Ukigumo.* He began work on it late in the spring of 1886 and rewrote the manuscript many times before Part One finally was published in June 1887. Part Two appeared in February 1888, and Part Three was serialized in *Miyako no hana* between July and August 1889. Part One brought Futabatei fame and recognition, and Part Two further established his reputation as a leading writer of the period. The two translations of Turgenev's stories appeared in the summer and fall of 1888, five months after Part Two of *Ukigumo* had been published and several months before Part Three reached the public. Not only was Futabatei's skill in handling the gembun itchi style universally recognized by the literary world, but an entirely new conception of how to translate fiction emerged.

Despite the fame his work brought him, Futabatei still lacked confidence in his ability. While the public awaited Part Three of *Ukigumo,* Futabatei was struggling with each chapter. By June of 1889 he had begun to doubt his choice of career. He questioned his ability to write a novel which would meet his own standards and wondered if he were suited to the literary life. After several months of worry and depression, he finally concluded that he had best take a position in the government. To this day we do not know whether Part Three of *Ukigumo* is complete or whether Futabatei abandoned it part way through when he took his new post.

On two occasions in this period Futabatei attempted to earn his living by means other than writing, but both attempts proved unsuccessful. Shortly after leaving school in January 1886, he went to work for a bank. He left in less than a month.[1] In 1888 he taught for several months at a private school, the Sakurai Girls' School,[2] lecturing to the most advanced students on literary theory. Futabatei reported to his friend Kuwabara that he was discouraged because his students seemed incapable of grasping the meaning of his lectures on realism and idealism, no matter how often he went over the material. Despairing of their ever under-

1. Kuwabara, p. 123.
2. Sakurai Jogakkō was founded in 1873 as a Christian school. It was one of many founded in that decade under the stimulus of foreign missionaries resident in Japan. By 1881 the school had expanded to the point where a new Western-style school building and dormitories were needed. In 1889 it merged with two other mission schools to form Joshi Gakuin.

standing literary criticism, he left the school after about six months.[3]

Futabatei's family hoped that he might follow in his father's footsteps and become a government employee rather than a writer.[4] He resisted the suggestion until 1889, but, suspecting that he might need another foreign language, besides Russian, to obtain a post in the government or elsewhere, he resumed the study of English. He worked largely on his own but also took lessons from an American scholar named Eastlake, who taught many of the young intellectual leaders of the period.[5] Futabatei found much to ridicule in the Japanese obsession for learning English, and humorous echoes of his experience with English language textbooks occur in *Ukigumo*. He became proficient in English, however, and his first position with the government was as a translator of English language newspapers.

Futabatei's First Attempts at Translation

Futabatei made his first serious literary attempts as a translator, and not as a creative writer. Throughout Futabatei's childhood and youth, many translations from Western

3. Kuwabara, p. 123.

4. Hasegawa Ryūko, p. 5.

5. Yamada Bimyō, p. 166. Frank Warrington Eastlake (1858–1905) went to Japan in 1884 after studying classical and modern languages in various schools, in America and Europe, and receiving a doctor of philology degree from Berlin in 1881. He knew French, German, Dutch, Latin, and Greek and specialized in Assyrian and Egyptian studies. After joining his father, who practiced dentistry in Japan for some years, Eastlake learned Japanese. He cooperated on a Japanese translation of Webster's Dictionary and translated works of classical and modern Japanese literature into English, including Mori Ōgai's *Maihime*. Remaining in Japan until his death, he published and edited two English language newspapers, founded learned societies for Japanese scholars of English, and wrote many grammars and texts for English students. For his biography and a bibliography of works by and about him, see *Kindai bungaku kenkyū sōsho*, ed. Shōwa Joshi Daigaku Kindai Bungaku Kenkyū Shitsu (Tokyo, 1958), VIII, 19–70. The poet Sasaki Nobutsuna (1872–1963), who also studied with Eastlake, gives a contemporary account of him in *Meiji bungaku no hen'ei*, p. 56.

languages were published in Japan. These included works of philosophy, history, natural sciences, and fine art as well as literature.[6] Translations from English predominated, but French and German works also appeared in considerable number. The earliest translations from the Russian language were completed in the first decade of the nineteenth century, but it was not until 1883 that a translation of a work of Russian literature was published.[7]

As Tsubouchi indicated in his introduction to *Gaiseishi den,* translations of Western fiction in the early Meiji period generally bore little resemblance to the original. Translators, eager to convert Western novels into recognizable Japanese stories, usually made no attempt to suggest the style employed by Western authors. Novels were generally pared down to the barest elements of the plot; descriptions of foreign cities might be rendered in some fashion, but passages analyzing the personality or motivation of the characters were often omitted. The concept of characterization through dialogue or description was rarely transmitted to the Japanese audience.

A very substantial part of the difficulty was linguistic. Some translators were not sufficiently familiar with the foreign language of their choice to understand colloquial fiction. Tsubouchi himself, an accomplished translator, admitted he had experienced great difficulty in understanding the texts he worked on in the 1880s. However, imprecise translations of literature were not solely the result of an inadequate understanding of the text. Even in instances where the Japanese translator was well aware of the meaning of the original, no written literary language existed suitable for

6. For a review of early Meiji translations see Okazaki Yoshie, pp. 123–31.

7. Pushkin's *The Captain's Daughter* (1836), translated by Takasu Jisuke, a former student at Gaigo Gakkō. The translation, entitled *Rokoku kibun: kashinchō shiroku* [a strange Russian tale: the record of the thoughts of a flowery-hearted butterfly], apparently was extremely free. A brief account of the history of the study of the Russian language, compilations of dictionaries, and the earliest translations is given in Berton, Langer, and Swearingen, pp. 4–8; 19–25.

translating European works. He was forced to choose between two equally unsatisfactory styles: the cold, terse, extremely difficult intellectual language of kambun-chō and the poetic, allusive, flowing gabuntai. The vogue which kambun-chō enjoyed in the mid-1880s stemmed from the fact that readers considered this style to be more suited to Western writing than the flowery gabuntai. The images and metaphors of gabuntai were so intimately linked with past Japanese literature that they seemed singularly inappropriate to foreign fiction. The wealth of associations conjured up by the mention of a familiar image or even word drawn from the traditional Japanese literary writing was likely to destroy the atmosphere of a foreign work. Such images and vocabulary had to be abandoned to forestall the possibility of irrelevant associations with past literature, but substitutions were hard to discover.

Futabatei's translations from Russian fiction were the first in Japanese even vaguely to resemble the original; more than that, they were the first which rendered a European literary work into colloquial Japanese. Futabatei experimented many months before he developed a satisfactory style. He labored over every word until he felt his Japanese version approximated the flavor of the original.

Even once he had decided to strike out in an entirely new path and not resort to the traditional literary forms, Futabatei was faced with many problems peculiar to the Japanese language. As we have seen, the spoken language varied greatly, not only according to the region but among the various classes of society. Which variety should be used to represent the speech of foreigners? Were the normal terms of respect employed by Japanese in addressing one another to be put in the mouths of Russian characters in a novel? Should foreign women use the humble language of their Japanese counterparts? These and similar problems made the translation of dialogue difficult, but the complexities were even greater when it came to writing narrative. Futabatei had to create a colloquial language to replace the poetry of gabuntai. His narrative had to be precise and clear to achieve the effect of realistic fiction, but it also had to be aesthetically pleasing.

Soon after meeting Tsubouchi, Futabatei showed him the translation he had made of part of a work by Gogol.[8] The translation, about thirty pages long, was written in the colloquial language. Futabatei, when making the translation, chose to imitate the speech of lower-class Japanese. Tsubouchi found this practice objectionable. The story, for example, contained a passage in which a middle-class woman engaged in a heated discussion. The coarse language Futabatei used in translating the argument made Tsubouchi suppose she was more vulgar and ignorant than Gogol had intended. He was disturbed because her speech contained none of the polite words used by Japanese middle-class women. Futabatei defended his choice on the grounds that the equality of women in the Western world made the deferential Japanese woman's language unsuitable. He failed to finish the translation, however, and all trace of it has been lost.

Futabatei next turned to translating Turgenev's *Fathers and Children*. Tsubouchi arranged for publication by an Osaka firm—Hino Shoten. About a quarter of the projected translation was completed and sent to Osaka on March 19, 1886; it bore the title *Kyomu-tō katagi* [character studies of Nihilists].[9] Tsubouchi described some of the problems Futabatei encountered in translating Turgenev's story:

8. Tsubouchi, the only person to make mention of the Gogol translation, did not indicate which novel or story Futabatei tried to translate.

9. Tsubouchi, "Futabatei no koto," pp. 23–24. *Katagi mono*, character books, were the innovation of Ejima Kiseki (1667–1736). Ejima wrote sketches satirizing particular social types and grouped them together under such titles as *Seken musuko katagi* [characters of worldly young men] (1715), *Seken musume katagi* [characters of worldly young women] (1717), and *Ukiyo oyaji katagi* [characters of old men of the floating world] (1720). Greatly influenced by Saikaku, Ejima continued a long tradition of type characterization in his brief, humorous sketches of townspeople. Katagi mono by other authors appeared throughout the eighteenth century, the most notable being *Seken tekake katagi* [characters of worldly mistresses] (1766) by Ueda Akinari (1734–1809). Hibbett, pp. 59–64; 100–51.

The katagi mono of Ejima and many of his successors were collections of

Futabatei suffered terribly with *Fathers and Children*. To begin with, there was a great dearth of words in Japanese suitable for translating such a novel. Today [1909] we share with the Western world any number of abstract concepts and material objects which were totally alien to us then. Spoken Japanese of that day could in no way be made to resemble dialogue between foreigners. . . . The major difficulty was the absence of words which would evoke a Western woman. Futabatei was such an extremely conscientious translator that he could never be satisfied with the results of his work. He labored over each word and each line, feeling he had lost the flavor here or missed the spirit there. Even after revising the manuscript three or four times, he was still not satisfied. In the end he did not finish it.[10]

While Futabatei was struggling with the translation, Tsubouchi suggested that he imitate the style of the yose performer San'yūtei Enchō (1839–1900).[11] Enchō, one of the great storytellers of the time, recounted his humorous anecdotes in vivid language that accurately captured the special flavor of the spoken language. Some of his stories, taken down as he delivered them in the yose hall, were later printed in pamphlet and book form. The first, *Botan dōrō* [peony lantern], was originally composed as early as 1862 or 1863. In 1884 Enchō allowed it to be transcribed; this was the first experiment in recording a yose performance. The stenographers had trouble keeping up with Enchō's rapid delivery, but the publication proved a great success.[12]

In 1885 Tsubouchi wrote an introduction to the second

vignettes, most often humorous but sometimes containing a note of tragedy. Marked by sharply realistic touches, they tended to emphasize the bizarre, erotic, or just mildly unusual events that might occur in the bustling city. They were not structured novels in the modern sense of the word. Tsubouchi's *Tōsei shosei katagi*, while retaining some of the same humorous, satirical quality, was closer to a well-organized novel. The choice of *Kyomu-tō katagi* as the title for *Fathers and Children*, however, seems singularly inappropriate.

10. "Futabatei Shimei," pp. 491–92.

11. Futabatei, "Yo ga gembun itchi no yurai," *Zenshū*, IX, 147.

12. Okuno Shintarō, "Kaisetsu," in San'yūtei Enchō, *Botan dōrō*, pp. 185–86.

edition of *Botan dōrō*. In terms similar to those used in *Shōsetsu shinzui*, he castigates novelists who, catering to the current vogues, wrote superficial tales; by contrast this is a story "which deeply probes the essence of man's emotions and portrays them well." *Botan dōrō*, Tsubouchi continues, is not the work of a literary man—at least not in the accepted sense of the word—but Enchō's use of colloquial spoken language is extremely skillful and deserves the attention of professional writers.[13]

The style Enchō used in his narrative was derived from upper-class Tokyo speech. Futabatei, abandoning his notion that lower-class speech could more vividly suggest the tone and manner of Western social conversation, took Enchō as his model. Tsubouchi considered Futabatei's translation of *Fathers and Children* superior to his translation of Gogol, but he felt that Futabatei's style was still far from mature.[14]

Futabatei frequently showed the *Kyomu-tō katagi* manuscript to Tsubouchi, who went over it carefully, suggesting stylistic modifications and other changes. One thorny problem centered on the choice of a Japanese word for the copula "is" or "equals." There were various possibilities: *de gozaru* or *de gozaimasu; de aru* or *de arimasu; desu;* or *da*. Although the meaning of each is identical, the level of politeness differs enormously. A remark with precisely the same content as another would therefore be given entirely different overtones, ranging from obsequiousness to gross rudeness, merely by the choice of the word for "is." Moreover, because most sentences end with the copula, the choice of one variant over another inevitably establishes the rhythm of the entire work. Writers had expressed concern about this question from the time of the earliest discussions of the new colloquial style. The choice affected essayists and journalists as well as novelists. In translating the dialogue, Futabatei based his decision on the social class, sex, and age of the speaker, and also on the immediate situation. Futabatei's real dilemma was the

13. Tsubouchi, "Jo," *Botan dōrō*, p. 3.
14. "Futabatei no koto," p. 24.

appropriate word to be used, not in conversational passages but in the narrative. If he chose *de gozaimasu,* the most polite word, his translation would acquire an entirely different tone than if he chose *da,* the least polite. At first, Futabatei thought he would compromise on *desu,* an intermediate level. Tsubouchi argued for *da* and finally persuaded Futabatei. In his subsequent translations and original works, Futabatei continued to use *da;* his gembun itchi style is associated with this word, although he at times experimented with *desu* and *de aru.* However, his choice was not universally accepted. Yamada Bimyō also began with *da* in his gembun itchi writing but quickly changed to *desu,* which he used from then on.[15] Twentieth-century colloquial narrative and expository writing ordinarily employs *de aru,* the most neutral form, although it is rarely used in actual conversation.

Hino Shoten paid a 30-yen advance on *Kyomu-tō katagi* on receipt of the first part of the manuscript, which consisted of between eighty and ninety handwritten pages. Tsubouchi gave the money to Futabatei on April 4, 1886. Futabatei wrote an advertisement for the translation which appeared in another book issued by the same publisher in April, describing the novel as a key to understanding Nihilism:

When the layman hears the word "Nihilism," he associates it with violence, but it appears that it is not such a superficial thing. . . . The hero of this novel advocates Nihilism. His views are in turn despised by a certain idealistic gentleman and their bitter rivalry gives rise, finally, to an incident. Further interest is provided by a lovely heroine who is involved with the hero, and by the arguments of foolish people who possess only a superficial understanding of Nihilism. While you are reading and enjoying this book, you will learn of the ideals of Nihilism and how people who believe in it speak and act, and, in the end, you will realize that violence is not the basis of their philosophy.

In the advertisement, Futabatei also referred to his style as

15. Yamada's friend Maruoka Kyūka recalled how Yamada struggled with the various possibilities in "Ken'yūsha to *Garakuta bunko* no yurai," pp. 15–16.

being based on gembun itchi, indicating the importance he placed on stylistic problems and the interest he assumed it would have to readers. ". . . The cynic may view my translation as a foolish imitation of Enchō; my admirers may see it as heralding a new literary style for Japan." [16] According to the advertisement, Turgenev's novel was translated by Futabatei with the assistance of Tsubouchi.

Despite the advance payment and the advertisement, Hino Shoten failed to publish *Kyomu-tō katagi,* for reasons never stated. Turgenev had not been translated into Japanese, but his name was well known in Japan because he was believed to have been associated with the Nihilist movement. "Nihilism" was one of the popular, jargon expressions of the day used by politically conscious intellectuals. A story by Turgenev entitled *Character Studies of Nihilists* would certainly have attracted a wide audience; it was precisely for that reason that Futabatei and Tsubouchi chose the title, and Futabatei's advertisement was obviously intended to stimulate interest in the political aspects of the novel. Tsubouchi, recalling events of the period, could not remember why the translation had not been published, but speculated that the Hino Shoten editors were disappointed when they realized that it was not as exciting a political tale as the title had promised. Perhaps they feared that the story would not sell and felt disinclined therefore to encourage Futabatei to continue.[17]

We may imagine too that the difficulties involved in translating the novel overwhelmed Futabatei. Tsubouchi's description of his fastidiousness in choosing words and expressions indicates how conscientiously Futabatei tried to render the original text into Japanese. Still uncertain of his style, he lacked the confidence to complete the translation of a novel he admired so greatly; when he met with discouragement from the publishers, he probably dropped the project with a sense of relief.

16. *Zenshū,* XV, 154–55.
17. Tsubouchi, "Futabatei Shimei," p. 511.

During the early months of 1886 Futabatei was also translating Russian literary criticism. He undertook these translations in order to help Tsubouchi and a few other friends
to understand the theories which so excited him. In April
1886 he published a short original essay on literary theory, a
condensation of ideas expressed in various works by Belinsky. In May and June of the same year his first translation of
literary theory was published serially. His essay and the
translation appeared in *Chūō gakujutsu zasshi,* a magazine to
which Tsubouchi frequently contributed. In these articles
Futabatei used the classical expository style known as *bungotai.* He did not attempt to incorporate gembun itchi into
his essays until a later date.

Ukigumo, Parts One and Two

Although neither of his early translations of fiction were
printed, these initial experiments provided Futabatei with
enough writing experience to begin his novel. Publication
of his own critical essay and his translation of literary criticism gave him some confidence in his ability to find a publisher for his writing. With Tsubouchi's encouragement, he
started *Ukigumo* early in the summer of 1886. After working on it for seven or eight months, Futabatei showed the
draft of Part One (chapters i through vi) to Tsubouchi. In
trying to reconstruct the sequence of events leading up to
the publication of *Ukigumo,* Tsubouchi wrote:

I cannot remember exactly when I first saw the unfinished manuscript, but it was probably around January of 1887. I don't
know how many times Futabatei revised that draft. He had
started it in the summer of 1886. I was very eager to see it printed
and finally arranged for its publication with a company called
Kinkōdō. We sent it off at last in July 1887.[18] Until then

18. Tsubouchi's diary for July 1887 says that "I sent *Ukigumo* to the
Kinkōdō last month." This would seem to indicate that it was finished in
June rather than July. However, Tsubouchi was moving to new quarters at

Futabatei was continually revising it; I was afraid he would never consent to its publication. Naturally, his feelings were not based entirely on the dissatisfaction he felt with his style, but that did play a considerable part in the difficulties.[19]

Part One appeared as a single, illustrated, paperbound volume of 165 pages. The cover and title page list the author as Tsubouchi Yūzō. Immediately following the title page is a preface signed "Futabatei Shimei," in which Futabatei expressed his debt to Harunoya (Tsubouchi). This is followed by an introduction signed "Harunoya shujin." The colophon also names Tsubouchi Yūzō as the author. To publish a book under another man's name was by no means unusual. As we have seen, several of Tsubouchi's early books were represented as the works of another author. Generally, this deception was intended to help sales; works by totally unknown authors could not be expected to command the attention given those by established authors. In the case of *Ukigumo,* the publishers were unwilling to print the novel unless Tsubouchi was named as the author. Unlike Futabatei, as yet unknown to the reading public, Tsubouchi was a famous writer. A new novel by the author of *Tōsei shosei katagi* was certain to sell many copies, and Tsubouchi could demand a high price for his work.

"When I first contacted Kinkōdō about *Ukigumo,*" Tsubouchi later recalled, "they indicated that they would publish it if it were issued in my name or in both our names. I conferred with Futabatei, and he agreed to the proposal." Kinkōdō contracted to pay at the rate of 1 yen a page of manuscript, an extremely high sum for the time. Had the book been published in Futabatei's name, he definitely would not have received as much money. The publisher paid a 30-yen advance on the manuscript, which Tsubouchi turned over to Futabatei. Upon publication, another 50 yen

the time and had stopped keeping a careful diary. He entered only a few lines for each month and was therefore not certain of the dating. "Futabatei Shimei," p. 514.

19. "Futabatei no koto," pp. 24–25.

was remitted to Tsubouchi, though 60 yen more was due on the 90-page manuscript.

When Tsubouchi tried to give the 50 yen to Futabatei, he was unwilling to accept. Tsubouchi was embarrassed by Futabatei's reticence and, upon reflection, even more embarrassed by the outcome of the episode.

When it came time to give him the 50 yen, the fastidious Futabatei would hear nothing of it. He argued that I had to be rewarded for the guidance I had given him. He pointed out that 1 yen a page was a very high price for a publisher to offer and that obviously Kinkōdō was paying for my name. He compared the price with what was normally offered for first novels or for translations, as for instance, the amount Hino Shoten had paid for the *Kyomu-tō katagi* manuscript. . . . He said he would accept only half the sum.

After discussing the problem with Yazaki, Tsubouchi kept 35 yen and gave 15 to Futabatei. The remaining 10 yen owed by Kinkōdō was left on deposit for Futabatei with the publishing company. "If it had happened three or four years later," Tsubouchi went on to say, "I should never have accepted the money under any circumstances, but at that time I was very conceited. Furthermore, nervous exhaustion had made me feel irritable and impatient. In the end, it seems, I grudgingly consented. When I think of it now, I can't help but blush." [20]

Most reviewers realized that the book was actually written by Futabatei and assumed that Tsubouchi had simply lent his help, but the reading public probably thought *Ukigumo* was another novel by Tsubouchi.

In the opening chapter of Part One, we learn that the hero, Utsumi Bunzō, has lost his job as a clerk in the government. The second and third chapters are devoted to an account of Bunzō's impoverished boyhood, his life as a young man in his Aunt Omasa's house, and the beginning of his love for his cousin, Osei. In the fourth chapter Bunzō

20. "Futabatei Shimei," pp. 514–15.

tries to summon up the courage to tell Omasa that he has been dismissed, but cannot discover a convenient occasion. In the fifth chapter, which takes place the next morning, he at last informs Omasa and makes her furious with him. She never liked Bunzō as a child and clearly resented having a dependent relative in her home. Bunzō's late father was her husband Magobei's brother, but Magobei is rarely in Tokyo, and it is left to Omasa, as head of the family, to look after Bunzō. Originally she felt much imposed upon by the addition of this boy to her family, but once he had taken a job with the government, he became more acceptable. Now when he loses his position, however, Omasa considers him a failure and wants no more of him. To complicate matters, her daughter, Osei, indicates a fondness for Bunzō, and Omasa is on the point of allowing the two to marry. But nothing had actually been said about an engagement, and Omasa can therefore conveniently pretend ignorance of such a plan. She orders Osei to keep her distance from Bunzō. In the final chapter of Part One, Bunzō's colleague Honda Noboru comes to visit Omasa. Noboru, far from being dismissed, has been promoted. At the close of the chapter, Omasa, attracted by Noboru's assertiveness and good looks, makes the contrast which plays a major part in the novel: Bunzō is a failure, Noboru a success.

The critical reception given the early chapters was by and large favorable, though some reservations were expressed about the prosaic nature of the plot. It should be remembered that most translations appearing at the time were of novels with exceedingly involved plots and that Japanese translators usually abbreviated Western novels until only the bare plot was left. Nineteenth-century Japanese novels were either heroic tales of fantastic adventures or vaguely pornographic stories of the demimonde. Fictional accounts of voyages to distant points of the globe also enjoyed a vogue. Few domestic novels like *Ukigumo* were being published— certainly none that aimed at such a degree of psychological analysis.

Even those critics who withheld judgment on the plot were quick to recognize the value of the colloquial narrative language. An unsigned review in *Chōya shimbun* of July 3, 1887, comments that "those interested in the reform of the written language and those who wish to learn in advance the literary style of the future would gain much by reading this book." Another unsigned review in the *Jiji shimpō* of July 5, 1887, says, in part, that "although the originality of the plot is still not apparent to the reader, the style is designed as a modification of the ordinary spoken language; it is easy to read and easy to understand. By its style alone, it is an outstanding novel." And *Kokumin no tomo* for August 15, 1887, comments: "*Ukigumo* is a novel about ordinary life. The plot is not particularly original but the style is extremely interesting because of the freshness of the diction and the words. An entirely new invention seems to have been introduced into the world of the novel." A review in *Chūō gakujutsu zasshi* of August 20, 1887, compares *Ukigumo* to other novels being written at the time:

The characters in most novels these days resemble figures in woodblock prints. The characters in *Ukigumo* however are people in oil paintings. When you read *Ukigumo*, you feel like a man on a desert island who suddenly meets a friend. However, the form of the novel is somewhat limited. . . . We must suggest that the author broaden his scope a little more from now on.[21]

In September and October of 1887 Ishibashi Ningetsu (1865–1926)[22] published a long, detailed review of *Ukigumo* in four issues of the magazine *Jogaku zasshi*. Although it is entitled "*Ukigumo* no homeotoshi" [praise and censure of

21. The four reviews are reprinted in *Zenshū*, I, 209, 210.
22. Ishibashi Ningetsu achieved fame as a critic between 1887 and 1891 while still a Tokyo University student. He was much under the influence of Lessing, Goethe, and Schiller, and his critical approach was accordingly based on nineteenth-century German idealism. Unlike Tsubouchi, he did not write any essays defining his critical views, but expressed his attitudes on fiction almost entirely through his reviews of other people's books. After being graduated from the university in 1891, he withdrew from the literary world.

Ukigumo], Ishibashi is much more spirited in his defense of the novel than in his criticism of it. In order to evaluate *Ukigumo* properly, Ishibashi begins by defining the novel:

A novel portrays human personality and ideas. Differences in social position and circumstances greatly affect the manifestations of personality and ideas, and the novel paints these variations. It records a society, or at least some segment of a society, and brings an understanding of one time and place to future generations. . . . Novelists must accept the realistic portrayal of man's emotions and his society as their primary duty. But strangely enough, contemporary novelists, with few exceptions, concentrate on plot at the expense of characterization. They portray only outward beauty and do not analyze personality and ideas. They create self-righteous, noble people and show only the outward manner men affect for the face they show the world. The novelists do not probe man's cruder and baser side at all. As a result, the reader is made to think society is wonderful and that all man's coarser qualities have been corrected. . . .

Ishibashi finds that the author of *Ukigumo,* by contrast, is aware of the true nature of fiction:

First: Because the author of *Ukigumo* understands the novel, he makes people the center of his story and the plot its decoration. He does not sacrifice characterization for the sake of plot. The focus of the novel is on the characters; the plot is merely a feeble skeleton.

Second: Because the author of *Ukigumo* understands the novel, he portrays personality and ideas. He is extremely careful to match differences in social position and circumstances to personality and ideas. The true superiority of this novel lies in this point.

Third: Because the author of *Ukigumo* understands the novel, he deliberately makes a mediocre, incomplete man his hero. He does not portray unrealistic self-righteous, noble creatures. This is not a novel which describes only superficial virtue and beauty or is sketchy in its study of man's emotions. Before the hero takes any action, he thinks about it, turning it over in his mind. He hesitates, wandering between decision and indecision. He wants to take a step and does not take it; he wants to put down his hand and does not put it down. The author's analysis of the thoughts of his hero at such times is the most striking aspect of this novel.[23]

Ishibashi goes on to point out the difference between *Ukigumo* and the political novels which were so much in fashion. No great political hero appears; the plot does not trace the precipitous career of a poor student who rises rapidly to become prime minister and marry the daughter of a noble family. This is, by contrast, the tale of a weak, vacillating young man of no particular talent.

In searching for a few points to criticize, Ishibashi suggests that the women in *Ukigumo* are too masculine and that the hero, Bunzō, is too feminine. He cannot see why a man so filled with moral ideals as Bunzō should love a brusque, rude girl like Osei. Bunzō shows the greatest love and respect for his mother, but Osei is impudent and insulting to Omasa. Ishibashi is also disturbed by the way Bunzō laughs at the clerks in the office when he goes there for the first time; this, to the critic, is an entirely inappropriate reaction for so sympathetic and sensitive a young man.[24]

Part Two, chapters vii through xii, was printed in the same format as Part One. It appeared in February 1888. Again, Tsubouchi Yūzō's name appears as the author on the cover. The title page lists Harunoya Shujin and Futabatei Shimei as coauthors, and the colophon gives their names as Tsubouchi Shōyō and Hasegawa Tatsunosuke. Tsubouchi made no statement concerning the financial arrangements for Part Two except to remark that the problem of dividing the money arose only in relation to Part One.[25] It is assumed, therefore, that Futabatei received the whole sum—probably between 80 and 90 yen, since the manuscript was approximately the same length as Part One.

In Part Two Osei becomes increasingly attracted to Noboru. Omasa, Osei, and Noboru take an excursion together. No-

23. "*Ukigumo* no homeotoshi," *Gendai bungakuron taikei*, I, 44, 45.
24. *Ibid.*, pp. 46–51.
25. Tsubouchi, "Futabatei Shimei," p. 515.

boru deserts them for a few minutes to greet his supervisor, his supervisor's wife, and her pretty sister. Osei is momentarily jealous of the girl, and Noboru uses her jealousy as a weapon to tease her. Bunzō begins to grow suspicious, but his love for Osei at first prevents him from believing she could be interested in a coarse person such as Noboru. Proud of his influence in the office, Noboru offers to help Bunzō get reinstated. He makes the offer in front of Omasa and Osei. Bunzō is insulted and refuses, unwilling to accept a favor from the man he now considers his rival. He watches the flirtation between Osei and Noboru develop with Omasa's encouragement. He tries to assert himself to Noboru; they quarrel and Bunzō comes off poorly in the exchange.

The next day Omasa, warning Bunzō not to quarrel with Noboru again, suggests he profit by Noboru's help to recover his position. She hints that she might let him court Osei again if he resumed his work. After much reflection, Bunzō decides that he cannot take Omasa's advice. He goes to Osei, hoping she will confirm him in his decision. The girl is instructed by her mother to persuade Bunzō to accept Noboru's help, and when she opposes Bunzō's contrary decision, he abuses Noboru, calling him a "lackey" and a "loathsome insect." Osei feels obliged to defend Noboru, and in the end admits she is fond of him. Bunzō swears he will never speak to her again. Omasa arrives shortly after their quarrel and extracts a promise from Osei that she will have no more to do with Bunzō.

Critics were even more enthusiastic in their evaluation of these later chapters. Tokutomi Sohō (1863–1957), an influential editor, wrote:

this novel is far superior to anything we have had in the contemporary world of fiction. There is nothing especially funny or amusing in the novel. It is not magnificent or elegant. It is a banal, domestic novel. But the author must be recognized as an amazingly talented writer in that he can make men grieve or hate, be surprised or fascinated in such a banal context. How can he accomplish this? Although the events in the novel seem extremely random, limited, trivial, and pedestrian, he observes them with his penetrating eye, portrays them, analyzes and explains them. This is how he accomplishes his effect. In another way of speaking, the light which shines from the author's eye illuminates the mundane world and in the end creates characters and events in the image of reality. This author knows a great deal about man's mind and emotions. He goes beyond knowledge. He observes and then analyzes. *Ukigumo* is a study of the human mind; its author is a master of analyzing human emotions.[26]

A review appearing in the magazine *Iratsume* in May 1888 states: "To summarize our reaction to the whole work in brief, this book is a study of mood without peer in modern times; the simplicity of its plot is unrivaled. As for its style, it is written in colloquial language so rare as to have few imitators; its smooth diction is almost without comparison." [27] Reviewers were not uncritical of specific aspects of the novel which they found inconsistent or poorly expressed, but their praise of the freshness and authenticity of the plot and characterization far outweighed any faults they found. They were virtually unanimous in praising Futabatei for having created the first gembun itchi novel, though some expressed regret that in some passages he used older styles and too many difficult Chinese-derived words.[28]

The publication of Parts One and Two brought Futabatei fame. Between 1886 and 1888 he established himself as a leading exponent both of realism and of the gembun itchi style. *Ukigumo* emerged into a literary world receptive to any story with a simple, straightforward plot told in colloquial language. The principles stated by Tsubouchi were already widely accepted. When Ishibashi Ningetsu said that the

26. Tokutomi, "*Ukigumo* no mampyō," a review published originally in *Kokumin no tomo* on February 17, 1889, under Tokutomi's penname, Ōe Itsuru. Reprinted in *Zenshū*, I, 210–11.

27. Reprinted in *Zenshū*, I, 212.

28. The reviewer in *Iratsume* wonders why Futabatei wrote his preface in gazoku setchū buntai when he specifically says in it that he is presenting a gembun itchi novel. *Zenshū*, I, 216–17. The review appeared in June 1888.

value of *Ukigumo* lies in Futabatei's grasp of the importance of characterization, he restated a view previously expressed by Tsubouchi. The reviewer who compared the characters to figures in oil paintings was paying tribute to the depth and perception Futabatei used in drawing his four major characters. Tsubouchi had declared that a fine novelist displayed his talent by his ability "to depict emotions, to investigate them carefully—minutely, exhaustively, leaving little out—to make hypothetical, imaginary people move within the structure of his plot until we can see them as real people." [29] Futabatei achieved this in his tale of the unhappy, neglected Bunzō. His hero's innermost doubts and fears are bared for the reader. Futabatei describes the whole range of Bunzō's way of thinking. "*Ukigumo* is a study of the human mind," Tokutomi Sohō wrote, "its author is a master of analyzing human emotions." [30] Tsubouchi defined the perfect novel as one which "depicts what is difficult to paint in a painting; makes palpable what is difficult to express in a poem; portrays the mysterious which is impossible to project on the stage." [31] By the time Ishibashi and Tokutomi were writing their reviews, Tsubouchi's definition had become widely accepted; perceptive critics, they recognized that Futabatei had fulfilled the requisites for a good novel.

Aibiki and *Meguriai*

In July and August of 1888 Futabatei published a translation of Turgenev's *The Rendezvous* (1850), a story from the *Sportsman's Sketches,* under the title *Aibiki,* a literal equivalent of the original. His translation appeared in the magazine *Kokumin no tomo.*

Futabatei maintained a close connection with *Kokumin no tomo* from 1887 until it ceased publication in 1898. In

29. In the introduction to *Gaiseishi den, Senshū, Bessatsu,* II, 450.
30. *Zenshū,* I, 211.
31. *Shōsetsu shinzui,* p. 32.

August 1887 Futabatei called on the magazine's editor, Tokutomi Sohō, one of the most famous social critics of the day. He was interested in Tokutomi's analysis of contemporary Japanese society and in his attempts to bring enlightenment to the people through his liberal magazine.

Tokutomi's belief in the educational mission of the press was expressed in the editorial statement which appeared in 1887 inside the title page of the first seven issues:

We believe that the time has come when we, the people of the nation, must pay the utmost concern to conditions existing in our country. It is now over twenty years since the Restoration; our Meiji society will soon have gone through a whole generation. The aged survivors of olden days will soon leave us; the young people of the new Japan are coming to join us. The ways of the East will disappear; the ways of the West will soon overtake us. The period for destroying the old will end and the time for building the new will be upon us. We must realize that we stand now at the crossroads for making decisions which will determine our nation's future; its security or peril, its rise or fall are in our hands. We hope that by publishing this magazine we will rouse our fellow countrymen to the burden we share.[32]

Futabatei made less of an impression on Tokutomi than he had on Tsubouchi; in fact, he had to call several times before he found Tokutomi at home, and even then Tokutomi had little to say.[33] Futabatei wrote a letter introducing himself after his first fruitless visit to Tokutomi's house. The letter explained Futabatei's reasons for seeking the older man's friendship and indicated how inadequate he felt about understanding his own society:

I wanted so much to see you so that I might have a long talk with you and ask you many questions I have on my mind. I seek your guidance as a teacher and adviser on the arts and social sciences, but particularly on matters relating to the state of affairs in our nation. . . . I studied Russian at Gaigo Gakkō. As you know, the books a language student must read deal with

32. *Kokumin no tomo,* No. 1 (February 1887).
33. Nakamura, *Futabatei Shimei den,* pp. 207–9.

art and literature and not with the social sciences. In the five years I was in school, the books I read were almost all novels or literary criticism. . . . Because the education I received for my career was thus incomplete, my understanding of the world is extremely inadequate.[34]

Although Tokutomi was unable to offer Futabatei the kind of intellectual companionship he sought, he appreciated his literary talent and readily helped him to have his work published. In April 1888, after Part Two had appeared, Futabatei's second translation from Russian literary criticism was printed in *Kokumin no tomo;* in July this was followed by *Aibiki.* According to Futabatei's introduction to *Aibiki,* he had translated it at Tokutomi's suggestion.[35] Tokutomi did not read Russian, but probably he wanted a Turgenev story for his magazine and left the choice to Futabatei.

Aibiki made a great impression on the reading public. Professional critics took issue with certain aspects of the gembun itchi style of the translation, but the youth of the country was enchanted. Kambara Ariake (1876–1952),[36] one of Japan's leading symbolist poets, recalled:

I first came to know Futabatei's name through *Aibiki.* I was then in middle school and my ability to evaluate literature was, of course, immature. I was still at the stage when *Kajin no kigū*[37] was my favorite reading matter. A translation from the works of the Russian novelist Turgenev sounded very exotic. I thought I

34. *Zenshū,* XIV, 5–6.
35. *Zenshū,* I, 156.
36. Kambara Ariake was a student of the poetry of Rossetti, Browning, and Swinburne, and he was deeply influenced by the French symbolist poets. In addition to writing his own tragic, forlorn poems, he published translations of European poetry. His first collection of poems appeared in 1902. He is considered the father of the symbolist movement in Japan and his poems are felt to be poignantly representative of the desolation, sickness, and loneliness besetting the city-bred modern poet.
37. *Kajin no kigū* [strange encounters with beautiful women] is a tale by Tōkai Sanshi (1852–1922). It was published in eight parts between 1885 and 1897. It is an episodic account of the adventures of a patriotic young Japanese who had opposed the Imperial forces at the time of the Restoration and is living in exile abroad. The novel is described by Sir George Sansom in *The Western World and Japan,* pp. 411–15.

would have a look at it. Futabatei's gembun itchi style with its masterly use of colloquial language—that unique style—sounded so fresh its echoes seemed to go on endlessly whispering in my ears. A nameless joy filled me. I was so moved that something deep down within me almost wanted to shut it out. . . . When I read the passages describing the forest, I could visualize the scene before my eyes. The changeable sky of late autumn, the light of the sun piercing through the forest, the rain lightly falling—it was as if I were looking at a scene in the country through which I had walked just the day before. I could hear the arrogant, cold, rough voice of the man, and the pleading, forlorn voice of the girl. The experience was all the more magical perhaps because I could not understand why I was so deeply moved. My reaction to the story filled my whole being; it was like music. Reading *Aibiki* was a completely new experience in my life.[38]

The novelist Tayama Katai (1871–1930)[39] also described his reaction to *Aibiki:*

It was such a marvelous new style. I may not have been able to appreciate it fully at that age, but still the subtle description of nature made my heart leap. "Aa. Aki da! Dare da ka mukō o tōru to miete, karaguruma no oto ga kokū ni hibikiwatatta—" [Yes, it is fall! Someone passes in the distance—the rattle of an empty wagon echoed in the clear air].[40] How often I thought of that line when I was in the fields of oak at home in the country or when I walked among the hazel trees on the hills outside Tokyo. This translation of *The Rendezvous* may be credited in large part with the fresh outlook toward nature which was to be revealed in Meiji literature.[41]

In September 1888 a review of *Aibiki* by Ishibashi Shian

---

38. Kambara, II, 194–95. An article written in 1909.

39. Tayama was a leading novelist of the Naturalist school. His most famous novel was *Futon* [the quilt] (1907). A translation of his story from his novel *Ippeisotsu* [one soldier] (1908) appears in Keene, *Modern Japanese Literature*, pp. 143–58.

40. Tayama has misquoted the passage slightly. It reads "Aa. Aki da! Dare da ka hageyama no mukō o tōru to miete" [Yes, it is fall! Someone passes on the other side of the bare mountain]. *Zenshū*, I, 167.

41. "Futabatei Shimei kun," *Zenshū*, II, 195. An article written in 1909.

(1867–1927), a novelist and critic active in the Ken'yūsha group, appeared in *Kokumin no tomo*. Ishibashi was delighted that Futabatei chose so simple and evocative a story to translate rather than "something gaudy and unclean." He was critical, however, of Futabatei's occasional use of difficult Chinese words and Bakin-chō sentences. He also disliked what he considered to be Futabatei's attempts to make the plain style of the original more interesting by the addition of "cloying" metaphors, the excessive use of modifying phrases and adjectives, and the repetition of phrases. Ishibashi believed this was a fault of the gembun itchi style in general and cited Yazaki as another offender.[42]

Ishibashi was obviously sincere in stating his own distaste for this quality, but he is mistaken in asserting that Futabatei added anything to the original. Futabatei was in fact trying to reproduce every phrase of the original text: the metaphors were chosen to match those used by Turgenev; the same repetitions appear in the original.

This close rendering of the original was the result of a deliberate effort on Futabatei's part to find colloquial Japanese equivalents for every word of Turgenev's text. He felt that to reproduce the rhythm of a foreign language, words had to be grouped as they were in the original; commas and periods had to match Russian usage despite the great differences between the two languages. As a result of Gray's methods in Gaigo Gakkō, Futabatei had learned the importance of the sound of Russian, and he strove to transfer that melody into Japanese. In an article written in 1906 entitled "Yo ga hon'yaku no hyōjun" [my standard for translations], Futabatei described the ideals he tried to attain in translating:

If you carefully savor Western writing, you will find it possesses a natural kind of melody which is not apparent when you read it to yourself. When read aloud, the inflection is revealed; it is like music. It is extremely delightful just to listen to someone reading. Although you can understand the true meaning of the

42. Ishibashi Shian, a writer of humorous, satirical fiction, was not related to the critic Ishibashi Ningetsu. The review is reprinted in *Zenshū*, II, 192–94.

words better when you read to yourself, points which were not clear at first become understandable and interesting when read aloud. This is certainly a characteristic of Western writing. . . . When you are going to translate foreign writing, you absolutely must transfer this rhythm. In regard to my own translations, this was my first guide to the form my translation would take. . . .

If you think solely of the meaning when translating a foreign language and attach excessive importance to it, you will take the risk of harming the original. I have always believed that you must saturate yourself with the rhythm of the original for some time, then transfer it to your own work. In my attempt to use Russian rhythms in my translations, I did not omit a single comma or period. If the original contained three commas and one period, the translation also had three commas and one period. Particularly when I first started to translate, this consideration induced me to try desperately to use the same number of words in my version as in the original and not to destroy the arrangement of the sentences. I worked as hard as I could on the form, but it did not always come out as I hoped; there were times when I simply could not meet my own standards. At such moments, I would feel I lacked the talent to live up to my own expectations, but I never really believed that my goal was impossible or that I would not eventually succeed. For many years afterward I held to this goal as my ideal as far as form was concerned. . . .

Futabatei realized that the reproduction of the individuality of a writer's style required the translator to capture the spirit of the author as well as the meaning of his words:

Style being inexorably tied to the poetic spirit of the particular author, the rhythm will vary with each writer. There is no reason to suppose, therefore, that a translation appropriate for one author will suit every other. The translator must be sensitive to the poetic spirit of each author—Turgenev is Turgenev, Gorky is Gorky—he must make his mind and body, his every action, identical with the original author's and conscientiously transfer this poetic spirit to his own version. This is truly the most basic and essential condition of translating.

Let us take Turgenev as an example. Turgenev's poetic spirit is not of autumn or winter, but of spring—not early spring, nor mid-spring, but late spring. It expresses that moment when the cherry blossoms, having burst into full bloom, are about to fall. It suggests the sensation of wandering along a narrow road lined with cherry trees on a night when the spring moon shines dimly, beautifully, far off in a clouded sky. A feeling of loneliness amidst beauty is evoked by Turgenev's spirit. This feeling runs throughout his novels, and if the translator loses it, if he does not become Turgenev when he writes, his translation will often be at odds with the original. He must not be tied to the outward forms alone; he must first saturate himself with the basic poetic spirit and then translate in such a way that he will not destroy either the poetry or the form.

Futabatei goes on to say that he felt he had failed to reproduce Turgenev's individuality in Japanese, not because he was unaware of it but because his command of Japanese was inadequate. He considered himself better able to handle Russian than Japanese.[43]

Although Futabatei felt dissatisfied with the results of his efforts, the translation of *Aibiki* differs categorically from the translations of his contemporaries. The differences become apparent if we compare *Aibiki* with, for instance, Tsubouchi's *Shumpū jōwa*. Tsubouchi's version of *The Bride of Lammermoor* has many omissions, but Futabatei includes every image and metaphor of *The Rendezvous*. Tsubouchi expands Scott's imagery to make it more in keeping with the style of traditional Japanese narrative; Futabatei does not add a single word. In contrast to Tsubouchi's *Bakin-chō,* so close to narrative poetry, the text is, for the most part, straightforward colloquial prose.

Futabatei's prose is distinguished by a cleanness and directness of line unprecedented in Japanese fiction. The delicacy and pathos of Turgenev's story, as it describes now a helpless lovelorn maiden, now a callous, indifferent young man, are fully conveyed in the Japanese. The justly famous translation of the scene in the forest has a stylistic ease and grace exceeding that even of *Ukigumo.* Futabatei's genius for writing dialogue is revealed again in the harsh, cold words of the man and the gentle pleas of the girl. The story is presented in such natural Japanese that it is difficult to believe that this is a translation and not an original story.

Futabatei's translation of Turgenev's *Three Meetings* (1851) was printed serially from October 1888 to January 1889 under the title *Meguriai* [chance meetings].[44] The first installment appeared in the first issue of a new literary magazine, *Miyako no hana,* published by Kinkōdō, and edited by Yamada Bimyō.

A glowing review of *Meguriai* by Ishibashi Ningetsu appeared in *Kokumin no tomo* in February 1889. Ishibashi begins:

> When I read it for the first time, I found nothing unusual in it. Only after repeated readings did I first become aware of the delicacy of the structure; each word glistened on the page like a precious jewel. How greatly I admired it! In its unforgettable beauty and stylistic perfection *Meguriai* far surpasses the ordinary run of novels. If someone were to ask me my choice as the best of current fiction, I would, without hesitation, answer *Meguriai*. The careful reader will discover exquisite felicities. The structure is truly incomparable, the descriptions amazing.

Although much of the remainder of Ishibashi's review deals with the excellence of the plot and not with the translation, he ends by quoting some examples from among "the countless number of jewel-like words woven into the book." [45]

The style of *Meguriai* resembles that of *Aibiki,* but the effect produced on the reader is not identical. Although Futabatei again achieved a systematically worked out, precise translation, *Meguriai,* a much longer story with a far more complicated plot, gave him more room to develop a consistent tone than did *Aibiki.* The style, more like that of the later chapters of *Ukigumo,* is tight, rapid to the point of

---

44. *Aibiki, Meguriai,* and *Katokoi* [unrequited love], Futabatei's translation of Turgenev's *Assya* (1857), were published together in book form in October 1896. The title of *Meguriai* was changed to *Kigū* [chance meetings]. Futabatei made some changes in both translations. The revised translations are reprinted in *Zenshū,* II, 64–97.

45. Reprinted in *Zenshū,* II, 195–96.

being almost staccato, and absolutely clear, but it possesses a stiffness absent from *Aibiki*. In approaching more closely a modern style shorn almost completely of the poetic qualities of Bakin-chō or jōruri, Futabatei lost something of the grace which made *Aibiki* so lovely. The result is a prose style colder and more monotonous than his earlier work. It is dangerous to assess a translation; one's reaction is necessarily influenced by the nature of the story. *Three Meetings* lacks the simplicity of *The Rendezvous*; its plot is filled with contrived situations and false mysteries readily explained by obvious facts. The poignant realism and touching nostalgia of *The Rendezvous* are missing. The coldness one finds in Futabatei's style probably resulted from a difference in his own attitude toward the two stories and may not mark any real change in his approach to writing in the gembun itchi style.

With *Aibiki* and *Meguriai* Futabatei revealed to the people of his nation the merits of European fiction. By not permitting himself to leave a single word untranslated and by writing in a style so close to the speech of his day, he communicated the true meaning of the modern, realistic short story as it was understood in Europe. These stories represent a realization of the ideal set forth by Tsubouchi in the introduction to *Gaiseishi den;* Japan at last had translations which could demonstrate the value of European fiction and help to inject a new vitality into Japanese literature. The reaction of young intellectuals to the new style is summarized in Tayama Katai's *Tōkyō no sanjūnen* [thirty years in Tokyo] (1917). In listing the various books and articles which most affected his circle in their student days, Tayama once again recalls how he felt when he read *Aibiki* in *Kokumin no tomo*:

Having been raised on the stiff Chinese classics and other ancient Chinese and Japanese texts, I was deeply moved by the precise, startling descriptive passages in this story. Could this be good style, I wondered. Yet I realized that such a clear-cut style was the strongest characteristic of Western writing and that, in the future, the style of Japanese literature would most certainly have to move in this same direction.[46]

Ukigumo, Part Three

The recognition Futabatei obtained from the publication of the first two parts of *Ukigumo* and the Turgenev translations failed to give him the confidence he needed to write Part Three easily. He struggled over it many months as earlier he had labored over the beginning of the novel and started to write Part Three in the fall or winter of 1888. His journal for 1888, which he entitled *Kuchiba shū: hitokagome* [a collection of dead leaves: first basketful], contains four outlines for the final chapters of *Ukigumo.*[47] These outlines appear near the end of the journal but are not dated. The novel as it emerged in July and August of 1889 differs considerably from any of the outlines; it would seem that Futabatei changed the plot as he wrote.

The discovery of these outlines after Futabatei's death led some recent critics to the conclusion that *Ukigumo* was left unfinished. Examination of the evidence supporting this conclusion, however, reveals certain errors and suggests instead the possibility that Futabatei may actually have considered his novel completed. On the other hand, there is no question but that he was thoroughly dissatisfied with the third part, and it greatly relieved him when he could stop.

Although he kept journals for both 1888 and 1889, he left no record of his daily activities during these years. His journals are filled primarily with drafts of articles, translations, or chapters from *Ukigumo,* although some personal notes relating to his state of mind are also included. If he

---

46. *Tōkyō no sanjūnen,* p. 287. Tayama and other writers of the Naturalist school were equally enthusiastic about *Ukigumo.* Nakamura Mitsuo discusses their reaction in *Futabatei Shimei,* pp. 78–82.

47. *Kuchiba shū: hitokagome, Zenshū,* XI, 31–36.

kept a diary in this period, it is no longer extant. His activities in 1888–89 must, therefore, be deduced from the limited sources available.

An article in the magazine *Jogaku zasshi* of January 26, 1889, mentions Futabatei was then engaged in writing Part Three of *Ukigumo* and had already completed two chapters.[48] In February 1889 Parts One and Two went into a second printing, and Kinkōdō's advertisement for them in *Kokumin no tomo* confirms that "Futabatei is in the midst of writing Part Three and should complete it shortly." [49]

The task proved more difficult than his publishers anticipated. Kinkōdō decided to publish Part Three in *Miyako no hana*, but Futabatei did not send them the manuscript of the early chapters until June. He was still engaged in writing chapter xviii in late June or early July 1889. A portion of a draft of the chapter is found in his journal, *Ochiba no hakiyose: futakagome* [a heap of fallen leaves: second basketful], following an entry dated June 26.[50] Although the portion of the chapter in this draft is quite similar in content to the final version, variations in wording and tempo indicate that Futabatei spent at least some time polishing the prose and developing the plot before he submitted the manuscript to the publisher.[51]

Chapters xiii, xiv, and xv appeared in the issue of *Miyako no hana* dated July 7, 1889. Futabatei did not receive his copy of the magazine until three days later. He had been waiting impatiently for it and turned immediately to his own story. The sight of his work in print came as a shock.

48. Reprinted in *Zenshū*, I, 218–19.

49. *Kokumin no tomo*, No. 40 (February 2, 1889), back page.

50. Very few of the entries in Futabatei's journals are listed under specific dates, and only a few more can be dated from internal evidence. In those cases where no date can be ascertained, I have accepted the dating ascribed to the entries by Nakamura in *Futabatei Shimei den*. I have also assumed that the entries follow some chronological order, since Futabatei was writing in a bound book and was not likely to have skipped pages and then gone back to fill them in at a later date.

51. *Ochiba no hakiyose: futakagome*, pp. 71–75; and *Ukigumo*, pp. 139–43.

When I found my own work in the magazine, I picked it up in my hands and read it pacing up and down the room. My fingers were shaking. I don't know whether they had been trembling before; I only became aware of them at that moment. Then suddenly I felt my face flush. I had not realized what a hopeless writer I was until then, but when I saw my work in print, I felt I simply couldn't read on. Even when I finally got through it, I remained extremely depressed. I kept wandering round and round my room, mumbling to myself. Finally, unable to bear the agony, I clasped my hands to my head in despair.[52]

The remaining chapters were published in consecutive issues of *Miyako no hana*. Chapters xvi and xvii appeared on July 21; chapter xviii on August 4. Chapter xix was published on August 18, and at the end of the chapter the word *owari* [end] appears. The writing of chapter xix left Futababei completely exhausted. His journal for the summer of 1889 contains several references to his annoyance and frustration with the novel, with writing in general, and with the literary world. On seeing the early chapters of Part Three in print, he concluded "I basically am not a novelist and I do not think I will ever become one," and "I shall probably not write another novel"; after finishing chapter xix in late July or early August, he realized "my endless brooding has been caused by the trouble I've had in writing this chapter"; and by the time he reached the end of chapter xix, he decided he must stop. He had been terribly depressed and even contemplated suicide, but he was much relieved to have fulfilled his obligations to Kinkōdō. "When I reflect on my feelings at this moment," he wrote in his journal:

I realize my misery comes from the troubles I've had in writing this novel. After I started, I found my material inadequate; I was incapable of resolving the plot as I wished. I have to smile

52. *Ochiba no hakiyose: futakagome*, pp. 77–78. Tsubouchi points out that although Futabatei wrote this passage in his own journal and was no doubt sincere in recording his frustration of that moment, he was also practicing writing a piece of self-analysis. It apparently was Futabatei's habit to indulge in periods of searching self-criticism and to talk about his feelings or write about them. "Futabatei no koto," p. 22.

when I think what a fool I am. But then I turn and look up at heaven; it is boundless. I look down at the earth; a million things are growing. It will be like this a hundred years from now, a thousand years from now, and tens of thousands of years from now. My life does not fill even a tiny niche in all eternity. Should I grieve because I am troubled? If I open my heart and relax my spirit, there will be joy within my troubles. If one's heart is closed and one's spirit strained, one will not find peace even with great fortune. Man's happiness or unhappiness depends greatly on his feelings. If I am to escape from my present feeling of depression, I must first reform my spirit.

And then, in the following entry, we learn how desperate he had been: "Only when you have thought of leaving this world do you realize its true worth." [53]

In the closing chapter of Part Two, Bunzō, having quarreled with Osei, vows never to speak to her again. Part Three, chapters xiii to xix, opens with Bunzō alone in his room immediately after the quarrel. He decides he must move from Omasa's house but, after finding an adequate room elsewhere, he still cannot arouse himself to make the change. He begins instead to regret his quarrel with Osei. The next day, seeing her weeping alone in her room, he resolves to make his peace with her. Two days later his first opportunity presents itself, but when he addresses Osei, she immediately leaves the room. At lunch, in the presence of Omasa and the maid, Onabe, she turns on Bunzō and attacks him mercilessly for having first insulted her and then attempting to make amends. Omasa commands her to leave and informs Bunzō that in the future he may not speak to her daughter. During the days that follow, he realizes that he can no longer justify his remaining with the Sonoda family: he has been insulted by both mother and daughter and cannot hope for a reconciliation with Osei. He begins to see that he was mistaken in his evaluation of Osei, that she is too superficial to appreciate him. Still he does not leave.

53. *Ochiba no hakiyose: futakagome*, pp. 78, 84, 85.

By chapter xvii, Omasa and Osei, drawn together by their mutual dislike of Bunzō, realize that they have become rather bored with their lives. Noboru has been so busy with giving English lessons to his chief's wife and sister-in-law that he hardly ever appears. One day Noboru stops for a visit; the delighted Osei joins freely with him in flirtatious interplay. Noboru's visits again become more frequent, but he is still more interested in discussing business with Omasa than in joking with Osei, who is frustrated in her attempts to join their adult conversations. Her only way of holding Noboru's attention is to engage him in childish banter. Omasa's suggestion that Noboru might make a good husband awakens Osei to the realization that she may be in love with him. Noboru senses the change in her attitude but fails to respond. He continues his light banter with her, though eventually it makes Osei grow cold. Depressed, Osei persuades her mother to allow her to take knitting lessons. Noboru stops coming to the house.

Finally, in chapter xix, the events of chapters xvii and xviii are related from Bunzō's point of view. He is horrified by Osei's flirtation with Noboru and convinced that she has fallen into evil ways. He decides he must warn her that she is destroying her life and tries in vain to find some means of conveying this warning. Instead, he spends his time in his room brooding about Osei's problems. Then, suddenly, Noboru's visits cease. Osei still maintains her silence toward Bunzō, but because she no longer glares at him, hope springs in Bunzō's heart. At the very end of the novel Osei favors Bunzō with a kind smile, suggesting to him that the time may have come for a reconciliation.

The outlines for Part Three transcribed by Futabatei in his journal, *Kuchiba shū: hitokagome,* differ in various respects from the novel in its present form. In the first, third, and fourth of the four outlines, Futabatei assigns dates to several of the chapters and briefly indicates the events to be included in each chapter. The second of the outlines is only five lines long and, although headed chapter xiii, appears to be a synopsis of several chapters.

All four of the outlines list events which do not occur in the novel: Bunzō's uncle Magobei is to return home and assume an active part in dealing with Osei; Bunzō is to receive word of a fire at his mother's house in Shizuoka accompanied by a plea for money; and Osei is to have an affair with Noboru, bringing despair to Bunzō and, later, to the rest of her family. The third plan called for the death of Bunzō's mother; the fourth, for Osei to be abandoned by Noboru, tormented by Omasa, and finally lose her mind and die in a mental hospital. The first outline includes a total of twenty-two chapters; the third and fourth twenty-three each.[54]

Futabatei jotted down a series of notes concerning the end of *Ukigumo* on the closing pages of the second volume of his journals, *Ochiba no hakiyose: futakagome*. This is the last entry in Futabatei's journal for 1889 and his last mention in writing about the closing chapters of *Ukigumo*. The entry, like most in his journals, is not dated, but the sequence of the material in the journal indicates that it was written after the publication of chapter xix and also after Futabatei had decided to take his government post. It is apparent from the irregularity of the style in these notes that he was merely jotting down disconnected thoughts as they occurred to him; as a result, the wording is highly ambiguous. He wrote, in part:

Osei's heart is difficult to recapture. She is like a boat caught on a wave, drifting out to sea.
Bunzō felt incapable of doing anything—he failed to do anything—he couldn't do anything.
Bunzō is depressed and uneasy—that is much the way I feel when I read over *Ukigumo!*
Bunzō foolishly puts his hope in the future. It is impossible for him to believe he has cut his ties with Osei.

54. *Kuchiba shū: hitokagome,* pp. 31–36.

Therefore, without questioning the fact that Osei is going for knitting lessons, he thought it was good that Noboru had stopped coming to the house. My!

Bunzō felt as if he had already warned Osei. Noticing with surprise that Osei had become more like her old self, he did not warn her.[55]

The only other time Futabatei is known to have referred to the plot of *Ukigumo* was in a rather casual, disorganized interview in 1897. He was asked if there had existed an over-all plan for the plot. Yes, he replied, "The general plan was that after winning Osei, Hondo Noboru would desert her and marry his supervisor's sister-in-law. Bunzō, though fully aware of what was happening, was to watch from the sidelines, suffering from his inability to do anything." [56]

Futabatei's journals were not published during his lifetime. Only after his death, when his wife gave them to Uchida Roan (1868–1929), did their existence become known, and not until 1953 were they published in entirety. Uchida, who became friendly with Futabatei in the fall of 1889, served as Futabatei's literary executor. He wrote his biographical article, "Futabatei no isshō" [the life of Futabatei], in June 1909, just after Futabatei's death. Uchida includes passages from the journals but not the final entry of the second volume relating to the conclusion of *Ukigumo*. He mentions the outlines found at the end of Futabatei's 1888 journal and notes that *Ukigumo* covers only a part of these outlines. He therefore assumes that Futabatei was obliged against his will to submit the last chapters in an unpolished form. Uchida, however, does not say that the novel was left incomplete.[57]

Tsubouchi also had access to the journals. He borrowed them from Futabatei's widow before she released them to

55. *Ochiba no hakiyose: futakagome*, p. 96.
56. Futabatei, "Sakka kushin dan," *Zenshū*, IX, 143.
57. Uchida revised his article in 1914 and included it in *Kinō kyō*, which was published in 1916. "Futabatei no isshō," p. 392.

Uchida, and had them copied.[58] Tsubouchi quotes extensively from the journals in his biographical article, "Futabatei no koto" [concerning Futabatei], but makes no mention either of the outlines or of this final entry, nor does he suggest that *Ukigumo* was incomplete. These writings provide striking—if negative—evidence that Futabatei's contemporaries thought of *Ukigumo* as a finished novel. Tsubouchi, better acquainted than anyone else with Futabatei during this period of his career, would surely have commented on the conclusion if he deemed that it offered special problems.

Readers of *Ukigumo* for fifty years after its first publication considered it to be a complete novel; the lack of resolution to the plot, far from disturbing Japanese critics, appealed to those tired of more conventional dramatic finales. Critics believed its fluid ending represented a remarkable innovation in modern Japanese literature, and the Naturalist writers of the early twentieth century adopted the same technique. Critics found in Futabatei's novel the forerunner of this vogue, but Japanese novels, whether ancient or modern, have frequently concluded on a note of uncertainty, and readers have never insisted that all loose ends be tied by the author. In any case, we may note that the standard prewar history of Meiji literature, *Meiji bungaku shi,* treated *Ukigumo* as a complete novel.[59]

58. Tsubouchi also began writing biographical articles about Futabatei in 1909."Futabatei no koto," which appeared in a book entitled *Kaki no heta* in 1933, is the last of a series of studies Tsubouchi made of his friend. Realizing that his copies of the journals contained errors, Tsubouchi tried to compare them with the original before publishing "Futabatei no koto," but he learned from Futabatei's widow that Uchida had not returned them with Futabatei's other papers. Tsubouchi's version of the excerpts from the journals differs therefore somewhat from the authentic text. (See *Kaki no heta,* p. 6.) In quoting from Futabatei's journals, both Uchida and Tsubouchi have added punctuation and, at some points, additional characters which help to make the journal entries more understandable. Tsubouchi's version is particularly helpful in this regard.

59. By Homma Hisao. The work was published in 1935. Homma's analysis of *Ukigumo* is a sensitive and detailed study indicating a careful reading of the text. Homma considers the fact that *Ukigumo* presents a picture of

Critical opinion largely changed, however, after the publication in 1937 of an article on *Ukigumo* by Yanagida Izumi (1894–), which stated unequivocally that the novel was unfinished and asserted that it is a serious error to interpret the ending in terms of the techniques of the Naturalist writers. Yanagida had no access to the manuscripts of the four outlines of *Ukigumo*; he based his conclusion on Futabatei's statement in 1897 cited above, and on a photograph of a page of the manuscript outline printed in 1910.[60] Yanagida supposed that the synopsis Futabatei mentioned in 1897 was identical with the outline in the photograph.[61]

The photograph Yanagida used was indistinct, and blots and strikeouts on the page made it difficult to decipher. The version he offered in his article as proof of his theory consequently differed from the actual text. Yanagida contended that *Ukigumo* followed this outline exactly up to the end of chapter xix, where Futabatei stopped. The outline Yanagida examined was the fourth of those included in *Kuchiba shū: hitokagome,* and failed to show the entry for chapter xxiii, on another page of the manuscript. Yanagida was mistaken in saying that the outline and the plot are the same: the outline calls for Osei to start knitting lessons (which may have been a pretext for her to leave the house) in chapter xv, but she actually starts at the end of chapter xviii. Her affair with Noboru was to begin in chapter xv, followed in chapter xvi by her reconciliation with Bunzō, but neither event occurs. Yanagida admitted that he could not decipher the entry for chapter xviii. The version of this chapter in the outline differs considerably from *Ukigumo*: in chapter xviii Magobei was to return home and Bunzō to receive news of the fire in Shizuoka.

The description of chapter xxiii in the fourth outline in-

one segment of a man's life and is not a story with a momentous beginning or end as its most valuable qualities. His discussion appears in Volume II, pp. 233–47, and his comments on this point on pp. 236 and 241.

60. In Volume I of the *Futabatei Shimei zenshū,* edited by Ikebe Kichitarō, facing p. 224.

61. Yanagida Izumi, pp. 22–26.

cludes the scene of Osei's losing her mind and dying in a hospital. Futabatei made no mention of this development in his 1897 résumé of the plot. Furthermore, in 1897 Futabatei said he intended Noboru to marry the chief's sister-in-law; this detail does not appear in the photograph of the fourth outline or anywhere else in the journal. The outline Yanagida examined cannot, therefore, have been identical with the synopsis to which Futabatei referred in 1897. Yanagida was clearly wrong, moreover, in his assertion that since *Ukigumo* follows the plot described in the outline until chapter xix, Futabatei merely stopped before he finished the work he previously planned.

Yanagida would surely have reached quite different conclusions if he had had access to the printed version made available in 1953. Seen side by side, it becomes obvious that all four outlines are tentative work sheets. In the successive outlines Futabatei shifted elements of the plot from one chapter to another and even made substantial changes in the plot itself. It would be mistaken to base any judgment about Part Three on these outlines; they were merely notes intended for Futabatei's own use, modified or discarded as he wrote.

The synopsis Futabatei described in 1897 was apparently still another plan for the novel which, although similar to the outlines in general, departed from them in certain details. The synopsis indicates that Futabatei had abandoned various complications in his plot: the fire in Shizuoka, Magobei's participation in the problems of the Sonoda household, and the death of Bunzō's mother. The melodramatic scene of having Osei's insanity and death in a hospital had also been discarded. The groundwork for the marriage of Noboru and the chief's sister-in-law, mentioned by Futabatei in 1897, had been laid in the novel. After she is first introduced in chapter vii, we learn in chapter xvii that Noboru has been giving the chief's wife and her sister English lessons, and the last line of chapter xviii states that "Noboru has been spending his time elsewhere of late," that is, else-

where than at the Sonoda house. The marriage does not occur in the novel, but the reader has been prepared for the
event.

In deciding whether Futabatei wrote his novel in accordance with the synopsis, a great deal depends on the expression "after winning Osei" ("Osei o te ni irete kara"). Although this expression in Japanese is ambiguous, most probably it refers to an affair and should not be interpreted as
meaning simply that Noboru had won Osei's affection. The
affair would have to occur after the middle of chapter xviii.
This chapter opens with a description of how Noboru and
Omasa ignore Osei while they are discussing business, treating her as a child, to her resentment. She flirts with Noboru,
teasing and coaxing him into indulging in childish antics
with her. Omasa tells the girl to behave in a more ladylike
fashion, and when a friend of Omasa's arrives with her newly
betrothed daughter, Osei realizes that she herself may be
ready for marriage. Omasa suggests Noboru as a husband;
Osei goes to her room to consider this suggestion. Suddenly
Osei has emerged into womanhood. Futabatei then describes
the events of subsequent days swiftly:

> For some days afterward, Osei was restless and uncomfortable
> in Noboru's presence, for she was trying to hide her feelings.
> She hoped to keep him from guessing that anything had changed
> between them by acting as childishly as always. Despite her best
> efforts, she gave herself away. A barely perceptible thickness crept
> into the tone of her voice when she spoke to him, she laughed at
> inappropriate moments, and kept bobbing in and out of the
> room. She carried on casual conversations with her mother, vainly
> pretending not to notice that Noboru was watching her. When
> their eyes met, she became flustered and turned quickly away.
> Omasa indiscreetly teased her about the way she was acting,
> hoping to call Noboru's attention to Osei's interest in him; she
> thereby caused her daughter even further embarrassment.
>
> But as the days passed and Noboru remained his old, joking,
> playful self, Osei's behavior changed. Gone was her bashfulness;
> her awkwardness before him vanished. She no longer cared
> whether he appeared or not, and his presence failed to cheer

her. On the contrary, the mere sight of him made her sad and pensive. She was cold and distant, treating him like an estranged relative. Had they quarreled or had she merely grown tired of him? Perhaps the novelty of her infatuation had worn off. It is impossible to tell.

Noboru continued his attempts at bantering with her from time to time, but he got no response—in fact, Osei ignored him. The edge went off his jokes; they fell absolutely flat.

When he was not in the house, Osei affected great cheerfulness, playing and joking merrily with whomever happened to be present. She made a great show of reciting poems and singing songs and dancing with Onabe, who could not imagine what was happening. Running, cavorting, laughing—Osei created a gay clatter about the house. But the moment Noboru came, her mood changed and she grew quiet and forlorn.

In the few remaining pages of chapter xviii, Osei is depicted as sweet and congenial to her mother. A few days later she persuades her mother to let her take knitting lessons in the evening. She goes off to her teacher's house regularly, dressed in her finest kimono and wearing the sort of heavy makeup she had once scorned as cheap and vulgar.

The total impression given by chapter xviii is that Osei, having decided she is in love with Noboru, finds him unresponsive; rejected for the first time in her life, she seeks amusement elsewhere. If Futabatei had intended to indicate that Osei and Noboru were having an affair, he would have had no reason to describe their relations in this way. The recounting of the same events in chapter xix leaves substantially the same impression; the difference lies only in the way Bunzō interprets the flirtatious exchanges between Noboru and Osei.

There is no question that chapter xviii is sketchy, and this may well have been an important factor in Futabatei's despair with the novel. The scene above was to be the culmination of the flirtation between Noboru and Osei which had been building up in importance since the end of chapter vi, and yet the romance is described in a few short lines. Osei's emergence from girlhood into womanhood is effectively suggested, but the balance of the chapter is flat and hurried.

The conclusion of chapter xix is ambiguous. Bunzō decides again, as so often in the novel, that he will try to make his peace with Osei; he goes upstairs to await an opportunity. His earlier decisions to talk with Osei had all ended in quarrels; it may well be true of this encounter too. Perhaps nothing will come of Bunzō's love, but, on the other hand, she may be ready for a reconciliation. The reader must decide this for himself. If Futabatei was trying to show that Bunzō would ultimately be rejected, as his notes in his 1889 journal and his comments in the interview of 1897 indicate, then he obviously failed.

We can only conclude that both chapters xviii and xix were written hastily and that the author did not know what he intended to do with his characters. The story had got out of hand; Futabatei was obviously confused. The final rush to complete the book and get it off to the publisher in time for the periodical's deadline probably kept Futabatei from working as carefully on the final chapters as on the earlier portions. A slow and deliberative writer, he was incapable of producing a satisfactory first version and had to rewrite all of his work, both novels and translations. It is apparent from his journal for the three months from June to August of 1889 that he was greatly distressed. He was in need of money, his family was making him very uncomfortable, and he was in despair over *Ukigumo*. Futabatei was in no condition to compose Part Three with the same care he had devoted to Parts One and Two.

He could easily have continued his novel. His interest in literature did not end when he took a government post; he gave up his career as a professional writer, but not his studies or translations. However, with Part Three already published in serial form, Futabatei could not revise his chapters to conform with the ending which apparently occurred to him later as he was writing. He evidently rejected the possibility of having an affair between Osei and Noboru in the course of writing his novel, but an alternative conclusion did not emerge readily. His despair over his failure no doubt prevented him from rewriting Part Three in later months. When the three parts of *Ukigumo* were published in book form in September 1891, Part Three was left exactly as in the serialized version.

Yanagida's arguments appeared to have been substantiated by the publication in 1953 of the outlines in Futabatei's journal, and since then, *Ukigumo* has almost always been described as an unfinished novel in textbooks, reference works, and critical essays. Critics generally refer to the outlines or to the 1897 description in discussing what Futabatei would have written in subsequent chapters if he had completed the novel. The ambiguity of the last chapter provides adequate evidence of Futabatei's inability to finish the novel. There is, however, a substantial difference between an incomplete novel and an unpolished one: *Ukigumo* should have been revised to make the conclusion more convincing, but altering earlier events to suit the new conclusion might have proved a more effective method than adding another chapter. Inconclusiveness, in any case, is characteristic of the endings of many Japanese novels, of recent times no less than of antiquity.

Futabatei's Decision to Take a Government Post

On August 19, 1889, Futabatei began work in the office of *Kampō*, the official gazette of the Japanese government. He obtained the position through Furukawa Tsuneichirō, his teacher in Gaigo Gakkō. Furukawa visited Futabatei in late June or early July 1889 and offered to help him to find a position in the government. "Although I had not intended to enter the government," Futabatei wrote in his journal, "this was not the time to refuse such an offer. If I could earn a little money and support my parents, I would be extremely happy, I told him. . . . After he left, I felt ashamed and depressed. The thought of men like Arai Hakuseki made cold sweat pour down my back." [62] Futabatei, an admirer of the philosopher Arai Hakuseki (1657–1725), recalled here how Hakuseki had sacrificed every comfort to pursue his ideals. Futabatei found that he could not sacrifice his life to his art; either he had to throw himself more actively into writing for magazines or editing, or he had to embark on some other career altogether. In asking Furukawa to help him find work, he admitted his failure to earn his living as a writer.

The income from his writing had been pitifully small, despite the recognition it brought him, and Futabatei was a burden to his family. The Hasegawas had been reasonably well off as long as Futabatei's father was working for the government. Upon retirement, Hasegawa Yoshikazu's income from his pension was 11 yen a month. Although he bought a large house in Tokyo and was not concerned with paying rent, this income was apparently not sufficient to enable the family to maintain their accustomed style of living. Futabatei's mother, dissatisfied with their reduced circumstances, made her son aware of his failure to contribute to the family's finances.[63]

The financial situation at home grew worse with each passing month. After Futabatei received his last payment for *Ukigumo* from Kinkōdō in May he was unable to contribute even the smallest sum to his family. In July Futabatei wrote:

Although there are four of us here, our only income is the 11 yen a month my father receives as a pension. Until the month before last, I had at least been able to contribute to my own expenses with the 10 yen sent by Kinkōdō each month for my manuscript. I stopped receiving money last month and am now

62. *Ochiba no hakiyose: futakagome,* p. 71.
63. Futabatei overheard his mother upbraiding his father for having sold some bonds without informing her ahead of time and listened as she bemoaned the family's continued poverty. Futabatei, recording the incident in his journal, spoke of his shame at not being able to earn a respectable income. *Ibid.,* pp. 91–93. Sakamoto Hiroshi uses this entry as evidence that Omasa in *Ukigumo* is a fictional representation of Futabatei's mother. *Futabatei Shimei,* pp. 39–42.

even more dependent on my father. My family's difficulties grow worse and worse.[64]

During the three years Futabatei was writing *Ukigumo,* his income appears to have averaged about 10 yen a month,[65] a sum inadequate for much more than incidental expenses. Futabatei's starting salary with the government was 30 yen a month. At one point in *Ukigumo,* Omasa says that 35 yen is a good salary for a low-ranking bureaucrat: we may infer that Futabatei considered that 30 or 35 yen was a reasonable, but not ample, salary.

Futabatei worked and studied in a small room on the second floor of a storehouse behind his father's house. Visitors were impressed by his large collection of books, representing a considerable expenditure. Contemporary photographs show Futabatei in a frock coat, though Western style clothing was expensive in Japan at that time. He liked to dress well in Japanese clothes too; Yazaki remarks that his taste "was somewhat on the fashionable and showy side, rather like the son of a wealthy business family." [66] Ten yen a month might have paid for Futabatei's books and clothing, but he could not have contributed much to the family budget. When even this income ran out, he had to make a decision about his future.

Even before he finished the eighteenth chapter of *Ukigumo,* Futabatei wrote in his journal:

I am in an extremely unsettled state. . . . I cannot even decide

64. *Ochiba no hakiyose: futakagome,* p. 83.
65. This estimate was made by Nakamura Mitsuo in *Futabatei Shimei den,* pp. 137–38. Other than the figures for the translation of *Kyomu-tō katagi* and Part One of *Ukigumo,* we have no precise information on the amounts of money he received for his writing. Nakamura assumed that Futabatei was not paid for the translations from Russian criticism published during this period, but he added in his calculation a sum for the translations of *The Rendezvous* and *Three Meetings.*
   The value of money at this time may be judged by the price of rice: 1 koku of rice cost 5.66 yen in 1886; 4.99 yen in 1887; 4.91 yen in 1888; and 6.05 yen in 1889. In 1962 the average retail price of rice was 24,819.30 yen per koku.
66. Quoted in Nakamura, *Futabatei Shimei den,* p. 138.

how I am to make a living from now on. Sometimes I feel that I should definitely abandon my current life, leave Tokyo, and teach English in some quiet spot. I would devote myself to reading books I have not yet read, studying philosophy, and disciplining myself in my search for truth. At other times, I feel I should go on writing novels and somehow earn enough to live and support my parents. I would read and observe the world and savor truth; I might even help others savor it too. The paths are different, but the goal remains the same; in either case what I seek is truth.

It really makes no difference which path I take in terms of the ultimate aim of my life. I stand at the crossroads and question which way I should go. What should I do? When I take up my pen to work on my novel and find that my knowledge is insufficient, my imagination inadequate, and that I have difficulty writing a single word, I feel that I am not suited for writing and that I should pursue scholarship instead. Still, when I put my pen down and reconsider, I realize that my English is not yet proficient. If I were to teach English now it would prove a very painful experience. It would do my students great harm if I taught them something wrong.[67]

Futabatei had tried teaching in Tokyo in 1888 but was dissatisfied with his classes: he had lectured on literary theory and found that his ideas were too advanced for his students. He does not mention the possibility of teaching Russian, presumably because there was no demand for Russian teachers at that time. English language teachers were needed, but Futabatei may not have known enough English to teach in Tokyo.

If he had so chosen, he could have earned more as a writer. Various publishers offered to print his next novel. On July 15, 1889, immediately after the first chapters of Part Three appeared, the head of the Yoshioka publishing company approached him and suggested he write a novel for their current series.[68] At first Futabatei was flattered. The series

---

67. *Ochiba no hakiyose: futakagome*, p. 66.
68. The series was called *Shincho hyakushu* [a hundred new works] and was published in eighteen paperbound books between April 1889 and May

had become quite famous, and he was pleased to be considered as a possible contributor. In the end he refused the offer, feeling incapable of writing another novel. The incident proved to Futabatei that he could make his way as a writer if only he had confidence in his ability. By refusing, he acknowledged that, unlike truly professional writers, he could not produce a novel on request.[69] Futabatei might also have supplemented his income by writing for magazines and newspapers. Many young authors lived entirely on the proceeds from writing and editing, and Futabatei's fame as the author of *Ukigumo, Aibiki,* and *Meguriai* should easily have won him a position in a publishing company.

Futabatei was uncomfortable in Japanese literary circles. He disliked associating with most writers and had few literary friends other than Tsubouchi, Yazaki, and the writers he met most frequently at Tsubouchi's house. Most members of the Japanese literary world knew each other well and formed a clearly defined clique.[70] Futabatei failed to obtain access to its inner circles despite Tsubouchi's help, partly because of his personality; his brooding, argumentative manner did not make him popular with writers. By June of 1889, having lost contact even with his school friends, he felt isolated and lonely.[71]

His isolation stemmed in part also from the difference between his approach to literature and that of other writers. In Gaigo Gakkō, Futabatei had studied the works of Russian critics who viewed literature as a means of revealing profound philosophic truths. They decried fiction or poetry written for amusement; art was an instrument for uncovering the mysterious, unknown forces of nature, the "Essence"

1891. The first volume, Ozaki Kōyō's *Irozange,* was very well received. By the time the head of the company, Yoshioka Tetsutarō, visited Futabatei, the series already included novels by Aeba Kōson, Ishibashi Shian, and others. In recalling the books he had read in his youth, Tayama Katai spoke particularly of this series, *Tōkyō no sanjūnen,* p. 288.

69. *Ochiba no hakiyose: futakagome,* p. 79.

70. The literary world of the period 1881–89 is described by Itō Sei in *Nihon bundan shi,* I, 156–289; II, 3–172.

71. *Ochiba no hakiyose: futakagome,* p. 60.

of life which they spoke of so frequently. Futabatei accepted this thesis and transferred to literature all the idealistic fervor he had felt toward politics as a youth. He was scornful of writers who considered only form and style, and thought his contemporaries were neglecting the true purpose of literature which lay in revealing this Essence to the world.[72] When Tsubouchi spoke of the difference between his view on literature and Futabatei's, he referred to this idealism. Futabatei's evaluation of literature, based on Russian standards, convinced him that a man should write books not to earn money but to learn and, in turn, to enlighten. A novel written for such an exalted purpose obviously had to be of the highest quality, but Futabatei considered that few novels by his contemporaries attained this standard.

In judging his own achievements, he was also evaluating them in terms of Russian literature. He wanted to write a Japanese novel which would meet the standards set by the masterpieces of Russian fiction, and he knew he had not succeeded. His despair over *Ukigumo* grew from his realization that he was incapable of portraying life with the skill of Turgenev, Dostoevsky, or Goncharov. He did not think to compare his novel with those of his contemporaries; he thought only in terms of the Russian masters. By such standards, *Ukigumo* was a failure.

In looking back later in life on this trying period, Futabatei described himself as having been caught in a great dilemma. He originally started to write *Ukigumo* to earn enough money to live independently, and he hated himself for it. His Confucian training and the ideals he acquired from his studies of Russian thought led him to a passionate conviction in the value of honesty. He wanted to live a life of which he could be proud and the thought of how he had begun his career filled him with disgust.

72. Itō Sei, II, 134–37, attributes part of Futabatei's despair to the fact that Ozaki Kōyō's *Irozange* had been favorably reviewed, indicating a revival of the gabuntai style. Itō believes that although Futabatei did not lose faith in the gembun itchi style or in the value of realism, the fact that other writers did not accept his opinion discouraged him.

It made no difference that, objectively speaking, *Ukigumo* had been fairly well received; I had a very low opinion of myself. I had no confidence whatever in my own ability as I have none now [1908]. On the one hand, I had "honesty" as my ideal and with it the greatest respect for art. But what was the result of the combination of my own humility, my love of honesty, and my respect for art? I began to think about the contradictions involved and I realized that it was an act of extreme audaciousness and an insult to art for me to have started my career at that time, no matter what might happen in the future. And yet, with my love of honesty, I could not take money from my parents. I had to be independent and go my own way; I could not be in debt to anyone. And so I wanted money, and wanting it, I had to write a novel—but this was incompatible with my feeling about art. I was unable to get my book published in my own name and I had to borrow Tsubouchi's; even then I barely managed to convince the publisher to print it. As a result, I made Tsubouchi do something dishonest for the sake of profit; I took terrible advantage of him. That was not all—what of the readers? I had cheated them as well. It was like selling dog's flesh under sheep's wool; it was a complete fraud. This was my dilemma. It was a conflict between idealism and practicality. . . .

He goes on to say that he turned to translating Turgenev to lighten the burden of his guilt.

I felt that even if I could not transmit the essence of his work, I could at least bring the outer form of his stories to Japan. Then people who could not read Russian might at least sense the beauty of the original to some degree. I struggled to make my translation exactly like the original, down to every word, comma, and period. When I think of it now, it was a very foolish attempt, but it was at least completely honest. Yet even in that there was a great contradiction. I was trying to become famous; I began to brace myself to take a leading position in the literary world. I was in the lowliest state possible.

I suffered terribly because I was corrupting my sense of honesty. Writing a novel was dishonest and there were other dishonesties involved as well. I violated my sense of honesty more and more as time passed. I was kept from working by this dreadful frame of mind, and I could not manage to support myself from writing. The fortunes of my family began to decline; the whole household was under a cloud of depression. My parents were continually worried, and there were other sorrows as well. All of our troubles came from not having any money. I wanted money very much and to get it I had to do something I considered immoral. But even then I could not really be of much help to them.[73]

Another course of life opened to Futabatei through Furukawa's suggestion: he could take a post in the government which would assure him of a steady income. No longer under any necessity to sell his art, he could write and study as he chose. He would be free to continue in his own fashion without having to cater to the whims of the reading public. Nor would he have to leave Tokyo, his family, and few close friends. This in fact was what happened: as soon as Futabatei assumed his post, his tension noticeably relaxed; and he became far more amiable toward others.[74] He mixed more in society and was often seen in bars and restaurants. In the office, where he translated English for the government, his work was efficient, and he was liked by his colleagues. Now that the burden of financial worries had been lifted and he no longer had to struggle with his novel, Futabatei became a much happier man.

Futabatei continued to study. He became engrossed in Western science and psychology. He read James Sully, Darwin, and Spencer. He translated Aristotle and wrote haiku. Soon he went back to Russian literature. In 1896 he completed a translation of Turgenev's *Assya* (1857) under the title of *Katakoi* [unrequited love]. It was published by Kinkōdō along with revised versions of *Aibiki* and *Meguriai* and achieved a great success. In subsequent years he published translations of stories by Turgenev, Gogol, Tolstoy, Gorky, and other Russian writers. The last five years of his life were

73. "Yo ga hansei no zange," pp. 38–40.
74. Tsubouchi, "Futabatei no koto," p. 67; Uchida, "Futabatei no isshō," pp. 400–8; Yamashita Yoshitarō, "Shippai shitaru keiseika to shite no Hasegawa kun," p. 5.

his most prolific. Except for a few scattered articles, his many essays on Japanese and Russian literature, social problems in Japan and abroad, and his autobiographical essays all date from 1904 until his death in 1909.

He did not attempt another work of fiction until 1906. From May until August of that year he worked on a novel entitled *Chasengami* (the name of a hair-style worn by widows). He made careful notes on the plot of the novel, which was to deal with the unhappy life of a war-widow who had lost her husband in the Russo-Japanese war. Futabatei was moved by the plight of the women left alone at the end of the war who were often prevented by Japanese social custom from remarrying. He completed only a portion of the manuscript. It was not published until after his death.[75]

Futabatei next turned to another novel, *Sono Omokage* [in his image], published in the *Tōkyō Asahi shimbun* between October and December 1906. This work, translated under the title *An Adopted Husband*,[76] deals with a browbeaten university professor, his nagging wife, domineering mother-in-law, and timid sister-in-law. The hero's education had been paid for on the condition that he marry his sponsor's daughter; with the death of his sponsor, he is left the sole support of the family. Dissatisfied with the provisions he makes for them, his in-laws make his life as uncomfortable as possible. He himself is beset by extreme inertia and permits his relatives to pursue their mercenary ends despite his awareness that what they do is cruel and heartless.[77]

Futabatei's last work of fiction was *Heibon* (*Mediocrity*),[78] a semiautobiographical study published in the *Asahi* from the end of October through late December 1907. One of many highly subjective novels published in the period, its

75. Nakamura, "Shōgai to sakuhin," pp. 37–42.
76. Translated by Buhachirō Mitsui and Gregg M. Sinclair (New York, 1919).
77. For a discussion of the similarities between the characters in *Sono Omokage* and *Ukigumo* see my "A Study of Futabatei Shimei," pp. 71–72.
78. Translated by Glenn W. Shaw under the title *Mediocrity* (Tokyo, 1927).

brooding, caustic hero who makes bitter comments on literary fashion and the superficiality of intellectuals reminds us of the earlier Futabatei.

Futabatei's decision to take a post in the government in August 1889 was not a sudden or particularly dramatic gesture, but it has since become one of the most frequently treated themes in discussions of his life and work.[79] The success of *Ukigumo* and his translations of Turgenev brought him considerable recognition, and such initial triumphs could normally have been followed by a successful career as a professional writer. Students of Futabatei's life have often speculated about which of the many factors was the most important in his decision to abandon his literary career. Many have suggested that it was his disdain of other writers, so strong that he could not continue to associate with them. In later life, even after he began to publish his writings with increasing frequency, Futabatei consistently refused to be identified with members of literary circles.[80] This has led to

79. The most perceptive analysis of the reasons for Futabatei's withdrawal from the literary world is Nakamura Mitsuo's study in *Futabatei Shimei*, pp. 19–62.

80. Futabatei frequently protested that he was not a writer and did not wish to be called one. For example, in 1906 Premier Saionji invited a group of leading writers to attend a conference, and Futabatei's name was included. He refused to go and was indignant at having been asked. When he met Saionji's private secretary, Yamashita Yoshitarō (1871–1923), who had been his colleague in the *Kampō* office, he protested, "'You know I'm not a writer. Why do you say I'm a writer? Why did you invite me?'" (Quoted in Yamashita, "Shippai shitaru keiseika to shite no Hasegawa kun," p. 8.) In 1906 Futabatei was concerned with political questions relating to the Asiatic continent and was also actively engaged in working for the expansion of the Esperanto movement.

In 1908 Futabatei traveled to Russia as a correspondent for the *Asahi shimbun*. His friends planned a farewell party but had difficulty in finding many writers who actually knew Futabatei. The translator and critic, Maeda Akira (1879–1961), recalled that "in the end we decided that it would not be a party of acquaintances but one at which the Japanese literary world would say farewell to a great Japanese writer." ('Futabatei shujin no koto," p. 5.) His friends also feared Futabatei would refuse to come and persuaded Tsubouchi to use his influence to make him appear. In his speech at the party Futabatei denied that he was a writer and asked that he be accepted

speculation that Futabatei, never seriously interested in a literary career, admired practical men of business or government more than litterateurs. Such a view appears to be substantiated by Futabatei's early interest in politics, his ambitions of entering the military academy, and his subsequent choice of Gaigo Gakkō as a place to prepare for a career in the Foreign Service.

Futabatei's genuine desire to be a great writer is proved beyond question, however, by Tsubouchi's description. The reminiscences of his classmates at school and the record of his achievements in Russian literature are further evidence of his profound interest in art. As we shall see in the following chapter, Futabatei reserved many hours in the years 1886–89 for the translation of Russian literary criticism, a task fraught with linguistic and analytic problems. Only the most dedicated student of literature would have devoted himself to the task of reading and translating such a critic as Belinsky. We are led to the conclusion that by 1886 Futabatei had decided to dedicate himself entirely to literature and that he did not deviate from that decision until 1889.

Futabatei did not admire most professional writers, but it would be a mistake to give undue emphasis to the part this attitude played in his decision to withdraw from literary circles in 1889. His most outspoken comments on this point belong to the period from 1897 to 1909, when his new publications made him a public figure of some prominence once again, and not to the period of his decision. Other factors were clearly of greater importance; these become apparent from a study of his journal for 1889 and his autobiographical essay, "Yo ga hansei no zange" (1908). The disgust he felt with his work, his discomfort at being unable to contribute to his family's income, and his inability to rise above the mundane concern of pleasing his publishers and the reading

for what he was. He maintained that he wanted to use his meager talents as a translator to help establish better understanding between Russians and Japanese. He appeared to be fearful of a new outbreak of hostilities between the two nations and hoped that he might do something to prevent it. ("Sōbetsu kai sekijō no tōji," *Zenshū*, X, 46.)

public all played a more important part in the decision than his attitude toward other writers.

Futabatei did not withdraw from literary circles because he thought literature unworthy of a man's lifelong devotion, but rather because he thought it too elevated an art to be contaminated by personal ambition or association with money. His idealism toward art was like a religion, and he could not allow it to be corrupted. The course which Futabatei chose enabled him to escape the conflicting emotions within him and to lead at least a somewhat happier life.

Chapter 4

Futabatei's Definition of Realism and the Superfluous Hero

PHILOSOPHIC SPECULATION in nineteenth-century Russia led the literary world into a protracted debate on certain key problems of aesthetic theory. This debate centered on the question of whether or not it was desirable or indeed even permissible for a novelist to make use of the vacillating, impotent hero portrayed by many great Russian writers beginning with Pushkin. This issue was fought in the salons and journals by critics and novelists. Virtually every leading writer was involved on one side or the other. The "superfluous" or alienated man of fiction was pitted against the "new" man, the positive hero. Each type symbolized the more significant issue underlying the debate: Was art to be allowed to remain free of political considerations or was it to be used for the expression and advancement of specific political goals? Writers on both sides favored extensive changes in the Russian social and economic system. Most had been imprisoned or exiled for their views. But men like Goncharov, Turgenev, and Dostoevsky demanded the right to depict life as they saw it; to reveal evil even in those whose political motives were commendable; to show the foolishness of revolutionary radicalism in a society which was not ready for it. These views were opposed by the radical, didactic critics, and their novels were frequently damned as empty and meaningless, if not positively dangerous.[1]

Futabatei read all the great writers of Russian fiction and many of the lesser known but equally influential journalists and critics as well. In Gaigo Gakkō he became familiar with Alexander Herzen (1812–70), an outspoken socialist who managed to avoid the Czarist censorship by publishing a successful *émigré* newspaper in England and circulating it inside Russia; Nikolai Chernyshevsky (1829–89), a proto-Marxist whose articles on economics and history anticipated many of the ideas of the Bolsheviks; and a host of others—some liberal, some reactionary, but few indifferent to politics. Futabatei was greatly interested in Russian theories of social reform, but he did not consider political problems as legitimate subjects for fiction. He discovered that by following the example of writers like Turgenev and Goncharov he could replace simple social protest with what was for him a more significant device. He learned that through describing Japanese society as accurately as he could, he might uncover truths no man had ever revealed before.

Objective realism, he believed, would portray the soul of Meiji Japan, and this picture of itself would serve to enlighten the reader. He felt it would be wrong to select only those aspects of reality which might prove a point of view desirable in the political or social sense. If an evil exists, it would be apparent from the total picture. In truth, no human being is entirely good or entirely evil. Each man must be analyzed and appreciated individually, and each literary type, while perhaps symbolizing a characteristic of broad social significance, must be human, vibrant, and, above all, believable.

Bunzō, the hero of *Ukigumo*, is a superfluous man, a direct literary descendant of the Russian type. The novel also has

1. The conflict between the writers and the radical critics is described by Rufus W. Mathewson, Jr., in *The Positive Hero in Russian Literature*, pp. 1–146.

its new man in the person of Honda Noboru. The four main characters of the novel each symbolize certain aspects of modern Japan as Futabatei saw them, but they are all eminently human and fallible. Furthermore, it would be as foolish to treat *Ukigumo* exclusively as a social allegory as it would be to describe *Crime and Punishment* solely as a symbolic representation of the dangers of irresponsible radicalism. *Ukigumo* reflects Japanese life in the 1880s, but more than that, it attempts to go beyond the limitations of nation and time and deal with universal questions that pertain to the entire society of man.

The Idea or Essence of Art

Futabatei's conception of the purpose and scope of a novel had its origin in Russian literary criticism, which in turn was based on German romantic philosophy. He was extremely interested in German philosophic reasoning and read and translated Russian works based on it. Of all the critics and theorists he studied, none fascinated him more than the brilliant, erratic Vissarion Belinsky (1811–48).

Belinsky symbolizes in literary history the dazzling group of intellectuals—critics, novelists, poets, political revolutionaries—who emerged in Russia between 1838 and 1848, the years so aptly named by one of their number "the marvelous decade." [2] Although Belinsky knew no German and did not travel abroad until shortly before his death, his theories of art and life were based on German philosophy, learned from his friends who had been to Berlin to study and had come back fanatic disciples of Hegel, Schelling, or one of the other leading romanticists. Belinsky and his colleagues to an almost astounding degree were obsessed with philosophy. They felt compelled to force their judgments on

2. For an excellent description of the impulses motivating the group see Isaiah Berlin, pp. 27–39.

every subject—whether poetry, music, or politics—into a prescribed mold and would not tolerate disagreement, even from their closest friends.[3]

Unfortunately there was no single set of rules in contemporary German thinking for defining and judging all life and behavior. A major point of controversy among the philosophers was the extent of any person's obligation to work for political and social reform. Abstract theory suggested two courses: the intellectual had only to study the stream of life which moved on its way toward eventual perfection without assistance from him; or he had to make use of his intelligence and observations to alter the conditions around him and thus further the course of history in its constant striving toward more perfect goals. This is the origin of the dispute over the nature of the hero in fiction, a dispute that was to have profound implications for aesthetic criticism.

Curiously enough, we can find a brilliant defense of either side of this basic philosophic argument in Belinsky's writing, for he never settled on a single consistent system of thought. His inconsistency accounts for the varying interpretations of his position which may be found in different sources, and naturally makes it difficult to determine his attitude on particular questions.[4] He was, however, a gifted writer, an astute critic, and, above all, an extraordinarily sincere and honest man. His literary reviews were extremely influential: he was among the first to recognize the talent of such writers as Gogol, Turgenev, and Goncharov, and the most outspoken in destroying the inflated reputations of lesser talents. He sought a true Russian literature, free of blind imitation of Western Europe, faithful to his own time and people, ex-

3. A vivid account of the heights this madness reached can be found in the memoirs of Alexander Herzen, pp. 516–21.

4. A careful analysis of his attitudes and opinions may be found in Herbert E. Bowman's *Vissarion Belinski*.

In the U.S.S.R. Belinsky is now considered the founder of Soviet utilitarian aesthetic theory. Mathewson demonstrates "that to discover consistency in Belinsky is to distort him" in his chapter on the Russian critic in *The Positive Hero*, pp. 29–56.

pressive of all classes of society. He based his critical theories chiefly on Hegelian philosophy and wrote several purely philosophic articles dealing with aesthetic theory.

Futabatei, captivated by Belinsky's writing, was anxious to have his work read and accepted in Japan. Early in 1886 he translated an essay by Belinsky entitled "The Idea of Art" in order to help Tsubouchi and his other friends understand the Russian critic's theories.[5] The translation, not published during his lifetime, was virtually incomprehensible to his contemporaries, not because it was poorly executed, but because the material is fundamentally so difficult.[6] Futabatei carefully reproduced every line of the text, with the exception of two poetic passages whose omission he noted, and was at least moderately successful in finding Japanese equivalents for the specialized Hegelian vocabulary Belinsky employed.[7] Still, Hegel is difficult for anyone in any society; it is not surprising that Futabatei's friends were dismayed by the essay.

Although "The Idea of Art" is fragmentary and disorganized, it is probably Belinsky's most positive statement on the nature of the primordial essence, variously called the Idea or the Essence or the Thought, which is the focal point of the Hegelian cosmology.[8] The Idea is said to have existed

5. Uchida, "Futabatei no isshō," p. 357.

6. Futabatei's manuscript was not dated. I have made use of the chronology suggested by Inagaki Tatsurō in "Futabatei no hyōron," *Futabatei annai*, pp. 77–78. Futabatei's title, "Bijutus no hongi," is a literal translation. It was not published until 1926, when part of it appeared in the magazine *Hankyō*. The entire essay was published for the first time in *Meiji bunka zenshū*, XII, 42–53 and is reprinted in *Zenshū*, IX, 115–34.

Tsubouchi was unable to understand it even with the benefit of Futabatei's oral explanation. "Futabatei no koto," pp. 51–52.

7. There was, of course, no well-established vocabulary for Western philosophic terminology by 1886, and Futabatei had to invent a good deal of it himself. The problem is discussed by the editors of the *Zenshū* in "Hyōron no hon'yaku ni tsuite," IX, 197–201.

8. Belinsky began "The Idea of Art" in 1841 but never finished it. It was not published in his lifetime. For the source of his ideas and an analysis of its relative position in the development of his theories see Bowman, pp. 152–54.

since the beginning of time and is contained in greater or lesser quantities in every material object. All of life, all of history, is an inexorable progression caused by the interaction of the Idea with the Material from which it is constantly trying to emerge. There are periods of quiescence when the struggle between the two is suspended, but they are only temporary. The movement will inevitably begin again and continue until at last it reaches its ultimate goal, the moment when the Idea finds complete expression: "the first movement of primordial matter striving to become . . . our planet and the last rational word of intelligent man are merely one and the same being at different moments of its evolution."

Man, said Belinsky, is the end product of a long evolutionary process, the result of continuous action and interaction within Nature. Through him, through his mind and his creations, history takes form and progresses. Like every other object, man is composed of the Idea within him, and the Material, his outer form. He has the great gift of being able to perceive the Idea in himself and in the whole universe. He can perceive this instantly, spontaneously, without the benefit of reason, but he can also discover it by rational processes. The great man is one who grasps the Idea clearly, instinctively, and lives in terms of his perception. He may be conscious of the need for his actions, but that is not what makes his actions great. It is his contact with the Idea, his awareness of it as it shines forth from his actions, which determines their worth. Actions which emerge from this awareness are creations; those which grow from calculation alone are base and mechanical. The products of inspired awareness, the creative, artistic products, are the perfect manifestations of the Idea; they need form to be expressed, just as man needs form to exist. In the universe "we perceive two apparently opposite but actually cognate and identical aspects: spirit and matter. The spirit is divine thought, the source of life; matter is the form without which thought cannot manifest itself. Obviously both these elements need each other: without thought all form is dead, without form thought is merely that which may be, but is not." [9]

Implicit in this discourse is a definition of the artist's function. Hegel had conceived of each phase of world history as having a specific configuration. As history progresses, so the form of every society progresses and everything within it changes. At any given moment in any one society there are distinct, discernible elements which are peculiar to that society. They will never be repeated; they are the embodiment of the Idea at that one time. The artist can perceive those elements more readily than ordinary men and can record them for posterity.

Belinsky and his successors accepted this as a creed for the artist; he not only was capable of perceiving, it was his moral duty. Given the talent or insight to analyze the special characteristics of his society, the writer had to devote his total energy to the study of the world around him. Only the artist who satisfied this requirement could be considered great. "Pushkin," Belinsky wrote in an earlier article, "was the perfect expression of his time. Endowed with a sublime poetic feeling and an amazing faculty of receiving and reflecting all possible sensations, he assayed all the timbres, all the tones and chords of his age; he paid all his due to all great contemporary events, phenomena and thoughts, to everything that then moved Russia. . . . He sang, and Russia stood amazed at the sounds of his songs, for, verily, she had never heard their like." A man's world is intimately bound to his nation; a writer must portray his country, its language, all its classes, all its customs. If he fails to do so, his work is painfully deficient. He must not blindly imitate Western European models; he must recreate the Russian scene. Only then will he succeed.[10]

These are the thoughts which formed the basis of Futabatei's first literary essay, "Shōsetsu sōron" [the elements of

9. V. G. Belinsky, pp. 182, 196.
10. *Ibid.,* pp. 65–66, 88–91.

the novel],[11] published in April of 1886 in the magazine *Chūō gakujutsu zasshi*. Futabatei wrote "Shōsetsu sōron" at Tsubouchi's suggestion, in an attempt to state Belinsky's theories in language simpler than he had used in his translation of "The Idea of Art."[12] Tsubouchi arranged for publication and wrote a brief introduction which describes the essay as forming part of a review of his novel *Tōsei shosei katagi*. Tsubouchi explained that since a long review of his novel by Takada Sanae had appeared in the previous number of the same magazine, the editors could print only a portion of Futabatei's review.[13] Futabatei's essay failed to impress other writers and apparently went virtually unnoticed.[14]

"Shōsetsu sōron" begins with an explanation of the Idea.[15] Futabatei states that the Idea is present in all material objects and abstract concepts, and that it expresses the true nature of those things. The Idea is eternal and immutable and would exist even without any Form. The outward Form assumed by objects or concepts, in fact, tends to disguise the Idea and prevents our being clearly aware of its universality. Man is compelled by his nature to search out the unchanging factor among all the changing Forms of the world; scientists and scholars do this with the aid of their intellect, artists with their emotions or instincts. Both methods are necessary for complete understanding, but it is the great gift of Art that it can make the existence of the universal Idea, buried as it

11. Many of the major concepts in "Shōsetsu sōron" can be traced to a theory of Belinsky's, as found either in "The Idea of Art" or in some other essay. The sources have been identified by R. Karlina in an article entitled "Belinsky and Japanese Literature," pp. 501–12. The article is available in Japanese in *Bungaku*, XXI, No. 10 (October 1953), 992–1005.

12. Tsubouchi, "Futabatei no koto," p. 52. Seki Ryōichi believes "Shōsetsu sōron" had influenced Tsubouchi's approach to aesthetic theory. He cites Tsubouchi's "Bi to wa nanzo ya" (September 1886) and "Bijutsu ron" (January 1887) as bearing the mark of Futabatei's theories. "Futabatei to Shōyō," pp. 19–21.

13. Tsubouchi's introduction is quoted in Inagaki, p. 81. The balance of Futabatei's review is no longer extant.

14. Uchida, "Futabatei no Isshō," p. 358.

15. Futabatei uses a character read *kokoro*, meaning heart, mind, or idea, followed by the English word "idea" written in *katakana*.

is in an infinite amount of Forms, clearly apparent to the most ordinary human being.

Futabatei then proceeded to demonstrate how these deductions apply to the construction of a novel. He rejected moral instruction as the purpose of fiction. Its function is rather to perceive the Idea in all the numberless Forms in the world directly, instantaneously, and to transmit this perception to mankind. Realism, the only technique which can achieve this, should be adopted. However, it is difficult to write a successful realistic novel. It requires much insight on the part of the writer to sense the Idea in the events of the everyday world and to incorporate this knowledge adequately into his book. He must write in a vital, dynamic style suited to his theme and develop his plot as logically and sensibly as it would have evolved in real life. Otherwise the Idea will not be revealed and the story will seem pointless and insipid, no matter how valid the original germs of the plot.[16]

In this short, terse statement of his views, Futabatei attempted to convey all the complexities of Hegel's aesthetic theories as transmitted through Belinsky. "The Idea of Art" is a complicated essay; even if it had been printed it is doubtful that many readers would have understood it. "Shōsetsu sōron" is much less involved; the vocabulary is closer to that ordinarily used by Japanese critics. Not only is it written in the classical expository style, bungotai, but Futabatei's inductive method is reminiscent of the methods of traditional Chinese and Japanese philosophers. Nevertheless, "Shōsetsu sōron" failed to attract attention. Tsubouchi praised Futabatei's theories as advanced, but only Futabatei's close friends ever became interested in them. This was partly because the time was not right for philosophy of this order.

Futabatei directed his arguments to writers; it was the novelist, as an artist, who was obliged to extract the all-pervasive, eternal Essence or Idea and convey it to the reader. Japanese writers in the 1880s, however, were not concerned with such abstract arguments. They were fascinated

16. "Shōsetsu sōron," *Zenshū*, IX, 6–10.

by Western material culture, Western literary forms, and practical political and economic theories, but not by abstract philosophic speculation. Nothing in "Shōsetsu sōron" was sufficiently novel or intriguing to hold their interest long enough for them to see its value.

The concept of realism had already been well expressed by Tsubouchi in his *Shōsetsu shinzui*, and those predisposed to accept realism had done so. On the surface, the only difference between Futabatei's arguments and Tsubouchi's was the theory of the Idea underlying Form. The obligation of the artist to reveal the Idea is the rationale for realism, but to a writer who had already accepted realism, such a rationale might easily seem unimportant. In any case, Futabatei's "Shōsetsu sōron" failed to find an interested audience, but he continued to study and translate Russian criticism which advanced similar theories.

Early in 1886 Futabatei also translated a portion of Belinsky's "The Division of Poetry into Genus and Species" (1841). The essay, a restatement of a chapter from Hegel's *Aesthetics,* deals with epic, lyric, and dramatic poetry.[17] Futabatei's translation, which he entitled "Denki no bunji," is from the section on dramatic poetry. Drama is seen as the synthesis of epic and lyric poetry. The discussion centers on a description of tragedy: the suffering of the hero, the conflict between his moral duty and his natural desires, and his helplessness in the face of overwhelming obstacles. Futabatei's translation appears unfinished. It is not dated and, like his translation of "The Idea of Art," it was not published in his lifetime.[18]

A month after "Shōsetsu sōron" appeared, Futabatei published a translation of an essay by the Russian journalist and

17. For a brief summary of Belinsky's essay see Bowman, pp. 152–53.
18. *Zenshū,* IX, 134–39. Belinsky's essay appears in his Collected Works, *Sobranie Sochinenii,* Vol. II, col. 1–70. The portion translated by Futabatei runs from column 54 to 58 and is thus only a small part of the whole essay. The translation does not offer any conclusive arguments and the discussion seems fragmentary. It appeared with "Bijutsu no hongi" in the magazine *Hankyō* in 1926 and was later reprinted in *Meiji bunka zenshū,* XII, 51–56.

editor Mikhail N. Katkov (1818–87). In his youth, as a
student and then as a teacher at Moscow University, Katkov
had been a friend of Belinsky's and was instrumental in introducing him to German philosophy.[19]

Futabatei's translation is entitled "Bijutsu zokkai" [a
popular explanation of art]. It was published in May and
June of 1886 in *Chūō gakujutsu zasshi*. The material Futabatei translated is apparently part of a longer article. Scholars
have not been able to locate the article in the vast body of
Katkov's writings, but it seems safe to assume that it dates
from the early part of his career.[20] Its importance to Futabatei
was obviously as a restatement of his conception of the Idea of
art.

Katkov wrote that art must do more than record the
phenomena of life, the superficial realities existing in the
world. It must help man in his eternal struggle to gain perception and understanding, exactly as the sciences do, by
stripping away the outer shell or forms which encase things
to lay bare the truth buried within. With increased knowledge, mankind will advance to a higher degree of nobility
than ever known before. The time-honored formula "art for
art's sake" cannot fully explain the artist's obligation to the
world. Art—especially literature—which merely diverts and
amuses is not true art. When poetry, either lyric or dramatic,
is written to display the author's skill at handling words, its
value is little more than temporary, for it cannot make the
reader a finer, purer person; it cannot reveal to him more
about life than he already knows. Art must open new hori-

19. Belinsky had copied a section of "The Idea of Art" from Katkov's
notebooks. Belinsky, *Selected Philosophical Works*, note to p. 198.

20. The ideas expressed here are similar to those held by the young
liberals at the university in the 1830s and 1840s and are quite different from
those Katkov advocated later in his career. As the years passed, Katkov
moved further to the right in his political and social theories. He used his
influential periodicals to denounce the teaching of science and philosophy
and to support the monarchy in the most virulent nationalistic terms. For
a biased but relatively full account of Katkov's career see Thomas G.
Masaryk, II, 191–98. For a discussion of the problem of dating this essay see
Bruno Lewin, pp. 30–31.

zons, broaden our understanding of the world, and teach us the path to virtue and intellectual development.[21]

The same philosophic conceptions are repeated in "The Distinction Between Science and Fine Art" by M. G. Pavlov, an article translated and published by Futabatei in April 1888, after the first two parts of *Ukigumo* had appeared.[22] Pavlov, who lived from 1793 to 1840, was a professor of natural science at Moscow University and teacher of many of the young men who were to shine in the "marvelous decade."

It being forbidden by law to offer a course in philosophy at the university, Pavlov was obliged to give his lectures on philosophy in a scientific disguise. He is not now remembered as an original thinker; virtually all his ideas were directly transferred from his German masters into the Russian language.[23] Nevertheless, he exercised a great influence on his students; "Pavlov stood at the door of the section of Physics and Mathematics, and stopped the students with the question: 'Do you want to acquire knowledge of nature? But what is nature? What is knowledge?' "[24] This often-quoted description by Herzen, one of Pavlov's most famous students, is indicative of the influence he exerted on his students. Many had never before been exposed to the magic of abstract thought; Pavlov was the person who opened their minds to contemplation and speculation for the first time.

In the essay translated by Futabatei, we find a restatement of the theory of the Idea expressed by both Belinsky and Katkov. The essay is a dry and turgid piece of writing in the Germanic style, each step in the proof interlocked in a tedious progression of valid, if not particularly original or striking, points. It describes the nature of conceptualization, from observation to conclusion, and its application to the scientific

21. "Kātokofu shi bijutsu zokkai," *Zenshū*, IX, 10–19.
22. Futabatei's title, "Gakujutsu to bijutsu to no sabetsu," is a literal translation. Pavlov's article was published originally in the scientific and literary journal *Athenaeum* which he began to edit in 1828. V. V. Zenkovsky, p. 122. Futabatei's translation appeared in *Kokumin no tomo*.
23. See Alexandre Koyré, pp. 126–36.
24. Herzen, p. 515.

process. Scientific understanding, it states, is not a creative but a selective process until the moment of conceptualization, when out of myriad possibilities an idea is created. In Art, on the other hand, the reverse process is in operation. Art is basically an expression of the Idea. Without the Idea, a work of Art could not exist; the Idea itself gives us pleasure. The aim of Art is to make manifest the Idea in a tangible object.

Science transforms objects and creates an Idea; Art transforms an Idea to make an object. Science transforms real objects to make imaginary things; Art transforms imaginary things to make something real. Although the intellect extracts science from phenomena, Art gives birth to phenomena spontaneously. . . . In science objects are reflected intellectually; in Art the intellect is reflected concretely. Science alters what is underneath and it comes to the surface. Art changes what is on the surface into something beneath the surface.[25]

In May 1889 another translation by Futabatei appeared, his last published work on aesthetic theory from the period while he was writing *Ukigumo*. It is a selection from a long review by the radical critic Nikolai Dobrolyubov (1836–61).[26] In his brief introduction to the translation Futabatei explained that he chose the portion most directly concerned with the author's main thesis, the relation between the common people and the development of Russian literature. "I made this translation because I felt this essay contained theories pertinent to evil conditions in Japan," he wrote.[27]

25. Futabatei, trans., "Gakujutsu to bijutsu to no sabetsu," *Zenshū*, IX, 23.
26. Dobrolyubov's review is entitled "What Strength Has Democracy Given the Development of Russian Literature?" It was written for the liberal magazine *The Contemporary* in 1858. It can be found in his Collected Works, *Sochinenia*, I, 464–516. The portion translated by Futabatei appears on pp. 466–77.
Futabatei entitled his translation "Bungaku no hon'shoku oyobi heimin to bungaku to no kankei" [the true nature of literature and the relation between literature and the people]. The translation was printed in *Kokumin no tomo*. In this translation Futabatei used colloquial syntax for the first time in his series of philosophic translations and essays.
27. Futabatei, *Zenshū*, IX, 24.

The concept of the importance of the "common people" in literature was an essential element of Dobrolyubov's philosophy. Dobrolyubov idolized Belinsky.[28] Not only was he educated on Belinsky, but he considered his own theories a logical outgrowth of those of his master. However, a striking difference divided the aesthetic views of the two men: Belinsky argued for the creation of realistic characters; he did not speak as if they existed outside the work of art. He did not expect the characters in a novel to maintain a fixed moral standard as if they themselves had some choice in the matter, nor did he set an ideal level of accomplishment and then demand that the characters attain it. In other words, his criticism did not tamper with the intrinsic unity of the work of art, which remains whole, each segment inseparable from the others. The integrity of a work of art was, in a real sense, sacred to him. This was not true of Dobrolyubov. His criticism attributed to the characters of a novel or play a life of their own. He held them morally responsible for their actions; he judged them as people and not as part of an artistic unit. This technique was displayed in his most famous essay, "What is Oblomovism?" in which he blamed the heroes of Russian fiction for their inadequacy in coping with problems they faced as a man might accuse an acquaintance of failing to live up to his obligations.[29]

In his other writing Dobrolyubov applied the same standards in judging historical figures and, by extension, groups of men and nations. Their worth is determined by the amount of constructive work they completed or at least attempted to complete. Constructive work, in Dobrolyubov's thinking, is often what we would define as progressive: social and economic reforms including education for more people, expanded economic opportunities, greater freedom for

28. See particularly N. A. Dobrolyubov, *Selected Philosophical Works*, pp. 177–78. Dobrolyubov was the literary critic on *Contemporary*, which had been the organ for Belinsky's writings a decade earlier.

29. The use of this technique by Dobrolyubov is described by Mathewson, pp. 58–77. For a translation of "What is Oblomovism?" see Ralph E. Matlaw, ed., pp. 133–75.

women, right of redress for wrongs, and the like. The evidence he accumulated in his militant attacks on past and contemporary societies is specious. His writing is filled with facile and often highly inaccurate generalizations about world history. Still it is difficult to deny his sincerity. He obviously wanted reform, change, and progress in whatever disguise. In championing action over inaction, he frequently drew the comparison between the producer and the parasite. It is the common people, the Russian peasant classes, who are active and productive; their social superiors are, with certain rare exceptions, the parasites. Dobrolyubov was not as idealistic on the subject of the virtues of the peasantry as some of his contemporaries, but he clearly saw in them the source of hope for future progress, excusing their boorishness by their condition of life.

The common people have been largely neglected in the history of world literature, Dobrolyubov asserts in the article translated by Futabatei. The exception to this was the literature of ancient Greece where, in keeping with the active role played by the populace in the government, the people actually participated in the drama and epics. By the time of the Roman Empire, however, the situation had changed. The people were no longer thought of as individuals but treated as possessions of the state. In literature they appeared only as followers or instruments of the heroes. Even in the medieval period, when poems and songs were created by commoner minstrels or troubadours, the literature was devoted to praising the upper classes.

Modern literature, Dobrolyubov goes on to state, is the product of privileged groups concerned only with portraying themselves and virtually never with the lower classes. This indifference to the common people was found not only in the arts but in the social sciences. No field of study is devoted to analyzing the accomplishments or failures of the common man; none describes the world from his point of view. Those social sciences like political economy, which pretend to deal with the people, are only concerned with them as they affect the capitalist class. Only two or three geniuses in the history of the world have been able to put aside their own interests and concern themselves truly with the question of the dignity of the whole human family and not of any one class.[30]

Although no mention of the neglect of the common man in literature occurred in Futabatei's earlier writings, he had undoubtedly been concerned with this question from his days in Gaigo Gakkō, as his interest in socialism indicates. With the exception of the brief mention of "evil conditions" in his introduction and his agreement with Dobrolyubov's theories implicit in the fact that he published the translation, Futabatei made no public statement on this question in these years. His choice of plot and characters in *Ukigumo*, however, has been interpreted as an attempt to bring the common people into literature by showing the conflict between the bureaucracy and the oppressed employee. Marxist critics have praised Futabatei's boldness in introducing the subject into a novel but have been disappointed that he showed more interest in investigating the psychology of his "common man," Bunzō, than in describing the cruel machinations of the government in more detail.[31]

Dobrolyubov's essay also contains a protracted attack on the belief that literature invents issues or causes and, further, that theories expressed in a work of literature can have any effect on the course of events in real life. The problems exposed in literature must have existed in his society before the author wrote about them. He could not have thought of them if they had not. Art does not create situations; it merely describes them. Careful observation of the conditions of real life and its accurate reproduction in a work of art are an author's greatest obligations. A writer likes to think of himself as a teacher. He wants to believe that his words will expose social evils and bring about their rectification, but he must not forget that what he says will affect only a very

30. "Bungaku no honshoku," *Zenshū*, IX, 24–38.
31. This is the position held by Kataoka Ryōichi in *Kindai Nihon no shōsetsu*, pp. 15–31.

small number of people, and they are most likely to be those who would have agreed with his point of view even before he expressed it.[32]

Futabatei voiced ideas similar to these earlier; in "Shōsetsu sōron" he speaks of the value of realism and attacks the didactic writers of the East who wrote novels to prove moral lessons. By translating this portion of Dobrolyubov's essay he reasserted his faith in the power of realism to describe a society thoroughly. Futabatei believed in fiction concerned with nonaristocratic men and women incapable of great acts of heroism. The "evils" in the society would be revealed by realism; no other device was necessary.

Futabatei's conception of art is expressed in these translations from Russian criticism and in "Shōsetsu sōron." It is essentially mystical, depending on intuition and insight for its success. The artist is to peel away the outer layers of reality, find beneath it the buried spirit which gives it its particular shape and meaning, and expose that spirit in the work of art. Because it contains that spirit, the completed work will lend both the artist and his audience understanding and enlightenment. The novelist is described as an observer, an especially sensitive, astute observer, equipped by his superior intelligence and special training to see more in the world about him than ordinary men. His duty is to portray reality, to capture his moment in time as exactly as possible.

The novelist should study his society and determine its essential characteristics; then he should construct his plot and define his characters so that they may illustrate these characteristics. "Present day novelists and critics," Futabatei wrote in his journal in June 1889, "occupy themselves with questions of stylistics and are forgetful of their obligation to depict the characteristics of men and paint the conditions of their country." The novelist, he felt, "Takes up his pen and depicts the characteristics, the customs, and the aspirations of the people of his nation. He paints the conditions of his country and personifies the lives of the people. In doing so,

32. "Bungaku no honshoku," pp. 28–34.

he discovers truth untouched by the scholar or novelist and helps his people through his suffering." [33]

Futabatei rejected Russian didacticism as he rejected Japanese didacticism and chose to study and investigate rather than teach. The lessons to be learned from literature would, he felt, emerge naturally. In this, he followed Tsubouchi's opinions. Tsubouchi stated in *Shōsetsu shinzui* that whatever advantages came from literature, they were merely the products of greater enlightenment. In writing *Ukigumo*, Futabatei used his four characters to symbolize his time and hoped to convey his feelings about contemporary Japanese society through their actions. As his title indicates, he saw the people of his nation as drifting clouds, torn loose by the force of Western ideas and material development from the foundations on which they had rested for hundreds of years, wavering uncertainly between clinging to the old and adopting the new, unsure of the value of their traditional moral code and not yet ready to accept Western philosophy and religion.

In some instances Futabatei's criticism of his society is lighthearted. He saw the foolishness of superficial Westernization; the vogue for learning foreign languages, wearing foreign dress, adopting foreign customs, all seemed to him ridiculous. Other flaws in Meiji Japan moved him more deeply. Futabatei was disturbed by the loss of the old standards of loyalty and courtesy, the disappearance of the respect for education which had for centuries characterized Japanese society, and the success of the vulgar man over his more restrained counterpart. He reveals these flaws through the plot of *Ukigumo;* by what his characters say and do, and even by what they fail to do.

Ukigumo as a Reflection of Meiji Life

In *Ukigumo* Futabatei describes a society where many of the traditional values are lost and a new ethic predominates.

33. *Ochiba no hakiyose: futakagome,* p. 61.

With his small cast of characters he attempts to symbolize the profound changes which had already taken place in Japan by 1886 and to forecast the path his nation would take in the future.[34] He did not admire the changes, but even at that early date he knew that there was no holding them back and that, for better or worse, the society he describes was permanently established.

All the major characters in *Ukigumo* are members of the samurai class or at least pretend to that distinction. It was the group in society which was most gravely affected by the political reforms following the Restoration of 1868, and therefore Futabatei's choice was particularly appropriate. In Tokugawa times the samurai together with the 140 families of the Imperial courtiers (*kuge*) constituted the hereditary aristocracy. The samurai were supported by stipends allotted to them by their domain lords or, in the case of those living on lands governed by the Tokugawa shoguns, by the shogunate itself. Beneath the shogun ranks within the samurai class ranged from the daimyo, the lord of the domain, often an extremely rich and powerful man, down to the low-ranking samurai, whose stipend barely supported a small family.[35]

During the 265 years of the Tokugawa period, many changes occurred within the structure of the samurai class. By 1868 samurai were often reduced to extreme poverty; some had lost their stipends entirely, others were forced to engage in trade in order to supplement their income. Whether rich or poor, however, in theory at least they

34. In an interview in 1897 Futabatei said he had hit upon this theme after reading Goncharov's novel *The Precipice* (1869). He went on to speak deprecatingly of *Ukigumo*, saying it was "nothing but an imitation" of Russian fiction. He said he was merely imitating *The Precipice* in writing his own novel. Critics have sometimes taken this statement seriously, but a comparison of the two novels reveals that they have little in common other than the general theme of transition from old to new. *The Precipice* has been partially translated by M. Bryant (New York, 1916). For Futabatei's statement see "Sakka kushin dan," p. 43.

35. Carmen Blacker describes the social and economic distinctions between upper-ranking and lower-ranking samurai in the Okudaira clan of Nakatsu in *The Japanese Enlightenment*, pp. 1–3.

shared a common ethical and moral code. This code had as its basic tenets a belief in loyalty to one's family and superiors, faith in the efficacy of education and hard work, devotion to propriety and restraint in social behavior. An insistence on modesty and humility ruled out all forms of display, and the study of both literary and martial arts was considered more important than the acquisition of practical knowledge which might result in greater material success.

In addition to his stipend a samurai enjoyed other privileges which set him apart from the rest of society. Most offices within the government were reserved for the samurai, either by law or by custom, and most officially sponsored schools were maintained exclusively for the children of the samurai. Samurai also had the privilege of wearing swords, symbolic of their duties—now largely fallen into abeyance— as soldiers, and emblematic of their superiority over the commoners. Membership in the class was largely hereditary, and the stipend of a samurai was transmitted to his son. With the advent of the Meiji period, the privileges of the class were stripped away. By 1876 the samurai ceased to receive stipends and were no longer permitted to carry swords. Generally, a samurai would not succeed to a post merely because his father had previously held it.

Among the commoners in the Tokugawa period, the wealthiest people were the merchants of the large towns and cities. Although they were in some danger of having their money confiscated or their trade ruined by restrictive laws, some amassed great fortunes and were, in fact, reasonably powerful in the society. There were numerous cases of merchant children marrying into samurai families, but the fiction of a separation between the samurai class and the commoner merchants was maintained until the 1870s. The samurai aristocracy believed itself superior to the merchants and claimed to scorn the aggressiveness, shrewdness, and avariciousness which it felt characterized the businessmen.

With the advent of the Meiji period, it became a practical

impossibility for the samurai to maintain this ethic. It was an age of opportunity unprecedented in Japanese history. The acquisition of a new, Western-style education—knowledge of Western languages, science, or mathematics—allowed a young man to rise quickly to fame and fortune. Changes in government administration were sudden and frequent; the clever man might seize his opportunity and find himself in a high-ranking position. Even in the far more rigid Tokugawa era there had been brilliant young men who rose through the ranks to positions of power,[36] but never before had it been so easy for so many to succeed. The new generation of samurai, or *shizoku* [gentlemen] as they were called, could no longer be content with a life of classical studies and simple devotion to family and superiors. There were to be few hereditary jobs in the new Japan; a man had to make his own arrangements for his livelihood. The vast range of opportunities awaiting in government and finance combined with the removal of hereditary posts and ranks forced the shizoku to come to grips at last with the competitive world.

The great symbol of the new Japan was Tokyo. The capital of the country, the center of education and industry, it represented advancement and progress to the entire nation. Reforms affecting the social, economic, and political life of every person in the country emanated from Tokyo and its influence was felt everywhere. Young men poured into the city seeking fame and fortune; enrollment in its schools swelled and its graduates staffed public and private institutions throughout the country. Being traditionally the best-educated and best-connected young men, the shizoku flocked

36. Probably the most striking example of this was the career of Tanuma Okitsugu (1719–88). In 1734 he inherited a 600-koku income from his father and received another 300-hyō salary as a page in the service of Tokugawa Ieshige. He rose rapidly to high position in the shogunal government and in 1785 had an income of 57,000 koku. By 1787, however, he had been stripped of his various offices in the shogunal government and had an income of only 10,000 koku. John Whitney Hall, pp. 35–40.

to Tokyo and sought to gain by influence and education a position comparable to or better than what they had once held by right of birth.

Ukigumo is in part the story of two branches of the same family; one is successful in adjusting to the life of the new Japan, the other fails. Magobei went to Tokyo and, after some initial difficulties, established himself as a businessman. His brother, Bunzō's father, remained in the family home in Shizuoka, used up his savings, and barely managed to eke out a living with his salary as a minor bureaucrat. His death left his wife and son destitute. Only Magobei's intervention offered Bunzō hope of salvation from a fate similar to his father's, but in the end, despite his Tokyo education and his knowledge of English, he too fails. Bunzō's brave and resolute mother is left alone in Shizuoka, waiting only for an opportunity to join her son and escape her loneliness.

Bunzō does not belong to the city. He cannot exchange his belief in sincerity, honesty, and restraint for sycophancy and aggressiveness. He is not witty and would not be able to join in an evening's festivities in a teahouse. He could not spend his time playing games or going to the theater. His are the traditional Confucian values: devotion to his family, hard work, and study. It is impossible for him to yield to the fashions of his time, and, as a consequence, he is crushed by the age.

Magobei never appears in the novel. His branch of the family is represented by Omasa, his second wife, a woman of the city. Shrewd, aggressive, calculating, Omasa conducts a successful business on her own. She deals in moneylending and real estate. Education, the most esteemed of all accomplishments in traditional Japan, is valueless to Omasa unless it can produce some material return. She is scornful of Bunzō because he is incapable of currying favor with anyone. By contrast, she admires Noboru; he is obviously going to be a great success in the new bureaucracy and he knows how to flatter her.

Noboru is in step with the modern world; he has the

qualities associated even in Tokugawa times with the *edokko,* or child of Edo. He loves to banter in puns or off-color jokes. He enjoys drinking and flirting with pretty women and can talk of money and business with considerable authority.

He is also of samurai stock, but he does not subscribe to any of the traditional beliefs. Having no family, he is free to pursue his own success ruthlessly. He spends his Sundays making himself useful to his superior and his superior's wife and sees an opportunity to establish himself permanently by marrying the chief's sister-in-law. Far from presenting a model of diligence for those who work under him, as Confucian morality would suggest, he is concerned only with pretending to his superiors that he is working. He even permits himself to play the fool, mimicking the chief at every turn to show the admiration in which he holds his model, acquiescing in every decision. Noboru never contradicts his superiors and leaves no stone unturned in attempting to win their favor. He ridicules Bunzō's bookishness. Furthermore, he lacks any sense of loyalty to his friends. It is apparent that he fails to help Bunzō's cause, for he could easily have prevented his dismissal. Sycophantic, opportunistic, materialistic, Noboru is the very antithesis of the Confucian gentleman. He has learned well the lesson taught by such monuments to success as Samuel Smiles's *Self Help.*[37]

Noboru represents success, Bunzō failure. Noboru never questions his actions. He believes that what he does is right because it is successful. Aiming only at material gain, he is not torn by any conflicts over the ethics of his way of life. Bunzō cannot accept success as a goal; money or position mean nothing to him except as a means to pay necessary expenses for himself, his future wife, and his mother. Not valuing wealth, he does not even consider sacrificing his moral code for it. It is only when he is in danger of losing the girl he loves that he is first tortured with doubts, and then the

37. Smiles's guide to self-advancement was translated into Japanese in 1870 and sold hundreds of thousands of copies. Keene, *Modern Japanese Literature,* p. 15. For a further discussion see Sansom, pp. 396–97.

struggle becomes profound. In the end he does not yield; he clings to his belief in the old virtues.

The head of the department in which Bunzō and Noboru work is another symbol of success. Here Futabatei paints a brief but bold picture of a fool. The chief has been abroad and spouts modern, democratic ideas while, in fact, being totally undemocratic in conducting his department's affairs. He is completely taken in by Noboru's sycophancy and greatly admires the young man. The reader knows him primarily through Noboru's confident remarks regarding his influence with the older man and through Bunzō's utter loathing of him. Success in the bureaucracy, then, can be obtained by a stupid man who has been abroad. Intelligence, ability, or hard work have little to do with making one's way in the bureaucratic world of Meiji Japan.

Using the bureaucracy as the focal point of his story gave Futabatei an opportunity to attack an institution dear to the hearts of his readers. As we have seen, it was an era of great political awareness; the political novel or allegory, either in translation or in original Japanese fiction, was enjoying a great vogue.[38] Western political concepts of liberalism and republicanism were part of the vocabulary of most Tokyo people, and some intellectuals voiced considerable opposition to the government. Whether for or against the administration, the young men of the time were passionately concerned with politics. This general interest provided Futabatei with a natural subject for his story.

For centuries the samurai were employed in the administration of the Tokugawa shogunate and of each han. In the Meiji period children of the samurai class naturally thought first of government service when they considered future careers. Futabatei himself had entered Gaigo Gakkō in anticipation of a career in the Foreign Service, and Tsubouchi's

38. For a further discussion of early translations from Western languages, see Sansom, pp. 396–404; and Feldman, "The Growth of the Meiji Novel," pp. 55–66.

family sent him to school in Tokyo in the hope he would eventually take a position in the government. Both men had chosen literary careers instead, but many of their school friends took jobs with the government or engaged in political activities. Futabatei made this cherished domain of the samurai the target of his biting satire and bared with his caustic comments the evils inherent in a system where success was the only goal and morality had been abandoned.

Futabatei said that he learned to despise the government bureaucracy through reading Russian fiction, and it was in imitation of Russian models that he revolved his plot around the evils of the bureaucracy.[39] Futabatei probably learned enough from his father about the ways of the bureaucracy to provide him with material for his story even without resorting to Russian examples. His reading of Russian fiction, however, reinforced his knowledge and gave him far greater sophistication than his contemporaries in appraising the Japanese situation. There are no set speeches inveighing against the bureaucracy in *Ukigumo*; for that matter, the advantages of a parliamentary system are not even mentioned. Futabatei chose to attack the system on a personal level and not in terms of theoretical ideals. His approach contrasts sharply with the obvious political allegories of Tsubouchi's early years and with the heroic political success stories so popular in the 1880s.[40]

Futabatei was also critical of the way his countrymen admired the Western world without understanding it. He touched upon this in the characterization of the chief but developed it more fully in the portrait of Ishida, Bunzō's old teacher, to whom he goes for help when he loses his job. Ishida has lived in England and claims to know Herbert

39. Futabatei, "Sakka kushin dan," p. 142.
40. Horace Feldman describes the development of the political novel in "The Meiji Political Novel: A Brief Survey." Feldman adds to this discussion in his section on the political novel in "The Growth of the Meiji Novel," pp. 66–86.

Spencer[41] and many other influential Englishmen. Ishida is an economist, by his own account, but he has been teaching English for eight years since his return to Japan and has not made any reputation for himself despite his foreign education.

Ishida, who may well be a fictional representation of Ichikawa, Futabatei's teacher at Gaigo Gakkō, is a pathetic figure. Not having achieved fame, it is difficult to resent his empty boasts of contacts in England, and his claim to knowing so much of the West because he can speak of boots and roll cigarettes is more touching than annoying. Through this highly exaggerated caricature, Futabatei captured another tragic but unavoidable failing in his nation. Futabatei felt that in trying so earnestly to learn, the Japanese were permitting themselves to accept virtually anything to which the word foreign could be applied. And the danger was that too many of his people would, like Ishida, avoid anything "preceded by the adjective 'Japanese,' be it object or idea." [42]

The hazard of exchanging the new for the old is exemplified by the course Osei's life takes as the novel develops. By the shift in her affections, she demonstrates how Japan was turning away from the traditional values and replacing them with the new formula for success. At first she is infatuated

41. Spencer's works were widely admired in Meiji Japan. His theories were used to justify both the liberal and conservative position: liberals thought of his philosophy as a defense of true competition and representative government, while conservatives thought of natural order as a science justifying maintenance of the *status quo*. Michio Nagai, pp. 55–64.

42. *Ukigumo*, p. 73. Critics, unwilling to credit Futabatei's perception of this failing in his society, have attributed Ishida's characterization to an imitation of Russian models, particularly of Pavel Piotrovich in *Fathers and Children*. They fail to remember that Futabatei had known Japanese at Gaigo Gakkō who had lived abroad and that he had had adequate opportunity to see the foolishness of idolizing the West. Kataoka Ryōichi makes this mistake in *Kindai Nihon no shōsetsu*, p. 29. Furthermore, Futabatei was not the first novelist to satirize the vogue. Characters in *Tōsei shosei katagi* are also used to mock the contemporary craze for things Western, while others express regret over the hurried adoption of Western social and political ideals. Seki, "Futabatei to Shōyō," pp. 23–24. Seki offers this as evidence that Futabatei was influenced by Tsubouchi's novel in writing *Ukigumo*.

with Bunzō and tries futilely to make him propose, but soon after his dismissal she turns to the cheerful, flattering Noboru. Although for a few days she clings to her defense of Bunzō when Omasa blames him for being fired, she soon loses interest in the whole problem and tries instead to capture Noboru's full attention. She forgets that she once thought of Noboru as crude and ignorant and is dazzled by his worldly manner. The shift is too rapid to be anything but metaphoric, but here Futabatei is describing the change his nation had made in a single generation.[43]

Osei also epitomizes the vogue for things Western. She follows the current fads—European languages, Western clothes, "progressive" ideas of female equality—and forgets each in turn. She is a spoiled and willful girl, cruel and insulting to her mother when the mood strikes her, soft and affectionate when she wants something. But she is suffering from growing pains, and as the novel progresses, her youth and immaturity become her predominating characteristics. Like her nation, Futabatei saw Osei as a naïve child, buffeted about by a confusion of ideas, lacking guidance from the previous generation, unable to distinguish between the superficial and the genuine.

Futabatei obviously sympathized most with his hero, Bunzō. He lavished the greatest attention on his portrait of this desolate child of the samurai and devoted a major part of his novel to exploring his mind. He knew, however, that the Bunzōs of this world were doomed to a life of obscurity and that men like Noboru would attain rank and fortune. Furthermore, he recognized that Noboru and his kind were in the majority. There would be few men who would dare

43. Yazaki Shinshirō said that Futabatei planned to make Osei represent the naïveté of contemporary Japanese. "Extremely naïve people like Osei move in whatever direction others lead them; Futabatei considered this characteristic of the Japanese people. They are not self-motivated but are pushed by others. If led by a good person, all goes well, but if tempted by evil, they turn bad. The guiding principle behind *Ukigumo* was that such was the nature of the Japanese people; Osei was made to represent her people." "*Ukigumo* no kushin to shisō," p. 168.

to defy the current customs; most would concede to necessity and behave as their positions demanded. In an interview Futabatei said:

I realized that people like Bunzō were actually more intelligent, but that men of Noboru's type were more numerous. They were the ones who enjoyed success and power in modern Japan. No matter how noble their ideas may have been while in school, the attitudes of most modern young people of the day were very superficial; as soon as they went out into the world, they became like Noboru.[44]

Futabatei was not blind to the faults in his hero. At times, he portrayed Bunzō's weaknesses with scathing humor. He showed his hero to be a blundering fool. His uncertainties and inaction are not admirable qualities even if they are pathetic. The Confucian gentleman was enjoined to act as well as to be sincere and honest, and for a considerable portion of the novel Bunzō is incapable of direct action. Futabatei's portrait of Bunzō has depth and dimension; he is at once admirable and foolish. Similarly, Omasa, although crude, vicious, and selfish, captured Futabatei's sympathy. He is openly critical of Osei's nasty manner toward her mother. The frustration Omasa experienced in having her plans for Osei's marriage to Bunzō thwarted is brilliantly depicted. Omasa's efforts to charm Noboru can be interpreted as simply her way of trying to secure a good marriage for Osei. The sympathetic characters in *Ukigumo* are not all good, and the unpleasant ones are not all bad. This is what gives the novel its merit.

The characters ranged on the successful side do not always win. Omasa suffers the most devastating defeat; she does not persuade Noboru to marry Osei and succeeds only in confusing her daughter. Through her mother's schemes, Osei is introduced to the cruelty of life for the first time. Rather than winning security for her beloved daughter, Omasa has led her to want something she cannot have. Osei is driven

44. "Sakka kushin dan," pp. 142–43.

to violent emotional outbursts in the confusion caused by her mother's ideas and ambitions. This is not what Omasa wanted for her child, and she has failed in her plans.

By dealing with issues easily understood by his audience, Futabatei was readily able to convey his major themes. No reader could fail to realize the ugliness inherent in sycophancy after finishing *Ukigumo,* nor could he escape the conclusion that the beliefs of the past were in grave danger of being totally destroyed. Through the novel, he saw the foibles of his society and, if he cared to heed the message, could have been led to the realization that blind imitation of the West was at least extremely foolish.

There had of course been sycophancy even in Tokugawa times. Aggressiveness and cruelty to one's peers was not an invention of the Meiji period. It did not take Samuel Smiles to tell the Japanese that God helps those who help themselves, and the admonitions of Confucianism had often before been honored in the breach. The Meiji period, however, was a time when the chances to break the rules were greater than they had ever been before, and it appeared to Futabatei at least that they would be so frequently broken that in time they might not be remembered at all.

This attitude on Futabatei's part can be seen as a direct result of his own intellectual and practical experience. His youthful idealism found its natural outlet in the simple plot of a good man crushed by the forces of evil. He himself was unable to accept authority and twice had been forced to leave schools, at least partially because he disagreed with the principals. Even while he was writing *Ukigumo,* he neglected to take advantage of his fame to engage in work which would have supplemented his income, apparently because he thought it would cheapen his art. However, his novel tells us that he had begun to realize how difficult it was to maintain an uncompromising position. It is impossible to admire Bunzō; he is clearly wrong in allowing himself to be so totally stymied by misfortune. Opportunity lay on every side for an intelligent man. Futabatei's hero is not in the mainstream of his time, and Futabatei was not advocating acceptance of Bunzō as a model of behavior. Many hundreds of shizoku attained the greatest possible rewards for their talents in the latter part of the nineteenth century. They became the leaders in politics, business, and education. Futabatei's hero is a man cut off from his society because he will not bend to the times.

Bunzō, the Alienated Man

Futabatei portrays Bunzō in many dimensions. He is shown alone with his thoughts; a timid, terrified young man, slow to reach decisions and even slower to act. We see him restrained and respectful with Omasa, and shy but somewhat more relaxed with Osei. Toward Noboru he is cold and finally openly belligerent. We also see him through the eyes of the other characters; quiet, retiring, and, in Osei's astute summation, "stodgy." In this many-sided portrait Futabatei depicts his version of the superfluous hero, the alienated man cut off from society. Futabatei learned of this literary type from his study of Russian fiction and, by transferring this hero to Japan, introduced a new facet into modern Japanese literature.[45]

45. The term "superfluous hero" as it is being used here must be restricted to characters in fiction of the period from the mid-nineteenth century to the present. It would be possible to categorize many earlier heroes of both European and Japanese literature as superfluous or positive, but such a consideration is outside the area encompassed by this study. We are dealing here only with the superfluous heroes invented by the Russian novelists and later introduced into world literature. For example, Kaoru of *Genji monogatari* is a man whose singular inability to carry out a love affair or be understood by his acquaintances would qualify him as a superfluous hero, but there is no evidence that Futabatei thought of Kaoru in relation to his novel or that he had even read the parts of *Genji monogatari* in which Kaoru appears. On a less lofty plane, the heroes of many jōruri dating from the eighteenth century could be classified as superfluous in that they are failures in life. They would also resemble more closely modern realistic heroes because they are average men with no rank or fortune. However, authors of jōruri and kabuki dealing with domestic life did not attempt an

Perhaps no literary type is as difficult to define as the superfluous hero; he must be described almost in terms of what he is not. The superfluous hero is seen most clearly when contrasted to the positive hero, the man of action, assertion, and aggressiveness. The positive hero, himself a conglomerate type, sets a goal for himself—economic, political, moral, or emotional—and proceeds to move toward attainment. He is usually completely successful.

In politics, the positive hero may be a revolutionary or at least a radical, but he may equally be an arch conservative. Whatever his position, he recognizes it, believes in it, and will stop at nothing to bring his objective to fruition. In the world of ideologies or philosophies, his devotion may be to a god or to a system of thought which has captured his faith and from which he will not be dissuaded. His goal may be success in the material sense, perhaps tied to political and philosophic ideals or else entirely unencumbered by intellectual considerations. He may be ruthless in achieving his goal or he may be kind and generous to his colleagues; in any case, it is power and recognition of his superiority which he seeks and often obtains. The positive hero frequently is a man of great physical strength. His strength, coupled with determination, often enables him to lead others. He may, on the other hand, excel only in his good looks and not possess notable strength. He invites devotion from his friends and from women; often they are prepared to sacrifice life and fortune for him.

The superfluous hero is a man who lacks these qualities. If he attempts to lead others, something is bound to thwart his success. When he falls in love, the love either falls short of fruition or dissolves into blind passion devoid of continued respect and admiration. No matter how sincerely he may believe in a cause or philosophic system, sooner or later he will reject it or find it deficient. Either his gods abandon him, or he turns his back on them. What had seemed most

extensive investigation of the psychology of their heroes; this remains Futabatei's unique contribution.

important in life will sooner or later slip into the background with no new faith to replace it. If he is a rich landowner, his attempts at modernization of his estates are often misguided; if he is a salaried clerk, the promotions he hopes for never materialize.

In some cases the superfluous hero is foolish, but usually he is both intelligent and sensitive and acts as a fictional representation of the artistic personality. Life buffets him and his intelligence rarely achieves maturity, but originally he possessed considerable talent. He was able then to think out his problems with reasonable clarity; he could see the foibles of those about him accurately and even perceptively. Misfortunes, however, are likely to frustrate his abilities. Failure, either material or spiritual, may so darken his outlook that he appears stupid to others and finally even to himself. He will not take the kind of action which for the positive hero would be obvious. He waits for his chance, but when it comes, he cannot seize it.

The term "superfluous hero" became popular after the publication of *The Diary of a Superfluous Man* by Ivan Turgenev. The story, written in 1850, tells of a low-ranking clerk in the Russian government. It is written as a diary composed by the hero, Chulkaturin, as he is dying. He reflects on his miserable, inadequate, unsuccessful life:

Superfluous, superfluous . . . I have thought of an excellent word. The further I penetrate into myself, the more closely I examine my past life, the more am I convinced of the stern truth of that expression. . . . All my life, I continually found my place occupied, perhaps because I sought that place where I should not have sought it. I was mistrustful, shy, peevish, like all ailing people; and, moreover, probably owing to excessive self-esteem or in consequence of some unsatisfactory allocation of my being between my feelings and thoughts—I came up against a senseless, incomprehensible and invincible obstacle.[46]

Chulkaturin was not the first superfluous hero in Russian literature; Onegin in Pushkin's poem (1821–31) is generally

46. Ivan Turgenev, p. 759.

considered the first of the class. Thereafter instances of the type abound. Some writers saw the superfluous hero as the perfect symbol of the Russian upper classes who would not awaken to the challenge of Western Europe after the Napoleonic wars. Others used him to portray the partly knowledgeable intellectual who quickly substitutes one set of ideals for another. Again, as the political issues within Russia became more sharply defined, the positive hero was shown to be the superfluous hero at his most extreme. Raskolnikov in *Crime and Punishment* is the absolutely determined hero devoted to a completely erroneous thesis; the activist who has deceived himself into believing that human life is dispensable. Raskolnikov is the positive hero in all but the one essential quality: he cannot really love. He cannot escape from himself and sympathize entirely with another human being.

Because the superfluous hero can exhibit so many different characteristics and approach so closely or remain so remote from a positive hero, no one definition suits him. No one character in fiction embodies all the qualities of a superfluous hero: he is everyone from the intelligent Nihilist Bazarov in *Fathers and Children* to the almost idiotic Makar of Dostoevsky's *Poor Folk* (1846). The one quality all the superfluous heroes share is that there is something they fail to be; some goal is not attained, even if that goal is no more glorious than committing a murder for which they will not be caught.

The superfluous hero has become a symbol of the sensitive, intellectual, or artistic man who lives outside the mainstream of modern life. He cannot find faith or philosophy or love in his world because the old beliefs have proved mortal and the new ones are not yet acceptable. The faith he seeks may be religious, intellectual, or emotional. The love he needs will take him from his confined universe, that is, from himself, and bring him closer to other people or even to one other person. He must learn to give—to a cause, to an ideal, or to a person. He must learn to sympathize, to see why the positive man wants what he wants. The superfluous man pictures all life as a reflection of himself, as if he were somehow looking at a distorted mirror in which his image filled every inch. As a consequence he cannot fully appreciate anyone else; in some cases he is led to reject everyone completely. Some superfluous heroes are merely quiet and ineffectual; others are completely mad, exhibiting the whole range of classic paranoiac symptoms favored by the literary world. Most are situated somewhere in between.

Bunzō is a superfluous hero. He is neither completely lazy nor utterly stupid nor insane, but he is weak, uncertain, unsuccessful, overly cautious, indirect, and not without neurotic symptoms. He is also gentle, tender, and completely sympathetic. Critics are fond of saying that Bunzō is an ordinary man, an average, everyday man, in contrast to the dashing heroes of earlier fiction. However, he is ordinary only in the sense that he is not extreme; he is neither very rich nor abysmally poor, brave nor exceedingly cowardly, fiercely intellectual nor totally ignorant. He is no more ordinary than any of the heroes of modern literature from Stephen Dedalus to Edward Albee's George; he in fact shares many qualities with his Western counterparts of the last hundred years.

Dozens of earlier Russian models may be found for Bunzō's endless brooding, his deep concern with others' opinions about himself, and his habit of ascribing the highest virtues to himself and the basest motives to others. Many similar figures abound in later nineteenth- and twentieth-century European, American, and Japanese fiction. Futabatei was not consciously copying any single Russian novel in writing *Ukigumo,* and little evidence suggests that later Japanese authors often modeled their heroes on Bunzō. Futabatei saw the applicability of the Russian type to Japanese fiction and adopted the pattern because of its appropriateness. In Japan, as in the West, this hero or antihero is so closely entwined with realism and naturalism that no one model should ever be cited. It is almost an accident that Futabatei was the first to portray him; another author would surely have created such a hero in any case. The amazing thing is that, being the first, Futabatei succeeded so well.

By centering his plot on Bunzō's difficulties in the bureaucracy, Futabatei established a setting for his superfluous hero already familiar from Russian literature. Bunzō's feelings toward his employers are not as overladen with emotion as those of some Russian heroes. In *Ukigumo*, however, the bureaucracy represents a major part of the cold, impersonal world which finally forces Bunzō into lonely isolation.

The symbolic treatment of the bureaucracy varied between two extremes in Russian fiction. In many Russian novels it assumes no particularly significant role. It is shown as inefficient, corrupt, and manned by fools, but it represents no important object of hate or fear to the hero. This is true, for instance, of the bureaucracy described in *Fathers and Children*. In other stories, however, the Russian government system plays an important part; it becomes the symbol of the larger, unknown, hostile world which the hero cannot enter. For example, in Dostoevsky's early story *The Double* (1846), the government service is represented as a vast, impersonal machine, deaf to the pleas of the desperate hero, who feels himself powerless to combat it. It symbolizes the uninterested modern world which has no place for the weak, discontented, or inept.

Bunzō's attitude toward the bureaucracy lies closer to the second of these extremes. Although Bunzō's hatred of the office where he works never reaches the intensity of emotion experienced by Golyadkin in *The Double,* he too scorns the pettiness and ignorance he finds there. Bunzō's position had been that of a lowly clerk. The work was simple for him, in fact considerably below his intellectual abilities. Unlike Oblomov in Goncharov's most famous novel or Makar in *Poor Folk,* Bunzō committed no foolish error which brought him to the attention of his superiors. His crime was simply that he was too retiring or too dull to interest influential people. Higher-ranking officials did not protect him, perhaps because they had not even noticed him; when someone was to be dismissed, he was the obvious choice.

Although it is apparent from Futabatei's description of conditions in Bunzō's office that an ability to flatter was an important element in an underling's success, Bunzō's belief that this was the only significant factor in his dismissal indicates the narrowness of his views. He does not entertain the possibility, for instance, that he was dismissed because he lacked seniority. Most of the employees in his office were older men who presumably had been working longer. Noboru, though only a few years his senior, started working in the same division two years earlier than Bunzō. One other man had also been dismissed; he, too, is apparently quite young. In the event of a general reduction in personnel, it would be natural to dismiss the newer employees before those with greater seniority, particularly if they had not attracted the interest of their superiors. However, Bunzō never conceives of any motive for his dismissal other than his aloofness from the petty demands of flattery and cajolery. He clearly sees himself as superior to those who cater to the chief's whims. His inability to toady is certainly commendable, but his snobbery indicates a serious failing in his personality.

In common with many of the heroes of Russian fiction, Bunzō finds it difficult to visualize a situation from any point of view other than his own. He does not recognize his essential selfishness because of his conviction that he is morally correct. Sycophancy, he is sure, is wicked; his aloofness, therefore, must be virtuous. He expects to be admired, only to meet with criticism and even ridicule for his stubbornness. Like Golyadkin, Bunzō often imagines himself to be the only man in his world who understands the true meaning of honesty and sincerity, and he convinces himself that he is being persecuted for his virtue.

Bunzō cannot understand the other characters in the novel. Noboru, Futabatei's positive hero, is the mirror opposite of Bunzō. Noboru is ruthless and calculating, and again Bunzō is morally correct in finding nothing to admire in him. However, he does not ever realize that he is jealous of Noboru. Noboru's success in the office is matched by his ability to win a woman's heart. Bunzō fails in both and will not even admit that it might be some inadequacy on his part that causes his failure. He assumes it is only because the world is stupid and vulgar that a man like Noboru can be so esteemed while he is ridiculed. Bunzō never considers that Noboru may, in fact, be a man of ability, or at least that his talent may have some value.

Similarly, Bunzō finds it very difficult to understand Omasa's behavior. Again he quite accurately perceives her lack of morality. She is dishonest in pretending that she had not planned his marriage to Osei. She wants nothing more than to be rid of him permanently and makes him extremely uncomfortable. Instead of offering him sympathy for his plight, she flies at him in fury. Omasa concedes to the traditional system of family loyalty only to the degree that she does not actually turn him out of the house. On the other hand, except for one brief flash of insight, Bunzō does not see why Omasa is driven to such extremes of anger. The reason is obvious to the reader. By wit and will, Omasa has raised herself to a position of respectability. She is determined to see her daughter married well so that her status will be maintained; a poor, unemployed relative is a blight in her home. Bunzō has disappointed her bitterly, and she is convinced that it is because he would not take her advice and be more yielding to the chief. No longer a suitable match for her daughter, he promises to be a persistent burden to her. Bunzō is morally correct in despising her overt materialism, but his failure to understand her position is a serious flaw in his personality.

Bunzō's evaluation of Osei moves drastically from one extreme to the other in the course of the novel, and in both instances he is not correct. At first thinking she is intelligent, enlightened, and sympathetic, he is unable to realize that her learning is painfully superficial and her sympathy as easily lost as it had been gained. He cannot appreciate her frivolousness or her girlish need for gaiety and romance. If he had told her his thoughts when she initially offered him sympathy regarding his dismissal, he might well have won her affection permanently, but his silence at that crucial point left her with no recourse but to seek amusement elsewhere. Bunzō fails to recognize that Osei is self-centered and stubborn and, as a consequence, cannot understand why she is so determined to defend Noboru. Bunzō sees her interest in Noboru as crude and distasteful and imagines that Osei has sunk to some horrible depths because she banters and jokes with him. Bunzō's exaggeration of Osei's merits is the natural reaction of a young man in love, but his distorted interpretation of her relations with Noboru is indicative of a more profound emotional disturbance.

Bunzō's inability to carry out any of his plans is his most dominant characteristic. Resolutions are broken one after the other. When he is rejected by the bureaucratic world, he determines to find other work, but, in fact, he makes only one feeble effort to gain employment in the many weeks encompassed by the novel. After his visit to Ishida four days after his dismissal, he does not contact anyone else, although he fully realizes that Ishida is not really interested in helping him. Early in the novel Bunzō also resolves to leave the Sonoda household. Initially his realization that he would be insulting his mother by being rude to his aunt combined with his affection for Osei prevent him from going. As the days pass, he reaffirms his resolution any number of times but still hesitates. Then he decides that he must save Osei from the degradation into which he is convinced she has fallen. He spends hours, even days, searching for a way to tell her how dreadfully she is behaving. In the end he merely exhausts himself in thinking about acting; he does nothing. In the closing chapters of the novel, Osei loses interest in Noboru and becomes more cheerful, but this owes nothing to Bunzō. He has failed to take any positive action at all.

In the few instances where he carries out one of his resolutions, he blunders badly, and his deeds become a kind of failure in themselves. He twice goes to Osei to seek her support in his despair, and both times she becomes extremely angry with him. He succeeds in telling Noboru that he wants no more of his so-called friendship, but in the course of their argument Bunzō is made a fool of, and subsequently both Osei and Omasa take Noboru's side. Bunzō then is a failure in virtually everything he tries to do in the novel.

Despite many striking similarities between Bunzō and the superfluous heroes of Russian fiction, Futabatei's transfer of the type into a Japanese context is complete. Bunzō's immediate problems, his relations with his mother, aunt, and cousin, as well as with his acquaintances, and the reaction he has to his situation are all consistent with conditions actually existing in Tokyo in the late 1880s. The reader is never conscious of an alien influence in the novel.

Although Futabatei found the theme for *Ukigumo* in Goncharov's work and, as we have seen, greatly admired his style, he did not adopt the Russian novelist's ideas indiscriminately. Oblomov and Alexander Aduyev in *A Common Story* (1847) are members of the landed aristocracy. Their difficulty in adjusting to modern society stems from their unwillingness to part with the comforts of their childhood. They had been brought up to believe that everything would be provided for them and that they would never have to work hard for anything. Both novels are filled with nostalgia for the ease and graciousness of the old life. Nothing of this appears in *Ukigumo*. Bunzō was always poor and, although his family were samurai, they were near the lowest level of the class. Bunzō, raised in the belief that hard work was his duty, never shirked this responsibility. Unlike Oblomov's self-induced pathological inertia, Bunzō's inaction is temporary and precipitated only by the loss of his job. He does not long for the past because, in fact, he has never known anything but poverty and uncertainty. It is death of an ethical system which Bunzō represents and not the end of a social class. Although the code which Bunzō believes in was kept alive by the samurai, it was not dependent for its survival on the continuance of the Tokugawa social structure.

Bunzō is protected against the worst extremes of poverty by the Japanese family system. As long as he stays in Magobei's house, he will be fed and his clothes cared for. He will not exhibit the visible signs of poverty which disgrace Dostoevsky's superfluous heroes. Without an income, Bunzō cannot send his mother any money nor bring her to live with him, and this is his greatest financial concern. However, although his mother's poverty worries him at first, he begins to think less and less about it as the novel progresses. It is possible to assume that Bunzō knows that she too will be cared for in some other way. Therefore Bunzō does not have to face unemployment with the terror which dominates many of the heroes of Russian fiction.

Bunzō is not insane. Although he feels oppressed and misunderstood, his is the variety of neurosis common to modern society. The Japanese bureaucratic world and the materialistic forces represented by Omasa fill Bunzō with disgust, but Futabatei did not follow the example of Dostoevsky and present a hero almost too sick to be brought back to the society of ordinary men.

Finally, it is important to note once again that *Ukigumo* contains no political message. It will be remembered that immediately before starting *Ukigumo,* Futabatei had been translating *Fathers and Children* and that he himself had been quite outspoken on political issues earlier in life. While the contrast between the strong man and the weak which is such a consistent theme in Turgenev's work is repeated in *Ukigumo,* it is impossible to read a political implication into the plot.[47]

The theme which *Ukigumo* shares in common with many Russian novels is the tragedy of separation or isolation.

47. Edmund Wilson considers the repetition of this theme in Turgenev's stories to be a reflection of the novelist's friendship with Belinsky. "Turgenev and the Life-Giving Drop," pp. 199–200.

Sympathy, love, or understanding—whatever aspect the emotion takes—is the unchanging, universal, all-pervasive force in human behavior; it is, in Futabatei's terminology, the Idea. *Ukigumo* deals with the absence of that emotion in the lives of its characters and, through the detailed analysis of Bunzō's situation, with the pathetic confusion which accompanies such a loss. Futabatei attempted to capture the qualities which made his time different from any other by telling the story of Noboru's success and Bunzō's failure in the bureaucratic world; he tried to capture the Essence of life by showing how Bunzō was unable to win the sympathy and understanding of Omasa and Osei.

The extent of Futabatei's contribution to Japanese literature is most apparent when *Ukigumo* is compared with "realistic" novels of the Tokugawa period. Shikitei Samba's *Ukiyoburo* and Jippensha Ikku's *Hizakurige* are often cited as predecessors of *Ukigumo*. These episodic, loosely constructed tales are not without value for providing sharp flashes of insight into the lives of Edo townsmen. Such brief characterizations, however brilliant, cannot be compared with the fully realized portrayals in *Ukigumo*. The dialogue in *Ukiyoburo* and *Hizakurige* is vivid and authentic, but the scenes are short and only vaguely related one to another. It is one thing to reveal personality in a brief incident by the use of clever dialogue; it is quite another to convey the many facets of a character's nature by what he says in scene after scene of expanding plot. The characters in *Ukigumo* develop before our eyes. Osei and Bunzō both grow up through their experiences, but they do not mature in any miraculous fashion. Their adult personalities are the natural outgrowth of their youthful selves.

Such development required time and space, and Futabatei allows for it in a way unknown in the Tokugawa and early Meiji novels of contemporary life. He restricts the outer limits of his plot to the simple circumstances of Bunzō's dismissal and its immediate ramifications. He does not attempt a montage of life such as we find in *Ukiyoburo, Hizakurige,* or the Meiji novels *Kajin no kigū* by Tōkai Sanshi or *Aguranabe* by Kanagaki Robun. Futabatei also avoids the complicated, intertwined plot found in Tamenaga Shunsui's *Shunshoku umegoyomi* and the idealistic fantasy of Tsubouchi's *Mirai no yume.* Futabatei describes a society he knows where men act and react as they have been known to the world over.

The superiority of *Ukigumo* to Tsubouchi's novels and to many other novels written in the same period lies in Futabatei's attempt to reveal aspects of the human condition which are buried beneath man's daily actions. He gives us a picture of a young man in his solitary hours, away from the probing, critical eyes of his family and friends, free to let his mind wander where it will. The portrait of weakness, vacillation, fear, and uncertainty is a vivid representation of modern man's dilemma. Despite Futabatei's despair over his novel and the unpolished state of Part Three, *Ukigumo* is a powerful, realistic novel.

With the models of the great Russian masters of realism to work from and with his own philosophic conviction in the merit of fiction as a serious form of art, Futabatei was able to create a novel whose plot and characterization symbolized some of the most important conflicts of his time. *Ukigumo* is a statement in fictional form of Futabatei's analysis of Meiji society. He was never successful in putting his literary theories into written form in expository writing; his novel is the positive expression of his views, and through it and his translations from Russian fiction he influenced generations of Japanese intellectuals. Futabatei was not a good literary critic, although his perception and understanding of Russian and Japanese literature were highly developed. The critical argument for realism was made by Tsubouchi in *Shōsetsu shinzui.* It remained for Futabatei to put that argument into practice. Between them, Tsubouchi and Futabatei established the model for realism which has remained the dominant pattern of Japanese fiction until today.

UKIGUMO

Translator's Note to Ukigumo

U K I G U M O has never before been translated in its entirety. A translation of approximately one half of chapter vii appears in Donald Keene's *Modern Japanese Literature* (pp. 59–69); several paragraphs from scattered parts of the novel are included in Horace Feldman's "The Growth of the Meiji Novel" (pp. 110–13); and a passage appears in French translation in Georges Bonneau's *Histoire de la Littérature Japonaise* (pp. 175–77). I have previously translated several pages of *Ukigumo* for an earlier study.[1]

In preparing this translation, I have used the text of *Ukigumo* included in *Futabatei Shimei zenshū* published by Iwanami Shoten in 1953–54. This text is considered authoritative by Japanese scholars;[2] to verify this point, I have compared Part One with a first edition of the text and have been satisfied that in those few places where they differ, the 1953–54 version is the more accurate. I have also compared the text of the novel in *Futabatei Shimei shū*, Volume X of *Gendai Nihon bungaku zenshū* (1928); and with the text published in the *Shinchō bunko* series (1960). In neither case have I found substantial variations.

1. "A Study of Futabatei Shimei," pp. 60–66.
2. For a discussion of the text of *Ukigumo* included in the 1953–54 *Zenshū*, see Tamai Kansuke and Kurita Hiroyuki, p. 80. The editing was supervised by Nakamura Mitsuo.

UKIGUMO, PART ONE

I T I S three o'clock in the afternoon of a late October day. A swirling mass of men stream out of the Kanda gate,* marching first in antlike formation, then scuttling busily off in every direction. Each and every one of these fine gentlemen is primarily interested in getting enough to eat.

Look carefully and you will see what an enormous variety of individual types are represented in the huge crowd. Start by examining the hair bristling on their faces: mustaches, side whiskers, Vandykes, and even extravagant imperial beards, Bismarck beards reminiscent of a Pekinese, bantam beards, badger's beards, meager beards that are barely visible, thick and thin they sprout in every conceivable way.

Now see how differently they are dressed. Here is a dandy in a fashionable black suit purchased at Shirokiya† set off by shoes of French calfskin. And now confident men oblivious of the ill-fit of their tweeds worn with stiff leather shoes— trousers that trail in the mud like the tail of a tortoise; suits bearing the indelible stamp of the ready-made clothes rack.

* The gate in Kanda was one of thirty-six surrounding the shogun's castle. It was to the northeast of the castle. The gates were originally sentry posts.

† Shirokiya was one of the first of the old, established drygoods stores to feature Western clothing. It opened its Western clothing department in the fall of 1886. Shibusawa, p. 29.

"I have a beard, fine clothing, what more do I need?" they seem to say. Glowing like embers on the fire, these enviable creatures swagger home, heads erect.

Now behind them come the less fortunate. Pitifully stooped, their hair grey, they stagger along with empty lunch boxes dangling from their waists. Despite their advanced years they still manage to hold a job, but their duties are so negligible they can easily work in old-fashioned Japanese clothes.

The crowd had thinned out by the time two young men engrossed in conversation came through the gate. The taller of the two was some twenty-three years old. His complexion was quite poor, pasty and sallow, but his thick eyebrows lent distinction to his face, and the bridge of his nose was straight. His mouth was not very shapely but it was firm and restrained. He had a pointed chin and prominent cheekbones. He was rather drawn and seemed nervous and not particularly appealing, his slenderness made him appear even taller than he was. He wore an old straw-colored pepper-and-salt tweed suit and a broad-brimmed hat of dark wool with a braid headband.

The other man was some two or three years his senior. He was quite good-looking, of average height and build, with a round face, fair complexion, shapely mouth, and alert eyes, but there was something too worldly and calculating about him. He seemed somewhat cheap. He was smartly clothed in a black wool morning coat with a vest of the same material and striped woolen trousers. Set low on his brow was a black hat shaped like the bottom of a pot, its brim turned up. His left hand was thrust in his pocket and he toyed with a thin cane in his other hand.

"But really," he said, turning to his companion, "it's obvious that the chief values my opinion. He must have been forced to do what he did. There are more than forty clerks, but they're either old as the hills, or just plain stupid. I know I shouldn't be the one to say this, but after all, just a few of us have read foreign books. We're the ones who really do the work. It's obvious that the chief relies on me. He must have had to do it."

"But what about Yamaguchi? He did as much work as anybody and still he was fired, wasn't he?"

"Oh, him. He's so stupid."

"What do you mean?"

"I mean the way he answered back. You have to be pretty stupid to do that."

"But the chief was completely in the wrong. He shouldn't have been so overbearing. His orders were completely un-reasonable."

"Unreasonable or not, you can't go against a superior. After all, what was Yamaguchi? He was an underling, wasn't he? He should have just said 'yes' and carried on with his work, whether he thought the orders made sense or not. Then he would have been doing his job. But the way he acted—telling the chief what to do and all."

"He didn't do anything of the kind. He just made a sug-gestion."

"Oh, now you're defending Yamaguchi, are you? Birds of a feather."

The tall man glanced in silent contempt at his companion. They turned up Nishikichō and went a few blocks further before the smaller man suddenly stopped and said, "Losing your job has its good side too."

"What might that be?"

"From now on you can stay with your sweetheart from morning till night."

"Don't be a fool!" His lips twisted into a distorted smile as he bid his companion a curt goodbye and went on alone toward Ogawamachi. Bit by bit the smile left his face and his steps grew slower until he barely crawled along. He went a few more blocks, his head hanging forlornly. Suddenly he stopped, looked around, then retreated two or three steps and went down a side street. He entered the third house from the corner, a two-story building with a lattice door. Shall we go in too?

He went in through the entrance-way. As he started along the hallway, a door slid open and a girl in her late teens popped her head out. She had a little button nose and round, plump, ruddy cheeks which betrayed her country origin.

"Hello," she said, wetting her lips.

"My aunt?"

"She's gone out with the young lady."

"Oh," the young man said. He went down the corridor, came to an adjoining staircase, and went up to the second floor.

It was a small room about ten by ten with a closet some three feet across at one end. Walled in on three sides, the room opened on the south with sliding windows. The painting in the alcove was a little ragged, and the few asters which had been thrust into the hanging flower vase were withered, their leaves all but dead. A low, antiquated writing table stood in the corner. On it were a stand filled with a writing brush, pen and toothbrush, and an inkstone lined up beside a box of toothpowder. Next to the desk were two bookcases, with a small lamp on top. Under the desk was a broken-rimmed firepan with the remains of some spent matches in it. A blanket was spread over the floor, a kimono hung on a clothes hanger, and a towel was hooked on a nail in the pillar. All the furnishings were neatly arranged, although they were old and had a musty, threadbare quality.

The young man changed into Japanese clothing. He made a futile attempt to fold the clothes he had taken off, then, with a grunt of disgust, shoved them into the closet.

The apple-cheeked girl came clattering upstairs. She was plump, stocky and sturdy—a true buxom beauty. She handed him a letter. "This came a little while ago."

"Where's it from?" He took the letter and looked at it. "Oh, from home."

"I really wish you could have seen the way the young lady was dressed today. She had on a yellow-striped silk kimono underneath and a gorgeous striped crepe over it. Her hair was coiled around in a bun, the way she usually wears it, but she had on that hairpin she got at the Izumo shop* the other day that looks like a rose." She outlined the shape with her hands. "She really and truly was beautiful. What I wouldn't give to have one sash-clip like that." The girl fell silent, brooding about something for a moment. "The young lady says she doesn't use any powder, but it certainly looked like she'd put on a little today. Her skin may be white but not like that. When I was home I used to wear a lot of powder. Since I came here I don't use any except at New Year's. There's nothing to stop me but I hate having the mistress talk about me. Once, in front of a guest, she said, 'When Onabe† puts on powder, it's rather like frost on a ball of charcoal.' Isn't that going too far? Don't you think that's going too far? No matter how plain I am?" As she talked her face grew all the redder from excitement. One would have thought her mistress was sitting there beside her.

Throughout her discourse the young man kept picking up his letter and trying to read it and then putting it down again in despair. He seemed very irritated. He grunted in response to her question to indicate his annoyance and refused to join in her chatter. This made the buxom beauty puff out her round cheeks until it seemed they would burst.‡ She went downstairs in a huff. He looked relieved to see her go and turned to the letter once again. It said:

Dear Son,

As winter approaches, it gets colder every day. My only concern is whether you are getting on with your work smoothly. You'll find that I've aged quite a bit lately and my hair has turned grey. I'm afraid I'm getting rather disagreeable. I know that I'll be able to come to your house by the end of the year,

---

* The shop was famous for having introduced a fashionable line of foreign style wigs and hairpieces and other accessories needed for Western style hairdos. *Shimbun shūsei Meiji hennen-shi,* VI, 466–67.

† *Nabe* [pot] was a form of address for maids and is not really the name of the girl.

‡ Japanese people characteristically puff out their cheeks in anger.

but somehow I am so impatient. I count each passing day on my fingers. I can't tell you how anxious I am to come and live with you as soon as possible. On the 24th your father's. . . .

The letter slipped to the floor. Folding his arms, the young man sighed deeply.

T H E M A N we have been calling "The tall young man" was named Utsumi Bunzō and he was from Shizuoka Prefecture. His father had served in the old feudal government receiving a stipend under it. But then the feudal order had fallen and the Imperial government was restored. The Meiji era began; there were none who did not yield to the change. Bunzō's father returned to his home in a small village in Shizuoka and simply vegetated for a while. He lived from day to day doing nothing until he had exhausted his resources. At last his savings had all but disappeared, and he became seriously concerned. Alas, the changes in political climate had left him like a fish out of water. A man's arm may be strengthened by the practice of kendō, yet he cannot necessarily use a spade; when his mouth is weighted down with the solemn language of the feudal order, it is no easy matter for him to say "yes, sir" like a shop clerk. Then peddling he felt would soil the good name of the family. He scurried about until, with great difficulty, he secured a post in the Shizuoka han administration. Although it was only a petty job and he could not better himself, he was happy for he was able to give his only child, Bunzō, an education by generously lavishing on it a goodly portion of his meager income.

The boy was sent off to school each morning with his lunch box strapped on his back. In the afternoon he went to a nearby private school for additional instruction and had little or no time for himself. This would have been much too rigorous a schedule for the average child, but Bunzō was rather reserved and took naturally to study. He seemed content to go to school every day. Sometimes he would wander off to play with a friend he saw chasing dragonflies, only to return forlornly to the house. But this happened only occasionally and as a rule his days were filled with his studies.

Bunzō's affection for learning grew as the years passed until he found himself willingly reading books that once he had rejected as dull or uninteresting. His parents were utterly delighted when strangers praised him for his intelligence, and they happily devoted their every waking hour to furthering his education. In the spring of the year when Bunzō was fourteen, he was graduated from school. He had done very well; his parents had every reason to be pleased with his accomplishments.

Almost immediately after Bunzō's graduation, his father caught a cold. He was so weak from years of worry and anxiety that it quickly turned into a serious illness. His family and friends desperately tried every remedy people recommended—medicines, charms, incantations, and prayers—but nothing seemed to help. He died a short time later, speaking of his son with his last words. It is impossible to describe the grief of his widow and child. They were unable to control their tears although they knew all too well how futile tears were. The body was sent to the family temple; a column of smoke arose from the crematorium.

The family's only source of income was cut off when Bunzō's father died. The medical expenses and the cost of the funeral seriously depleted their small savings. Fortunately Bunzō's mother was a resolute and determined woman. She sewed shirts in whatever time she could spare from her work in the kitchen. Through her tireless efforts and with the help of the interest on her husband's pension, they were able to avoid utter destitution and somehow managed to scrape together enough to eat simply.

Bunzō had been aware of his family's financial difficulties even when his father was still alive, but he was still just a child and felt that somehow things would be all right. Sometimes, out of his love for his parents, he would promise to do this or that to help them and would sadden them by saying things too old for his years. But he was still, after all, just a boy, and the days and months drifted by without his doing anything to help. After his father's death he was terribly saddened when he saw how his mother struggled. As if waking from a dream, he realized, for the first time, the cruelties of life. He considered becoming an office boy so that he could at least support himself although he realized this would not enable him to help his mother financially.

While he and his mother were thinking about this idea, kindly providence intervened; an uncle in Tokyo offered to take the boy in. Bunzō and his mother very much regretted being separated but there was nothing to be done about it, and, in the spring of 1878, when he was fifteen, he left Shizuoka and went to live in Tokyo.

Bunzō's uncle was his father's younger brother. He was named Sonoda Magobei.* He was sympathetic, honest, and upright, and people liked him, unfortunately he was a little too easygoing. After the Meiji revolution he had substituted brush and ink for the swords of the samurai, and night and day practiced flipping the abacus. The fact that he was not accustomed to the business world proved a serious handicap at first; he quickly used up everything he earned and sank heavily into debt. Still he struggled to find a solution to his financial difficulties and in time things improved. He accumulated a little capital, bought some land, and lent small sums. He had a home in Tokyo and ran a teahouse in Yokohama. He was not particularly wealthy, but he lived comfortably.

* It appears that Magobei was adopted into the Sonoda family, hence the difference in their names. He is described as Bunzō's father's real brother.

When Magobei was away in Yokohama, his Tokyo affairs were managed by a woman named Omasa who had been his mistress and became his second wife. Her background is a little hazy; she claimed to be of a respectable samurai family but well, one wonders. At any rate she was shrewd; in fact, shrewd enough to collect rent and press people for the payments on their loans, besides caring for her family. Her flaws were minor: she drank too much, was rather wanton in her ways, and hated to sew. Her neighbors made much of her faults, the way people will. They said she was the reincarnation of a lustful snake and hinted that there might be others in her life.

The couple had two children: their daughter Osei and their son Isami. When Bunzō went to live with the family, Osei, who was twelve, was at home, while Isami, a naughty little boy who was still wiping his nose on his sleeve, was away at school. If Bunzō had been able to get along with his aunt everything would have gone smoothly in the little household. Unfortunately the boy was constitutionally incapable of currying favor with anyone. In his heart of hearts he wanted to be loyal and devoted to her as if she were his own mother, and he tried desperately to please her, but she made things very difficult by constantly scolding him and calling him stupid. Each time she reprimanded him, he remembered how good and kind his mother was, and he longed to be home again. He often wept when he was alone. Living with his aunt required a great deal of patience and self-control on his part.

For several months he attended classes in a neighborhood academy in the little time he had to spare from his chores at home. Then one day he heard that scholarships were being offered to a new preparatory school, and, eager to escape from his unhappy position in his uncle's house, he took the examination. He received a scholarship and went off to school.

Bunzō was so happy he could have danced for joy. He had been terribly overworked by his aunt since coming to her house and had, in addition, very much disliked his role as a dependent nephew. Now that he was back in school, he was able to devote his full time and energy to his studies without any distractions.

But even at school he was continually reminded of his poverty and loneliness. He had no one to spoil and pamper him as the other boys had, no one to give him an allowance. He channeled all his youthful energies into his studies. He was inspired by an overwhelming desire to bring joy to his destitute mother and to repay his great debt to his uncle by being successful at school. And he was. He took either first or second place—but never lower—in every examination. He was the pride of his teachers. His rich and lazy fellow students were very jealous of him, but the boy ignored them and never stopped studying. After several years he received the coveted diploma and went back to live at his uncle's house while he looked for a government job.

Bunzō was confident that he would find a position readily. Unfortunately there were no openings at the time and he had to wait six long months for any sort of opportunity to come along. This arduous waiting period was made even more terrible by his aunt's contemptuous attitude which grew more obvious as time passed. Only his realization that his own failure to secure a position was to blame for her anger enabled him to control his temper.

He finally obtained a temporary post as a government clerk through the assistance of someone he knew. He was delighted to be able to remove the cause of his differences with his aunt, but still he felt a little ill at ease when he finally did start to work. On the first day he was given a document to check, and when he was settled at his desk he surveyed the room. Around him were men engaged in all kinds of work: copyists with their heads tilted importantly to one side; checkers who studied the work before them like monkeys searching for fleas; accountants turning over the pages of their books with a busy air, their brushes between their teeth.

Just opposite Bunzō was a man of about fifty with a deeply

furrowed brow who flipped the beads of an abacus without pausing, rapidly blinking his eyes. Suddenly he held his hands still and, fingering the beads, said, ". . . Six by five is seventy-two—no—six by five . . . ," as if the welfare of the entire world depended on this one calculation. He looked up at Bunzō over his glasses, his mouth hanging open. ". . . makes eighty-two?" He raised his voice in a high pitched chant and began pushing away at the abacus, giving it his undivided attention.

The situation was so funny that Bunzō could not help laughing. Almost immediately he realized with a pang that there was little difference between the man who was laughing and the one being laughed at. How painful it was to try to accept the idea that he had taken a job where he would completely waste the learning he had acquired with such sacrifice. For a time he just sat there stupidly, paralyzed with despair, until at last he forced himself to get down to work. For four or five days he sighed each time he looked at that old man, but as time passed, his sadness lessened.

From then on he helped his mother by sending her money every month. He paid back his debt to his uncle in monthly installments and his aunt's attitude toward him improved markedly. At the end of the year he was promoted a grade and made a permanent employee. In the summer of the year before the beginning of our story he had gone home for a visit for the first time in a long while. His joys seemed to multiply. The wrinkles on his brow disappeared and he felt life had taken a change for the better. At this juncture we have a little romantic episode to tell, but before we do, let's have a short biography of Magobei's daughter, Osei.

Magobei was by nature an indulgent father and Omasa a mother who could see no wrong in her own children, although she was cold enough to others. As a result Osei had been lovingly fondled all her life like a precious hair ornament or a jewel wrapped in silk and she grew to expect to have everything her own way. In short, she ended up a very spoiled child.

She started going to grammar school at the age of seven*
to suit her father and took kiyomoto† lessons to satisfy her
mother. Being naturally clever, Osei grasped her studies
easily, if only superficially. To her mother it seemed she was
a prodigy in both her schoolwork and her music lessons.
Omasa could not restrain herself from praising her daughter
extravagantly, even to people who had not asked about her.

A government official, his wife, and their daughter moved
into the house next door and in due course exchanged greet-
ings with their neighbors. As the parents got to know each
other better, the girls became close friends and began to visit
each other almost every day. The neighbor's daughter was
two or three years older than Osei. She was gentle and ladylike. Although she was only a child, she liked her studies and
did quite well in school, perhaps because her father had been
something of a Confucian scholar.

Osei was a faddist by nature and found it necessary to
mimic others even when she grew up—how much more so
when she was still a child. She immediately fell under the influence of her new friend and imitated her movements, her
behavior, and even her way of saying things. She quickly
tossed aside her samisen and placed a quill on her writing
table. Omasa had no particular fondness for anything as
disciplined as schoolwork, but whatever her beloved daughter wanted to do was all right with her and she did not interfere.

Now it happened that the neighbor's girl was to enter a
private finishing school in Shiba at about the time Osei
was graduated from her school. Of course, Osei immediately
wanted more than anything to enroll there too, and she tried

---

* Literally, "after they had celebrated the *himotoki* ceremony," in which
a seven-year-old girl (or five-year-old boy) is dressed in a proper kimono and
obi for the first time. Until then the children tie their kimono with a
string sewed on the garment itself.

† A style of singing to the accompaniment of a samisen dating from the
early nineteenth century. Both the voice and the instrument are tuned to
a relatively high pitch, resulting in a rather sweet tone. It is often used to
accompany love scenes in a kabuki play. Malm, *Japanese Music*, p. 199.

desperately to persuade her parents to let her go. She talked of it in her sleep and even went on a hunger strike. They, in turn, felt that it was absolutely out of the question to send such a poor, defenseless girl off to school and tried to stand their ground just this one time. Osei moaned and groaned and said that there was no point in living if she could not go to school. In short, she made a great display of her misery. In the end her parents had to give in. With great misgivings, they allowed her to be enrolled in the school and sent her off with the neighbor's daughter. This all took place two years before the time of our story.

The headmistress of Osei's school was a fine figure of a woman who arrogantly aired knowledge she had acquired secondhand from the newspapers. A loathsome creature, she was quite forgetful of kindnesses received but always remembered any insult done her. She invariably managed a thinly veiled insult when she met someone she disliked. Although Osei was outspoken enough to her parents, she was a meek little lamb to everyone else, and being unable to bear the woman's caustic comments, won her over by being obsequious. Under the influence of that great lady, the girl changed so completely that she was barely recognizable, which certainly shows what a precocious young girl she must have been. She dropped her neighbor friend before long.

Things went from bad to worse after she started studying English at the school. She switched from a Japanese underrobe to an undershirt and adopted a Western style hairdo, strangled herself with a scarf, and donned eyeglasses which ruined her perfect vision. Her self-approved transformation was perfectly ridiculous.

At the end of the year preceding our story, the headmistress got a job as a teacher elsewhere and left the school. One by one her clever young charges departed. As a result Osei conceived a great affection for her own home. It seemed that it was awfully hard for her to admit it, however, and so she said she was leaving school because her Chinese studies were completed. That was in the spring, about the time when the cherry blossoms were falling.

As we have said, when Bunzō came to Tokyo, Osei was a child of twelve, still wearing a little girl's narrow obi and not quite grown up. She was very shy with her cousin at first, perhaps because she thought Omasa might have meant it when she jokingly told visitors he was Osei's future husband. But children get over such things quickly, and the two young people were soon sharing sweets with one another. In no time they were fast friends.

After Bunzō enrolled in school, he and Osei rarely saw each other; they did not spend more than a few hours at a time together. Then the girl went off to school too, and it was not until she was home for winter vacation that year that they saw each other for any extended period. By that time they were of a marriageable age, and they had to behave differently. Bunzō treated Osei coldly, with his characteristic reserve, and did not speak freely to her as he had when they were children. And yet when she went back to school at the end of the holidays, he was quite lonely for the first few days, as if he had lost an old friend. Soon he forgot her again.

When Osei finally left school, they found themselves living in the same house once more. Bunzō discovered that he felt gay and festive when she spoke to him in a friendly way. It was more than the pleasure of having another young person around—his whole mood changed peculiarly when he sat in the same room with her. He would straighten his rounded back and adjust his neck and become very self-conscious and awkward looking. Distracted and uncomfortable, he found it difficult to concentrate. Everything seemed enveloped in a haze of unreality, and he lost his ability to distinguish fact from fantasy. There was only one object he could see clearly —still it was too early for him to understand what was troubling him.

Early in the summer before the beginning of our story, the family had asked Bunzō to teach Osei English, and after they had begun the lessons he found he could speak to her a little more readily. He began to talk to her about the status of Japanese women, the advantages of Western hairdos, or social relations between men and women. Osei answered him freely without considering that her cousin was a man. But strangely enough, as time passed, she grew rather quiet and demure during such discussions and she seemed much more gentle and feminine.

One day Bunzō noticed that she was not wearing her glasses or scarf. When he asked her why, she replied, "You told me they were bad for healthy people." He could not help being pleased.

Osei thus turned into a young lady, but Bunzō, by contrast, was extremely restless. While he was at the office, he kept thinking of Osei and waiting impatiently for the end of the day, and he was extremely disappointed if she was not home when he got there. He began to wonder if he might not have fallen in love with her. The mere thought of it made him blush.

Since Osei had come home to live, worms had been breeding inside poor, unsuspecting Bunzō's heart. At first they were very small and did not occupy enough space to give him trouble. But once they started actively crawling around, he felt as though he were peacefully departing from this world and entering a blissful paradise. It was like lying among exquisite flowers and glittering leaves on a spring day, wafting on scent-filled air, dozing, half awake and half asleep, hearing the drone of a fly growing ever more distant. It was an indescribably glorious sensation.

But all too soon the worms grew fat and powerful. By the time Bunzō had begun to suspect that he was infatuated with Osei, they were enormous and were crawling about, anxious to be mated. They depended on her encouragement for their survival, and if she had been cold they would surely have died. But as it was, they were being half killed. The worms seem to have found this state of affairs horribly painful—

they wriggled around and chewed away at his insides, making him utterly miserable.

Bunzō tried to guess what his aunt thought about his marrying Osei. It appeared to him that she was aware of what was happening between them and was simply pretending not to see anything, perhaps to save him any embarrassment. If that was the case, he might assume he had Omasa's approval and could confess his feelings to Osei without hesitation. But he was checked by another voice within him which warned that he might very well be refused. He knew he had to go on suffering for a while longer.

Let's go on to the important part.

I T   W A S the summer before the beginning of our tale. One
night when Bunzō came home from a walk, he found that
the only light in the house shone in Osei's room. His aunt
had not returned from an errand she had had that evening
and Onabe had apparently gone out to the bath. Bunzō
started to go directly upstairs but stopped part way up and
retreated a step, lost in thought. He hesitated and then went
down another step. All at once he started up again, when
he heard a voice call out from Osei's room. "Who's there?"
she said.

"Bunzō," he replied, drawing up his shoulders.

"I was just wondering who it might be and here it's
Bunzō. Why don't you come in and keep me company?"

"Thank you but let's make it a little later."

"Have you got something to do?"

"No, nothing."

"Then why not? Come on in."

Bunzō hesitated a second, came all the way down, and
went to the entrance of Osei's room. He did not go in, but
stood in the doorway.

"Do come in."

He remained standing uncertainly at the door. He obviously wanted to go in and yet felt he should not.

"Why are you being so reserved tonight?"

"You're alone. It looks a little odd."

"That doesn't sound like you at all. Now who was it who said we can't put our theories into practice if we're weak?" she asked tilting her lovely head.

Bunzō was trapped by her smile. He went into the room and sat down. "There's nothing I can say to that."

"Won't you use this?" she said, offering him a fan. "Now, what's this all about?"

"It's just that gossip is so terrible."

"No matter what we do, people will gossip. And anyway, it doesn't matter as long as we haven't done anything to be ashamed of. You have to expect some difficulty when you destroy the traditions of two thousand years."

"I think so too, but I still hate to be talked about."

"That's true enough. The other day I got angry when Onabe was teasing me, and I tried to explain about freedom between the sexes* even though I knew it would be hard for her to accept such an idea. She told me I used too many difficult words so she couldn't understand a thing I said. What can you expect from someone who has no education?"

"She is very funny, isn't she? But it seems to me that she's not the only one who's been suspicious. What about your mother?"

"Oh, she just teases me all the time. That's the way lower-class people are. Lately I've been trying to persuade her to stop and she doesn't do it as much as she used to."

"What does she tease you about?"

"Well, she says if we're going to be so friendly, I really ought to—ought to marry you."

Bunzō stared at her in astonishment.

---

* In the text Osei says she tried to tell Onabe about *Danjo kōsai ron* [An essay on the relations between men and women]. Written by Fukuzawa Yukichi, a leading writer and educator, it explains the dangers inherent in the traditional Japanese system where women lead virtually separate lives from men, and champions free intellectual and social interchange between the sexes. It was published in June 1886. *Fukuzawa Yukichi zenshū*, V, 581–605.

She pretended it was nothing and went on calmly. "The trouble is it's not just people who have no education. My friends aren't really what you'd call educated but they've had the usual schooling, and yet only a few of them really understand Western thought. Even they just pay attention to liberal ideas while they're in school. Once they're out, they allow themselves to be dominated by their parents and they go off to their husbands' families or marry someone adopted into their family. I find it discouraging to think I'm the only one left who's really liberal. But now that I've made friends with you I feel much more confident about my ideas."

Bunzō lowered his head. "You're so kind."

"Not at all. It's true."

"Then it makes me all the happier. Unfortunately it's impossible for us to be friends."

"Why?"

"I don't understand you and you don't understand me. So we can't be close friends."

"I think I understand you pretty well. You are learned and well behaved and you're devoted to your mother."

"That shows how little you understand me. You say I'm devoted to my mother, but I'm not really. There is something more important to me than my mother," he said brokenly and lowered his eyes.

Osei watched him with a puzzled expression on her face. "There is something more important to me than my parents, too," she said.

Bunzō raised his head. "To you, too?"

"Yes."

"Who—who is it?"

"Oh, it's not a person. It's truth."

"Truth!" Bunzō trembled, bit his lip, and was silent for a moment. Then he took a deep breath. "You're so pure, so innocent. To say that truth is more important than one's parents, that is innocence. But emotion is a strange thing. It makes a fool of a man. It makes him laugh and cry and tosses him about like a plaything. Even though you realize you are being toyed with, you can't control it." He paused to think and then went on excitedly. "I cannot forget her. I cannot possibly forget her. Osei, you're so innocent that you may not understand what I mean but—but there is someone more important to me than truth. My emotions have been dominated by her for six months and I can't forget her even when I'm asleep. I feel worse than death itself, but she doesn't understand how I feel at all. I might be able to put her out of my mind if she were cold but . . ." his voice be-- came fuzzy, ". . . and when I find she relies on me like a good friend, I feel. . . ."

"The moon. It looks like it's rising right out of the bamboo grove. Look!"

The cool moon rose, outlining the leaves of ten slim bamboo trees which stood in the corner of the garden. There was not a single cloud and its powerful, radiant, white light lit up the face of the sky. Glistening drops of light poured down to the earth below. At first the bamboo fence between the houses held back the moonbeams and they extended only halfway across the garden. As the moon rose in the sky, the moonbeams crept up to the verandah and poured into the room. The water in the miniature garden there shim- mered in the light; the windbell glittered and tinkled. Then the moonlight silhouetted the two young people and stole the brightness of the single lamp in the room. Finally it climbed up the wall.

Each time the cool, refreshing breezes blew, the shadows of the moonflowers clambering up the garden fence danced and fluttered, and pearls of dew clinging to the tips of lily leaves turned to fireflies and skipped away. With the rustling of wind through the foliage, excitement grew within the hearts of the young people. As the wind subsided, every- thing was hushed. The only sound was the chirping of in- sects gathered in the rush of the eaves. It was a beautiful scene, but Bunzō and Osei were so preoccupied with their own thoughts that they did not really see it.

"How lovely," the girl said. She smiled sweetly and turned

her head, pretending to gaze at the moon. Her features were actually no more beautiful than at any other time, but to Bunzō she seemed utterly enchanting, with her lovely oval face glowing in the moonlight, and two or three loose strands of hair playing about her cheeks, stirred by the breeze from her fan. He could not take his eyes from her face. The profile of his enchantress turned slowly toward him. Her cool, wide eyes swept around and their eyes met. Coquettishly, she hid the smile which filled her pouting lips with the fan she held in her five slender, delicate, white fingers. Bunzō's eyes brightened.

"Osei!" His voice trembled.

"Yes," she replied in a little voice.

"Osei, you are very, very—cruel. I am . . . I am so much . . . ," he said, and putting his hand to his face, he fell silent. The shadow reflected on the wall trembled. Now, one word—the barrier of one word—if you cross it you will enter the mountain of matrimony.* Ever since Bunzō had begun to love this girl who was so close to him every day, her image had hovered before his eyes constantly. He could not drive her from his thoughts no matter how hard he tried. He had no way of knowing whether she shared his feeling; he was alone in his struggle with confusion and doubt. If he could speak out now, if he could but say one word. . . .

* The passage which begins here and continues until Bunzō's thoughts are interrupted is particularly rich in poetic imagery. For example, what has been translated as "the mountain of matrimony" is *imoseyama* [man and woman mountains]. Imoyama and Seyama have symbolized courtship and love from the earliest days of Japanese poetry. (See *Man'yō-shū* 544, 1195, etc.) The mountains originally referred to are either two of that name in modern Wakayama prefecture or two in Nara prefecture.

Osei's close physical proximity to Bunzō is expressed as *ashigaki no majikai* [close together as strands of rush woven to form a fence], a metaphor used as early as the *Kokin-shū* (506). Bunzō cannot banish her from his thoughts as you cannot drive away the moon's reflection from the *kinuta* [fulling-board]. The kinuta has been associated with undying love since the eleventh century (*Genji monogatari*, "Yugao"). When he struggles in silence, unable to decide whether or not to tell her of his love, a line from the second of a pair of famous courting poems from the *Man'yō-shū* (1992, 1993) is used.

Just at that moment the front door rattled open. Startled, Bunzō and Osei looked at each other. He rose quickly. Stumbling, he left the room.

They did not see each other again until the next morning. Bunzō was working through the summer holidays that year because things were so busy at the office, and he barely mumbled a few embarrassed words to the girl before hurrying off. He came back about noon, had his lunch, and went up to his room. As he sat fanning himself, Osei came clattering up the stairs. She asked him two or three questions about English usage. She lingered for a moment after the questions were answered, her eyes lowered shyly. Finally she said, while toying with a pencil, "What was the matter last night?"

There was no reply.

"What was it? You said something about my being cruel and you were very angry. What do you mean by my being cruel?" She lifted a smiling face and peeked at Bunzō. He turned away in great confusion.

"You know what it is, and yet you talk like that," he said.

"But I don't know what you're talking about."

"Then it doesn't matter."

"How strange."

After that, each time Osei saw Bunzō she tried to get him to utter the unspoken word, teasing and nagging him, until she finally threatened to tickle him if he would not tell her what it was. But the formal Bunzō, who had missed his first opportunity to tell her casually of his love, continued to try to broach the subject properly. Whenever he got ready to speak again, Osei would turn away and pretend not to notice his seriousness. Feeling rebuffed, Bunzō would not pursue the matter any further, and it was left to Osei to start flirting with him openly again.

Poor, somber Bunzō was quite confused by her teasing. Gradually it came to him that she might really care for him. Sin and retribution were forgotten; life had no greater meaning. He was completely infatuated and nearly lost his reason. He moved restlessly about his room, unable to sit still. He would stick out his tongue and shrug his shoulders and smile at something he remembered and do things in a most peculiar way. He was out of his mind with joy. But in front of Osei he maintained his self-control and continued to treat her with proper ceremony.

One day they had been chatting pleasantly together, becoming more and more relaxed, when he suddenly felt almost overwhelmed by desire for her, and had to close his eyes and stop speaking to steady himself. Still laughing, she coyly tried to coax him out of his silence and reached out and tickled him. He pushed her away angrily. "I must control myself. Please go downstairs, Osei." Osei was furious about this.

As time wore on Osei seemed to tire of the game. She became much more thoughtful and subdued and no longer laughed as freely as she had in the past. But still she had perhaps not entirely given up hoping to interest him for she would sometimes talk to him in a rather intimate way.

And so the bud of love, which had begun to bloom, closed again, touched by an unexpected frost. It was a relationship sharply twisted in the threads of entangled ties, suspended without touching sea or river. Perhaps it was a game of the god of matrimony. It was, nevertheless, a very odd beginning to a love story.

It was almost two years since Bunzō had gone to work in the office, although it seemed like only yesterday. He had managed to accumulate a little savings, and he decided to bring his mother to Tokyo and to take a house for the two of them, because he felt very guilty about her living in the country by herself. He wrote and told her his plan, and she was naturally very happy to hear of it. She did not know that he had his heart set on Osei. This was her letter:

It would mean so much to me to see my first grandchild. I do hope you'll find a nice girl soon. You really should have a wife to take care of the household if you really want me to come and live with you. I've grown very fond of the younger daughter of

some relatives of ours and I thought perhaps you might care to
see what she's like. She's very well-mannered and so pretty.

Bunzō's mother had enclosed a photograph of the girl.

Bunzō was very upset by her letter. He told Omasa about
it in the course of passing on other news. His aunt was also
quite disturbed by this turn of events.

When Osei had first returned home from school, Magobei
had said to his wife, "We have Isami to take over the household and we will have to give Osei to someone for a bride.
Shall we let her marry Bunzō?"

At the time Omasa had not committed herself and had let
the months slip by. Then, seeing how close the two young
people became, she eventually began to accept the idea that
they would marry.

One day her husband said, "It's nice to see the pleasant
relationship those two have, but they're both terribly young
and we can't be sure that everything they do will be for
their own good. You'd better be careful that they don't do
anything foolish."

"Oh, it's all right," she had answered knowledgeably. "It
doesn't matter if there is a little something between them.
They're going to get together eventually anyway."

Having thus determined her daughter's future in her own
mind, it was natural that Omasa should now be chagrined by
Bunzō's news. However, the frown gradually left her face
and she nodded approvingly as Bunzō went on speaking.

"I probably will have to get married if I'm to have my own
house, as Mother says, but I don't want to marry somebody
I don't know. I think I'll say no to her suggestion," he said
with unusual decisiveness.

"You have to like the girl you marry just as much as your
mother does," Omasa responded. "But it was very nice of
you to confide in me. To tell the truth, we've been thinking
a little about this matter ourselves. It would be helpful if
you'd let me know whenever your mother mentions this
again. As I say, we've been giving it some thought and I'm
sure my husband will speak to you before long. By the way,

I'm rather curious to see what kind of girl your mother would like you to marry. May I have a look at that picture?" Bunzō was very embarrassed. "I—I haven't got it right now. Osei took it from me a few minutes ago."

So it was that mother, aunt, and uncle all awaited the end of the year, each with his own wishes and expectations. And yet today (to return to the events related in the first chapter) Bunzō, upon whom everyone's expectations rested, had been asked to leave his post. An old-fashioned person would attribute it all to an evil fate.

FIVE O'CLOCK. The day would soon end. It was impossible to tell when his aunt and Osei would come home and there seemed to be no point in waiting, so Bunzō ate supper alone. He sat on the little balcony that ran along the second story and leaned against the wooden railing, watching the sky darken. The sun had already dropped behind the tops of the houses, but the last reflections of its fire lingered on, dyeing the western half of the sky a faint crimson hue. Turning to the east, he saw that it was pale blue, ever so faintly sprinkled with the first stars of evening. Evening crows chattered noisily as they hurried to their nests, urged on by the dim tolling of the bell of the Denzūin.*

Suddenly the day ended. Darkness gathered on all sides. The last traces of color had disappeared from the sky above. The great ocean of heaven glittered and twinkled with stars. The garden of the neighboring house, which could be seen until just a moment before, disappeared in the darkness of the night. It was so dark that he could place the trees only by the gentle wind which blew. The walls of the storehouse had become a blotch of greyish whiteness. Wings fluttered close

* A Buddhist temple located in Omote-chō, Bunkyō-ku. It was founded in 1415.

by under the eaves. Looking about him, Bunzō could distinguish nothing; all was darkness.

Even the heartless learn of sorrow in an evening in fall. How much more painful it was to Bunzō whose plight was like that of a loose kite* drifting at the mercy of the wind, only to be caught perhaps on a plum tree or a clothes line. In the ten years since his father's death he had been tossed about endlessly on the great waves of the sea of this uncertain life. He had found no calm between the storms as he struggled on the ocean of officialdom, and he had tried to keep in mind that he might one day lose his job and become lost and helpless, like a small boat adrift on the boundless sea. But, like all of us, he had developed a false sense of security and thought he was safer than he proved to be.

His mind strayed to thoughts of his mother. He wanted very much to send for her at the end of the year, to bring her some joy in her old age. He felt he could not go home empty-handed, and he began to wonder what sort of presents he should take. As he was working out these relatively carefree calculations on the abacus inside him, it came to him all at once that it was life itself that was really so difficult to calculate, and this thought brought him abruptly back to bitter reality.† "How wretched I am!" he exclaimed.

Suddenly there was light in the west. Bunzō turned, his reveries interrupted. His neighbors had forgotten to close their second-floor shutters and the shoji were exposed to view.

---

* The kite referred to is a *yakkodoko,* which is made in the shape of a ridiculous-looking man in a tight-sleeved kimono. The wording of the simile is very close to one used in *Igagoe dōchū sugoroku,* a play of revenge written for the puppet theater and first produced in 1783. *Jōruri meisaku-shū,* LXVII, 148.

† Literally, "he awakened in an instant from Rosei's dream, which he had been witnessing until now." This is an allusion to a scene from a Nō play, based on an ancient Chinese story, in which a traveler seeking wisdom and knowledge dreams he has become a wealthy prince while sleeping on a magic pillow. He awakens to find that he has dreamed all this in the length of time it has taken the innkeeper to boil some millet, and he comes to realize how vain it is to seek material wealth. *Yōkyoku taikan,* II, 775–90, esp. 788.

A human shadow was reflected through the paper. The form bulged grotesquely and turned into a monster. All at once the shadow disappeared and everything was dark again.

Bunzō sighed and looked down into the garden of his own house. The densely crowded flowers and trees were filled with the lonely drone of insects. The trees emerged from the darkness. They reflected the dim light which came through the glass doors below and looked like so many figures lurking there, spying on the house. The night wind rustled through the foliage and blew against Bunzō's face. He shivered. He stood up, went into the house, and, groping about, lit the lamp. With his hands clasped on his knee, he sat staring off into space. Then he poured hot water from the kettle at his side into a teacup and drank it down in one gulp. He stretched out, resting his head on his arm, and stared at the flicker of light from the lamp reflected in a circle on the ceiling. He smiled, chuckling to himself; but then his open mouth became twisted and distorted and an expression of grief appeared on his face.

"Oh, what on earth shall I do? I certainly have to say something. I must make up my mind to tell them when they come home tonight and get it over with. My aunt will make a very nasty face, I'm sure. But why should I make myself miserable over something like this? It's not like borrowing money; there's nothing to be ashamed of. I'll tell them tonight and that's all there is to it. But it will be very hard to say if Osei's there. It will be terrible to have her hear my aunt reproaching me. I'd better wait until she's not around. But why? Why should it be so hard to say it? Why in heaven's name should a grown man be ashamed of having a little temporary setback? What a coward. Damn it, I'll get it over with tonight. Of course Osei will be disappointed when she hears I've lost my job. She's obviously been looking forward to our future together although she's never said anything about it. But I know she's not fickle. She won't change her mind because of this. She's different from the ordinary; she's an educated girl. There's no reason to worry about her reaction, I'm sure. But my aunt—there's my aunt to consider. When she hears I've been fired, she won't like the idea of my marrying Osei. For all I know she may make her marry somebody else altogether. We haven't made any definite agreement so I can't even complain if she does. Oh, what a mess, what a mess. No matter how I try to work it out, it's a mess.

"Why did they have to fire me? I don't think I flatter myself when I say that I'm perfectly capable of doing my job. The fellows still working there aren't especially competent. I must have been fired because I wouldn't play up to the boss. The boss is a bastard. And my fellow workers—they're so damned obsequious. It's downright obsequious to be so submissive and grovel for the sake of a little pay.

"But wait a minute. Haven't there been times when they've taken a man back after firing him? After all this commotion, tomorrow a recall notice may very well—no, it won't come. But what if it does? Should I accept? This time I'll be the one to turn them down. No matter what anybody says I'll definitely turn them down. On the other hand maybe I am being a bit too hasty. I wonder if I should go back to work there if they ask me. Idiot! I really am an idiot. Why am I worrying about something that may never happen? Instead of thinking about that I should be concentrating on—what was it now? Oh yes—telling my aunt that I've been fired. She's sure to be angry. But I have to do it. I've got to make up my mind to tell her tonight. Still, in front of Osei. It doesn't matter. I'll tell my aunt anyway. What if she says terrible things in front of Osei? I don't care. I'll tell Osei—no, not Osei. I'll tell my aunt . . . a terrible face . . . tell that terrible face . . . tell that offensive mouth. . . . Oh, I'm all mixed up." He shook his head back and forth.

A rickshaw came clattering along and stopped abruptly in front of the house. The front door opened with a rattle and he heard chattering voices. Steeling himself, Bunzō tried to straighten up. Using his arms for support, he raised his body but fell back again. He tried again. The hinges of his hips were quite up to the task, but the hinges of his heart were stayed by his inability to decide whether or not to tell them. Suddenly he rose and went to the head of the stairs. He stopped. He hesitated. Then determined to get it over with at once, he rushed downstairs and went into the sitting room.

Beside the long hibachi was a woman of forty; slender with sallow skin. She was chic and rather spirited; a faded but attractive flower. She wore her hair up, swept exotically around a comb. A plain cotton kimono served as her undergarment. Over it she wore plaid silk. A black satin obi lined with a checked brownish yellow silk twill was tied carelessly about her waist. This was Bunzō's aunt Omasa. She was slightly intoxicated and leaned oddly to the side. She had a toothpick in her mouth. Bunzō greeted her. "Good evening," she said, "we're rather late, aren't we?"

"Where did you go today?"

"We planned to walk from Sugachō over to Misujimachi, but when we got to Sugachō there was some 'Actor's'—what's it called? 'Actor's—?' "

" 'Amity Club.' "

"That's it. Well, my friend Ohama suggested we stop in there. I would have been interested in seeing the show at the Shintomiza or at the theater over on Nichōme.* I didn't especially care about any Amity Club or Calamity Club, but Osei naturally insisted on going. So I went along to keep her company. It wasn't what I'd thought at all. I expected a lot of amateurs, but it turned out to be a first rate yose. Next time you come too, Bunzō. It costs 50 sen."

"Yes, I'd be happy to," he said, and thought to himself, "this would be a good time to say it, when Osei isn't here. I'll get it over with right this minute." He was about to open

---

* The Shintomiza, a kabuki theater, was built in 1872 in Shintomichō in what is now Chūōku. The building was destroyed in the earthquake in 1923. The theater on Nichōme was the Ichimuraza, which was founded in the mid-seventeenth century and moved to this location in Saruwakachō, Asakusa (modern Taitōku) in the year 1842. It was moved again in 1889.

his mouth when footsteps came pattering along the hall and the door behind him slid open. He turned and there was Osei.

She was a lovely girl of eighteen, in the full bloom of life. Her classic oval face was beautifully framed by a widow's peak. The sharp line of her brows added strength to her sparkling eyes. There was restraint and elegance in the tight smile of her pursed mouth. Her back was slender, her small waist supple and graceful, moving like an autumn weed waving in the wind.* One might have wished her hairline more tidy but, as the saying goes, a fair complexion makes up for everything, and she was an angel with pure white skin. She bore no resemblance to her sallow mother. Her glossy black hair was severely bound up in a bun in the Western manner and the only jewelry she wore was the rose-shaped hair pin. She used neither rouge nor powder and was simply dressed in a silk kimono bound with a printed muslin obi lined with purple satin. In fact the very simplicity of her attire made her appearance striking. She had none of the unpleasant flavor of a distorted artificial flower. To Bunzō she was a radiant princess in the most beautiful garments.† His judgment may have been influenced by his love, but in any case she really was more beautiful than any ten women.

As she came into the room, she exchanged smiling glances

* An allusion to a passage in the introduction to the *Kokin-shū* by Ki no Tsurayuki. When the author suggests that reciting poetry helps to soothe despair, one of the things he mentions as reminding us of the swift passage of life is the swaying *ominaeshi* plant, whose yellow flower blooms for a short period in the fall. It has come to symbolize femininity and youth. *Kokin waka-shū*, VIII, 97–98.

† Bunzō sees Osei as "Sotōri-hime," the younger sister of the wife of Emperor Ingyō (reigned A.D. *ca.* 438). Her beauty was reputed to be so great that it shone radiantly through her clothing. She was a poetess. Aston, pp. 318–22.

To Bunzō she is dressed like "Komachi." The word is now used as a general term for a beautiful woman as we use "Venus." Ono no Komachi, with whom the name originated, was a famous beauty and poetess who lived in the ninth century. The introduction to the *Kokin-shū* places her in the same poetic tradition as Sotōri-hime. *Kokin waka-shū*, VIII, 101.

with Bunzō, bowed briefly, shuffled over to the side of the hibachi, and gracefully slipped into her place.

Strangely enough, when Bunzō saw Osei, he had a change of heart. He completely swallowed the word "dismissed" which had risen in his throat and adopted a nonchalant expression. He told himself he would wait just a little longer.

"Mother, I'm so thirsty. May I have a cup of tea?"

Omasa looked at the tea things. "Goodness, the cups are all dirty. Onabe!" she called.

As the apple-cheeked girl came in, the dirty dishes were thrust out at her. She took the tray and left, wagging her hips. She washed them, brought them back, and poured the tea. Mother and daughter began to chatter away about the music they had heard that day, and there was no opportunity for Bunzō to announce that he had been fired. He was compelled to listen to this conversation although he had no desire to hear it. Eventually they began to talk about the comparative merits of kiyomoto and nagauta.*

"You can sing kiyomoto yourself, Mother, so you say that. But nagauta is better."

"Okayasu isn't too bad but Matsunaga† sounds so jumbled

---

* In contrast to kiyomoto, which is usually classified as a *katarimono* [song primarily concerned with narration], *nagauta* is the most highly developed of the *utaimono* [songs primarily concerned with melody]. Both use the samisen and voice, but the nagauta has evolved into a complex musical form, employing drums and flute as well. It was first created in the mid-eighteenth century to accompany the sustained dances of the kabuki plays. Words and music are filled with subtle allusions, and the voice is used more as an instrument than as a device for telling a story. Malm, *Japanese Music*, pp. 188, 199, 205–12.

† Although there were several nagauta performers named Matsunaga in the 1880s, Omasa is probably referring here to Matsunaga Wafū (1839–1916), who was the leading nagauta singer of the period. Wafū had an extraordinary singing voice and, interestingly, had acquired his graceful delivery by being trained in kiyomoto.

There was no singer of comparable eminence with the name of Okayasu. The head of the Okayasu school at that time was Okayasu Kisaburō IV (1849–1906). He was, however, noted as a musician and not as a singer. *Engeki hyakka dai-jiten*, I, 417–18.

and dull. Kiyomoto has much more style. 'When we first met
in Yotsuya/How sweet I thought you were/But, alas, the
wheel of fate . . .' " Omasa sang a short passage from her
favorite song. "It's so lovely," she added.

"It's vulgar. I hate it."

There she goes again. What a shrew. She always has to
contradict everybody."

"But vulgar things are terrible."

"If you're so elegant, you shouldn't want to eat that cheap
oden." *

"When did I ever say I wanted any?"

"Night before last."

"You're always making things up," the girl replied, but
it was obvious that she had been caught and all three of them
burst out laughing.

Omasa turned to Bunzō. "A letter came from your mother
as we were going out. Did you get it?"

"Yes. I'd almost forgotten. Mother didn't enclose a letter
for you this time but she sends her regards."

"Oh, thank you. How is she?"

"Fine, thank you."

"That's good. I'm sure she mentioned how happy she'll
be at the end of the year."

"She said she was counting the days, but. . . ."

"I'm sure. Coming to live with her dear boy. You can
hardly call it sweet and proper to catch your mother up on
every little slip of the tongue and make a fool of her, like
someone we know. But you're so considerate, Bunzō, that
your mother must be terribly fond of you." She directed
these insinuations at Osei, tossing her a glance. Bunzō smiled
helplessly. "Did your mother have anything to say about
that other matter?" Omasa asked.

"Yes, she did. She said I might as well wait till I've met
her before I make up my mind one way or the other."

"What are you talking about, Mother?"

---

* A slow-cooking vegetable stew with a seaweed base. It is considered a
low-class dish.

"Well, I told you the other day, Osei."

Osei nodded eagerly.

"So your mother said that, did she? Well, I wish my husband would come home soon and look into the matter. You see, he's been thinking about your marriage too, as I told you the other day. I know all about it and I could just as well talk it over with you now." She paused a minute. "When are you going to answer the letter?"

"I have already."

"Really? My, that's not like you at all. It certainly would have been better if you'd waited until you'd said something to me." Bunzō tried unsuccessfully to interrupt. "Well, at any rate, what did you say?" Omasa asked.

"That I really can't manage to get married now anyway."

"That's sure to get your mother worried. You should have said. . . ."

"I haven't had a chance to tell you yet but. . . ."

"Just listen to me. You could have said that your uncle seems to have something in mind and you want to wait until you've had a chance to talk to him first or that you have someone here that you like."

"But Mother, does Bunzō really have someone he likes?"

"That's not the point. He should tell his mother how he really feels to set her mind at rest. I suppose you have to be a mother yourself to understand these things. You can't imagine how complicated it can be to choose the right husband for a child. Even with an ungrateful girl like Osei, I worry all the time because I know she can't stay home indefinitely. The other day I said to her, 'You have to get married one of these days. You can't go on acting like a baby forever. Unless you're lucky enough to marry into an easygoing household like mine, you just wait and see what happens when you have a mother-in-law living with you. You won't be able to act so spoiled and selfish. You'd better make up your mind to that right now.' I told her that for her own sake—I hate to think of her having a hard time of it later on. But—listen to this, Bunzō—she said, 'I have my own ideas on the subject. It's up to me to decide if I'll marry or not.' So I said, 'You don't want to get married?' 'That's right. I will remain pure.' What do you think of that, Bunzō? Who ever heard of anybody, except maybe a nun, living alone without a husband?"

What she said had some basis in fact. Several days before, in the course of nagging Osei about something, she had said, "This really is no joke. Think how old you are. Eighteen, isn't it? It's about time you started thinking about making a good marriage and yet you go on being so stubborn. I wish you would get married soon. If you have a nagging mother-in-law, maybe you'll get to appreciate me a little." The conversation Omasa had related to Bunzō had been only slightly embellished.

"But after all," Omasa now continued, "she talks like that because she's still a baby. By the time we were her age, we used to dress up and go out and find ourselves a little romance."

"Must you talk like that?" Osei scowled.

"Anyway it's true. Maybe we did flirt a little, but this girl here is grown up in size only. She's really just a baby. She'll go on giving me trouble forever."

"The minute you get a little tipsy you start saying such terrible things—things no mother should say to a child."

"It seems to me you've got things upside down. You ought to be watching what you say instead of correcting me. Your behavior is dreadful." Omasa turned to Bunzō. "You see how she makes a fool of me. She's no docile young lady who does what she's told. Give her a good talking to, Bunzō, and make her listen. If you tell her, maybe she'll pay attention." She glanced at Osei.

Just then they heard a voice on the other side of the wall. "Such a lovely clasp . . . such a. . . ."

The three of them looked at each other in surprise. They laughed when they realized that it was Onabe talking in her sleep. Omasa turned to the wall clock. "Heavens, it's eleven o'clock already. No wonder she's talking in her sleep. Well, shall we go to bed? If we stay up too late, we won't be able to do a thing tomorrow. And Bunzō, let's talk about that matter again some time—perhaps tomorrow."

"Yes. I have something I must tell you. Maybe tomorrow. Well, goodnight." Bunzō bowed and left the room. When he got to the foot of the stairs, Osei called after him.

"Bunzō, have you got today's paper in your room?"

"Yes."

"Have you read it?"

"Yes."

"May I borrow it?" she said and went up the stairs behind him. He took the newspaper from on top of the desk and gave it to her.

"Bunzō."

"Yes."

Osei just laughed without going on.

"What is it?"

"Shall I return that picture you gave me, just for tonight?"

"Why?"

"I thought you looked lonesome." She laughed and ran down the stairs.

Bunzō watched her leave with relief. "It gets more and more difficult to tell them," he sighed.

An hour passed. Bunzō changed his clothes and got into his bedding but could not sleep. He lay there, wide awake, with his eyes open, thinking about the past and the future. He tried to make himself go to sleep by shutting his eyes and settling himself comfortably, but he was unsuccessful. He tossed helplessly and sighed and had dreams although he was still awake. The first cock crowed and then the second. Daylight was approaching. He had just resigned himself to not sleeping that night when his eyes grew heavy and his thoughts became jumbled. The image of his white-haired mother which had been flickering before his eyes grew a speckled black beard and became the head of his chief. Soon that terrifying head, swirling around and around like a water wheel, gradually grew smaller and smaller . . . its features changed . . . gradually a rose-shaped hair pin . . . Osei's head. . . .

STARTLED FROM an unfinished dream by the maid's voice, Bunzō raised his head and saw the reflection of the morning sun piercing obliquely through the shoji. "I've overslept," he thought, but at once the word "dismissed" came to his mind and his heart shrank. He rose stiffly and dressed. Without bothering to fold the bedding, he stuck a toothbrush in his mouth and an old towel in his belt and went downstairs quickly. "Hurry, Bunzō, or you'll be late!" Omasa called. Her voice startled him although it was not especially harsh. He was at a loss for an answer and managed to escape by mumbling something, his words blurred by the toothbrush.

He washed his face quickly and sat down to breakfast. His heart felt stifled; he found it very hard to eat. He had only two bowls of rice instead of his customary three and then modestly put the small table, on which he had eaten, to one side rather than pushing it forward as he usually did. His very body seemed to have grown smaller.

He got up, walked around the house, and furtively looked into the sitting room. Omasa was alone; Osei was not in the room. She was probably in Surugadai for her morning English lesson. Fearfully, Bunzō entered the room.

Omasa was in the midst of polishing the hibachi. She stopped suddenly, obviously startled at Bunzō's appearance.

His face was pale and devoid of strength; a mixture of sadness, bitterness, and shame played on his features. "What's the matter? You look terrible."

"Nothing really."

"Well then hurry up. It's almost eight o'clock."

"I—I haven't had a chance to tell you yet, but the fact of the matter is that yesterday—yesterday. . . ." He felt suffocated and cold sweat poured down him. His face became red. He could not speak. After a moment he tried again. "I was dismissed from my job," he declared with an effort. He lowered his head.

The hand holding the polishing rag froze in mid-air. Her body stiffened and Omasa cried out just once in surprise. For a few seconds she sat there, speechless with astonishment, staring at Bunzō. Then she busily put aside the cloth and moved closer to him. "You were dismissed? Why?"

"Why indeed? I don't know. There was some sort of reduction in personnel."

"How terrible. So you lost your job. Isn't that a pity," she said, crestfallen. "Well, in that case," she went on, "what are your plans?"

"I thought I'd have Mother stay in the country a while longer and I'd look for another government opening somewhere. There's nothing else I can do now."

"I suppose it won't make too much difference if you find one easily, but otherwise things will be pretty miserable, won't they? But don't say I didn't warn you. I told you over and over to go and call on your supervisor, but you're so stubborn, you wouldn't go. Now this has happened."

"It surely can't be because of that."

"It must be. If not they would never have let an innocent young man go, no matter how many people they were discharging. Or have you done something wrong?"

"No, I haven't."

"Well then." They were silent for a moment. "What about Noboru?" *

* "He will be discussed in Chapter Six" appears here in brackets in the original text.

"He came through all right."

"You see how everything works out if you're lucky? It's more than luck in his case, though. He's clever and shrewd and he's always alert. I know he goes to call on the supervisor all the time, and that must be why he didn't lose his job. This wouldn't have happened to you either if you had just listened to me and played up to the chief a little. But you never listen to anybody. Now look what's happened."

"That may very well be, but I couldn't possibly do something as disgusting as that."

"Don't be so proud! That's why the chief dislikes you— because you're so proud. Even a man like Noboru doesn't miss a chance to get in his good graces because he's afraid of getting fired. You should have tried twice as hard. If you only had yourself to think about, you could afford to be so superior. But you have your mother to consider."

She realized she had discovered a good instrument of torture. She tapped on the tatami with her pipe. "Don't you feel sorry for your mother? She lost your father early in life and now she has only you to rely on. She must feel so helpless. She could hardly like living down there all alone in the country, but she's patient and lives for your success. If you had thought about what you were doing, you would have realized that you had to make your way in the world no matter what. But you're so vain and selfish. No, you couldn't bear to play up to somebody. Now you've ended up driving your mother to utter destitution. Oh, what a bad day this is. You've brought this all on yourself. You deserve whatever happens to you. But don't you care what happens to your poor mother?" Throughout her tirade Bunzō sat with his head bowed and did not answer.

"Your mother has been waiting and waiting for her chance to be happy. How miserable she'll be when she hears you've lost your job. What hardships she has to endure in her old age."

"I know I've failed my mother. I feel terrible about it."

"I should certainly hope so. You're twenty-three years old

and you can't even support your mother decently. What a son!" Feigning indifference, she blew smoke rings.

Bunzō glared at his aunt's profile and was about to explode angrily, but he managed to control himself. He tried unsuccessfully to smile. His voice trembled as he said, "I feel terrible about it, but what's done is done."

"What's that?" She turned slowly toward him. Blue veins stood out on her forehead. The corners of her eyes turned up in fury and her lips became twisted. "What did you say? What's done is done? Who did it? Who's fault is it that you were fired? Isn't it all because of your own stubbornness? You're always causing people trouble and now you're not even sorry that you lost your job. What do you mean by saying that what's done is done? You really are too much. You walk all over people. What do you think I am? You may think I'm an old witch and treat me like a complete stranger, but I'm still your aunt. If I were an outsider, I wouldn't care whether you were fired or not. I wouldn't have to bother with you at all. But we are related. I am your aunt and you are my nephew.

"I've taken care of you all these years all by myself. Maybe I shouldn't have interfered in your life, but I think of you as my own son, even though I have children of my own. Do you know what that means? Not a day has gone by that I haven't thought how much I wanted you to be a success so that you could bring your mother to Tokyo. When you tell me this horrible news, I am naturally upset and worried for your sake, imagining how ashamed it would make you. I'd never feel that way about a stranger. I expected you at least to say you are sorry you lost your job because you haven't listened to my advice. I don't even really care if you don't apologize. But to get fired and then say 'what's done is done'! I just can't believe it. What a waste of sympathy. When I think how I've watched over you and cared for you all these years and you think nothing of it."

"That's not true. I'm very poor at expressing myself, as

you perfectly well know, but there are things in my heart which I. . . ."

"Oh, no. I won't listen to any excuses. You treat me like a stranger. I'm just an old witch to you. I never dreamed you could be so ungrateful. Here I've been wasting my time worrying about your marriage. I planned to talk to your mother about it. I thought I'd try to find some nice girl for you. I wanted to make all kinds of preparations for your wedding because it was to be my own beloved nephew who was getting married and not some stranger. I've been doing nothing but plotting and planning. I thought I'd stitch up that heavy silk obi and do over the striped crepe and fix up one thing and another. But I should have known better. I don't care so much that you've been fired, but not to feel ashamed of yourself after all I've done for you—to just shrug the whole thing off. I won't say another word. It won't do any good. I'm nothing but a stranger to you.

"And what's more, you should have told me you were fired last night," she went on after a minute. "You never said a word about it and I went to all sorts of trouble to fix lunch for you today. I was worried about you because you work so hard and I decided to put an omelette in your lunch box for a little variety. But Onabe doesn't know how to make it so I had to fix it for you specially myself. The one time I put myself out, this is what I get. I should have kept out of it. Nobody even asked me. Onabe!"

"Yes."

"Throw Bunzō's lunch out!"

Onabe thrust her wide face through the door. She looked very confused.

"Bunzō was fired yesterday."

"Really?"

"These intelligent men are certainly extraordinary." Before Omasa could go on Bunzō got up, white with anger. He walked straight out of the room and returned to his own quarters. He sat down before his desk. Tears of vexation dropped on his knees. He wiped his falling tears away with a handkerchief, but he could not erase the fury that kept swelling up within him. The more he thought about it, the more angry he became, until he was completely lost in resentment and mortification.

His aunt's criticisms were plausible enough, but he knew that they only covered up what she really thought. Her attitude toward him obviously changed just as soon as she learned he had lost his job. The superficiality of her affection came as no surprise; he had endured the knowledge of it before and could do so again. What he could not endure was that she had all but called him a coward to his face. He was too angry to stop to consider why she had jeered at him or why she considered him a coward. He was so furious and so hurt that it seemed his heart would break. "All right then, if that's the way she's going to be. I let her say whatever she wanted because she's my aunt. But if we're going to cut all our ties, I can do whatever I please, just as if I were no relation to her at all. I know what I'll do. I'll move to a boardinghouse just to spite her."

Even as he said this, Osei's image darted before his eyes. He wavered. His hesitation ended when he remembered his aunt's vile face. He became angry once more. "Damn it. Even if she forbids it, I won't stay here!" he declared with rare resolution. The idea of remaining in that house another minute seemed horrible. He began to dislike his room when he thought of it as rented. He was irritated with everything in it, even the firepan with the broken rim, when he realized that nothing was his own.

He looked at the clock. It was already eleven. He decided to pack his belongings at once and move to a boardinghouse that very day. Muttering to himself over and over that he would not stay no matter what his aunt said, he began to assemble things in a great fury. He was searching for something when he happened to open the desk drawer. The photograph of a white-haired woman caught his eye. He stared at it. It was a picture of his mother.

Bunzō loved his mother very much and seeing her photograph forcibly reminded him that he had endured the hardships of the world all this time for her sake as well as his own. All his old feelings of obligation welled up within him and he felt utterly crushed and broken. His determination to leave that hateful house deserted him.

Then the vile face of his aunt flashed before his mind's eye and he became angry again. He tightened his fist and clenched his teeth. No, he told himself, he must not stay in that house. He was just about to start packing once more when the maid's voice called out from downstairs that lunch was ready. He deliberately made her call him several times before answering and then went down reluctantly. He looked annoyed and irritated and rather frightening. Opening the door of the sitting room, he saw Osei.

Bunzō had been so preoccupied with his misery that he had barely thought of her until now. He had, in fact, nearly forgotten her. When their eyes met and he saw her tender, smiling mouth, his frozen heart relented as a light snow thaws when it is greeted by the sun. He was amazed at what had been going on in his mind. He had buried the joy of his love deep in his heart, and had allowed bitterness and anger to dominate him. At the sight of her a smile almost came to his lips, rising from deep within him, but he forced it back. There was laughter in his heart but only sullenness on his face.

Bunzō had his lunch and went back upstairs. He made an attempt to resume the task of packing his things but somehow his earlier determination had deserted him. He tried to work up some spirit by coaxing himself on in a soft voice, but nothing happened. He made another effort, speaking out in more strident tones. He even clenched his teeth fiercely again. "Would I ever change my mind once I've decided on something? No, never. Even if she forbids me to go, I will not stay here." At the same time it occurred to him that it would mean giving up Osei. He loved her dearly; this would be a terrible sacrifice. On the other hand, he hated the idea of apologizing to his aunt, which he would have to do if he stayed on. His thoughts became twisted and confused; either alternative was unpleasant. All was turmoil within him. He already had half a mind not to leave.

Without really having managed to reach a decision one way or the other, he started to pack, but he was so preoccupied that it took much longer than he had anticipated. At two o'clock he finally finished putting his things together.

Just then footsteps sounded on the stairs. Bunzō was perhaps able to tell who it was by the sound of the steps alone, for the smile he had held back earlier came to his lips. He turned to the door.

It was Osei. She smiled when she saw Bunzō. She looked around and said, "You've certainly straightened up your room."

"I had to. It was terribly messy." The words slipped out before he realized what he was saying. He surprised himself. He found it hard to understand why he had lied.

Osei apparently accepted his explanation. She sat down. "Mother says you've lost your job."

"I was dismissed yesterday." His manner and tone were entirely different from what they had been that morning. "I feel very badly about it but there's no point in crying over spilt milk. I told your mother about it this morning but she —well, she was very angry." He gnashed his teeth and lowered his eyes.

"So I gathered."

"She said I couldn't manage to support my mother even though I'm twenty-three. She as much as called me a weakling." Osei murmured sympathetically. "I know I'm a weakling. But it's terrible even for an aunt to say something like that."

"Mother talks like that because she's so unreasonable. I had an argument with her myself just now. I couldn't bear the way she was acting, as if she were so superior. It really wasn't an argument. Actually she didn't understand what I was talking about at all—she never does—she just gets furious. What can you expect from someone who has no education?"

Bunzō's head shot up. "You argued with your mother?"

"Yes."

"Because of me?"

"Yes. We quarreled because of you."

He looked down again. Tears fell on his knees.

"What's the matter, Bunzō?"

He lifted his head and smiled. His eyes were moist. "Nothing. You—you've made me so happy. As your mother says, I can't even support my own mother decently at my age and yet you defended me. You argued with your mother over me."

"She doesn't understand what I'm talking about and yet she gets furious. What can I do?" she said, feeling rather superior.

"I—I didn't know you thought so much of me. I have to admit that I've been keeping a secret from you. Let me tell you about it right now. I was considering moving to a boardinghouse."

"To a boardinghouse?"

"I had thought I might but I certainly won't now. I'm just an outsider here and yet you've taken my part against your mother. Now that I know how you feel I couldn't possibly go even if you told me to. I must apologize to your mother for the way I acted."

"Oh, don't bother. It doesn't matter what an ignorant woman like that thinks anyway."

"That's not so. That wouldn't do at all. I certainly must apologize. And, Osei, your motives are fine, but please stop quarreling with your mother. Don't become a bad daughter because of me."

"Osei!" Omasa called from below.

"Your mother is calling you."

"She doesn't need me for anything."

"Osei!" Omasa called again.

"Go ahead and answer her."

"Osei! Osei!"

"Yes," the girl said at last. "What a bother," she added, standing up.

"Don't tell your mother what I said just now," Bunzō said, cautioning her to secrecy with a gesture. Osei merely nodded and went down to the sitting room.

Omasa was awaiting her eagerly, the corners of her eyes turned up in anger. Even before the girl was in the room, she unleashed a stream of fury, revealing the rancor which rose within her. "Osei, can't you hear when I call you? You're not deaf. You should answer properly when you're called. What did you go upstairs for?"

Osei remained perfectly calm. "Nothing special."

"Then why did you go up? You still don't seem to understand what I mean when I tell you you must not go up anytime you feel like it any more. You aren't a dog in heat. All you ever want to do is run to Bunzō."

"It's always been all right for me to go upstairs—now, all of a sudden, it's wrong. How can you be so illogical?"

"You don't understand at all. Bunzō is in an altogether different position now. Don't you understand what it means to be fired?"

"What's so terrible about that? Is he going to bite people now? Well, is he?"

"What on earth are you talking about? Osei, you really are too much. You're always making a f—f—fool out of me."

"I'm not making a f—f—fool out of you. I'm just being logical," she said, curving her lips.

As soon as she heard her daughter's words, Omasa's face changed color. She flung the long bamboo pipe she had been holding to the floor and grit her teeth in a paroxysm of fury. Osei gave her a sharp, sidelong glance and calmly left the room.

If we were to dismiss this as a quarrel between a mother and child, we would fail to do justice to the real motives of our heroine. Why even call it a quarrel? It is rather a fine example of the conflict between the marvelous new ways of future Japanese culture and the old habits of bygone times. We would do well to ponder it carefully.

That night Bunzō resigned himself to apologizing to his aunt. Omasa was adamant in her fury. She began by chastizing him over and over again, carrying her nastiness far beyond what it had been that morning. She even attributed Osei's disobedience of her to the young man. Bunzō managed to suppress his emotions and continued to beg her forgiveness. Omasa's song of nastiness became tinged with a shadow of disappointment. Just as he thought it was all over, the flames were ignited once again by something he said, and they burned more brightly than before. The black smoke enveloping her face made it seem unlikely that the fire could ever be put out, but Bunzō patiently continued to pour out his apologies and gradually the flames grew smaller, the fire smoldered and finally sputtered out. Bunzō sighed with relief. Well aware that anything might happen in another minute, he quickly bade her farewell and left the room before she could change her mind. Behind him he heard Omasa say, "I thought I was well rid of him. Am I going to be saddled with him again?"

I T W A S three o'clock in the afternoon. The autumn sun began to sink in the sky and the shadow of the tree in the garden grew longer. Omasa sat alone, leaning on the hibachi. She was idly tracing letters in the ashes with a pair of tongs, her mind occupied with her thoughts. She sighed from time to time with annoyance and vexation.

The front door opened with a rattle. Someone entered the house and looked in at the doorway. "Hello," he said. His face will be familiar to the reader; it belongs to the man we saw passing through the Kanda gate with Bunzō the day he was dismissed.

He was wearing a plain, blue striped kimono of sturdy fabric with a silk pongee haori over it. The chain of his pocket watch was coiled around a rather sorry-looking obi of coarse silk. In his hand he carried a Turkish fez.* He had obviously changed his clothes after coming from the office.

"Well, this is a rare pleasure. We see so little of you these days. I'm sure you'll be sorry to find just an old lady like me here."

"No, no, that's quite all right. Oh, dear, that sounds terrible, doesn't it? Well, anyway, is Utsumi in?"

* The practice of wearing exotic headgear with Japanese costume enjoyed great popularity in the Meiji period.

"Yes."

"I'll go and talk to him for a minute. Then I'll be right back to get even with you for the last time."

"You may be sorry."

"Maybe." After exchanging a few more words, he went upstairs.

Before he returned, we should have a brief biography of this young man, but unfortunately his past is lost in a haze and we know little of his parentage, the kind of education he received, or how he lived as a boy. One set of rumors has it that he lost his parents as a child and drifted about among relatives and friends, a poor, homeless waif, and had been driven to taking employment as a servant. But such idle rumors should be discounted; they rarely prove reliable and are shorter lived than the morning dew. Someone who had actually seen the records reported that the young man was born in Tokyo into a family vaguely connected with the samurai class. This much at least was not a lie.

The young man's name was Honda Noboru. He had been appointed to a post in the lower ranks of the government service two years before Bunzō was hired. With luck he had quickly improved his position. As our story begins, he is in the sixth rank,* still a bachelor, and living quite comfortably indeed.

Noboru was what is known as a "clever fellow"; resourceful and proud of his talents. There was no limit to the power of his eloquence; he might, in fact, have rivaled a street entertainer. Unfortunately at times this very gift led him to exaggerate and boast. As for his other talents, he managed to do all sorts of things reasonably well, although it could not be said that he excelled at any one thing. Idleness was his nature and inconstancy his illness.

Suave and charming, Noboru was extremely adept at flattery. He was particularly attentive to people when he first

---

* Bunzō and Noboru were both *hannin*, the lowest group in the bureaucratic hierarchy. The subclassifications within the hannin category ranged from eight up to one.

met them, making himself agreeable to everyone, even women and old people. But strangely enough, after he got to know someone better, his cordiality disappeared and he became haughty. He teased his friends and said things which offended them until they grew angry and turned on him. If it was someone less clever than he, Noboru would give another twist to the screw, but if it was someone with more skill, he would laugh it off at the time and wait for a chance to get even later. To express it in a vulgar way, he threw dogs' dung into the face of his enemies.

At any rate Noboru was a clever man and served his chief at the bureau very well.

That worthy gentleman, the chief, had once made a trip abroad. Maintaining that he felt the greatest contempt for the old feudalistic hierarchy, he loudly voiced criticism of the arrogant ways of his fellow bureaucrats. On the other hand, he was known to be a very difficult and unreasonable man himself and would fall into a towering rage over anything that displeased him. In short, he was an old-fashioned despot who made a show of advocating liberalism. This contradiction between the ideas he expressed and his own true nature resulted in tremendous confusion among those who worked with him. Most did not know how to please him.

Only Noboru knew. He copied the gentleman's speech and gestures and even assumed the way he cleared his throat and his manner of sneezing. The imitation was almost perfect except that the chief laughed in the same way no matter who he was with, while Noboru varied his tone depending on his audience. When the older man spoke to him, Noboru rushed over to his desk and listened respectfully, his head cocked knowingly to one side. After he had finished speaking, the young man would smile broadly and reply most humbly. He maintained just the right tone. He was neither too distant nor too friendly. Everything was done in accordance with the chief's wishes; he was never contradicted. Moreover—and this is the most important point—Noboru took note of the mistakes made by other division heads as a device for praising the man. He, in turn, considered Noboru very promising and was quite partial to him. The other young men in the office did not speak well of Noboru, but he attributed it to their jealousy.

In short, Noboru was a clever man. He went to work diligently and carried out his chores in the office most expeditiously. His face remained pleasant; his manner unruffled. This was particularly impressive because he produced more work in half a day than others could in a full day. Actually, most of his work was done by browbeaten pages and office boys while he merely made a great show of being terribly busy.

At the end of each day he returned to his boardinghouse, changed his clothes, and immediately went out again. He rarely settled down and stayed in his room. On Sunday he would pay his respects at the home of his supervisor and play Go with him or run errands.

Once the chief's wife expressed a desire to have a Pekinese for a pet. No sooner said than done. Before a day passed, Noboru had got hold of one and presented it for her inspection. The chief looked at the dog and remarked that it seemed to him to have a rather strange face. Noboru agreed that it indeed had a strange face. The chief's wife suggested that it was considered desirable for a Pekinese to have such a ratlike face. Noboru said that to be sure it was thought to be better if a Pekinese had such a ratlike face, just as the lady had said, and he had complacently patted the dog's head.

Even the talented Noboru makes mistakes at times. They say that once he managed somehow to incur the chief's displeasure, and for a day or two he was so upset that he found it difficult to eat. He soon won the chief's wife over to his cause, and then it was only a matter of a short time until he was able to soothe the anger of the great man himself. How much better he felt when it was all over. He was indeed a young man of considerable talent.

Bunzō and Noboru lived in the same neighborhood. As a consequence Noboru had always made it a practice to call on his colleague quite frequently, but after Osei had returned home from her boarding school he was to be seen there even more often. In fact, he came at least twice a week.

As was the case in his dealings with other people, Noboru's relationship with Bunzō underwent certain marked changes in the years they knew each other. Once they were well acquainted, Noboru often offended Bunzō by what he said. He spent much of their time together enumerating the faults of the other men who worked in their office and eulogizing his own virtues by way of comparison. He frequently held forth on his favorite theme: there is no point in plodding on in the usual sober, steady way.

However, he rarely spent his time talking to Bunzo. More often he chatted with Omasa in the sitting room. At times he joined her in a game of cards and perhaps, as a crowning gesture, treated her to some delicacies. She was extremely fond of Noboru and made much of him. There were even some who, out of jealousy, thought her perhaps too fond of him. But for a woman in her forties . . . and with a lovely daughter like Osei . . . hush, he's coming.

"How terrible this is for poor Utsumi," said Noboru as he entered the room. "I feel so sorry for him. I tried to cheer him up a little, but I'm afraid I didn't help much."

"Oh, don't let it bother you. It's all his own doing. It's just as well if he does suffer a little."

"I'm sure you're right, but still it's a shame. If I'd known this was going to happen, I might have been able to do something about it."

"Didn't he tell you anything?"

"About what?"

"About me."

"Nothing special."

"I can't trust you either, can I? You side with a fellow like that against me."

"I'm not siding with him. Really."

"Oh?" she said, pouring some tea. She took some sweets from the cupboard and offered them to Noboru and then sent Onabe for Osei. Not having noticed that Bunzō was being ostracized that day, the maid asked uncertainly if she should go upstairs and call him.

"If he wanted tea, he should have . . . no, it isn't necessary," Omasa answered. Isn't that just like a woman.

"What's the matter?" said Noboru. "Have you two been squabbling?"

"I wouldn't mind a little quarrel. But to be treated that way, and by Bunzō."

"Well, what's it all about?"

"Just listen to this." Then began an endless tirade in which Omasa embellished over and over the terrible wrongs Bunzō had done her on the previous day. Her words poured out with the force of a great river overflowing its banks. She neither faltered nor paused. Complaints which had been accumulating within her for many years formed themselves into one long, merciless attack.

She was in the process of making Bunzō into a fierce monster when Osei wandered into the room reading a copy of *Jogaku zasshi*.* She nodded briefly to Noboru and accepted the teacup her mother had filled for her without a word of thanks. Omasa went right on talking. Osei swallowed the tea, put down the cup, and took up the magazine she had been reading again with an air of complete indifference. She usually acted like this when Noboru came to visit.

"And that's the way it ended up. Well now, Noboru, who do you think was to blame?"

"Utsumi was in the wrong, of course."

"And to make matters worse, someone I could mention took that wicked boy's part against me."

"I did no such thing," exclaimed Osei.

* Literally "the magazine for women's education," it was first published in 1885 and appeared as late as the first decade of this century. Originally intended as a vehicle for presenting ideas of Christian morality, it soon became an outlet for literary critics, novelists, and translators of European literature. Okazaki, pp. 62, 615.

"Oh, no? I tell you, Noboru, I was simply furious. But you know how weak I am—I felt there was no point in saying anything since her guardian angel Bunzō was involved. I controlled myself and didn't say a word."

"You're always telling fibs!" Osei cried.

"It's no fib; it's the absolute truth. Isn't this terrible? Can you imagine a girl turning on her own mother to defend a total stranger? And after all I've done for her. Am I not right, Noboru? It hasn't been easy bringing her up, heaven knows. They say you cry seventy-five times when you have a child. I must have wept hundreds of times over this girl already. She doesn't feel the slightest gratitude for all the care she's had. She attacks me for the least little thing I say. What have I done to deserve such a cruel child? Just to think of it makes me miserable."

"You simply go on saying anything you please because I don't object. But really it's gone too far. I'm not a three-year-old child. I know about the love parents have for their children, all right. Logically. . . ."

"I understand, I understand. Don't say another word. That's enough now. I understand," said Noboru, silencing Osei's angry outburst with a gesture. He turned to Omasa. "I think you've missed the point. How unlike you! I'm disappointed. Osei can't very well sit back while you have a quarrel with Utsumi. She has her reasons." He ended in a loud laugh in which no one joined him.

Osei continued to stare at Noboru, frowning, but not saying anything. Omasa had an artificial smile on her lips. She too was silent. A chill fell on the group.

"That was just a little joke, but really, you do expect too much. Osei is such an accomplished girl."

"What's she accomplished?"

"A great deal. If you don't think so, just compare her with ordinary girls her age. If they're good looking, they don't bother with serious things like studying; they're too busy getting into mischief. Pretty as she is, Osei behaves just perfectly. Not that that's surprising, considering who brought her up. She never flirts or does anything silly. She just studies very hard all the time. She knows Chinese—and now even English. What are you reading these days, Osei?"

"*The National Fourth Reader** and Swinton's *Outlines of the World's History.*" †

"*National Fourth*. That must be quite difficult. Even some men couldn't read it. You're so young and just a woman and yet you study so hard." He turned to Omasa. "Excuse me for mentioning it, but everybody says how amazing it is that you have such an extraordinary child. Think about it. What could you do if she carried on and disgraced her family? But here everyone envies you because she is so accomplished. That should make you very proud. There's a lot to be said for a daughter who makes people speak well of her family. You should be completely happy with Osei. If you're not, it's because you expect too much."

"I wouldn't care what people said about her if only she were a little nicer to me. But she is so cruel. She doesn't treat me like her mother at all. I hate her." She narrowed her eyes and looked at Osei, but her expression melted as she gazed proudly at her lovely daughter.

---

* By Richard G. Parker and J. Madison Watson, it was first published in New York in 1858 as one of A. S. Barnes & Co.'s "National Series." Its contents include lessons in elocution and exercises in reading and declamation as well as notes explaining the classical and historical allusions in the text. "Parker, Richard Green," *A Catalog of Books Represented by Library of Congress Printed Cards* (Ann Arbor, 1942–46).

The "National Series" enjoyed enormous popularity in Meiji Japan as textbooks for teaching English. The demand for copies of the books was so great that in 1887 the government was forced to issue a warning to over fifty producers of pirated editions that they were violating copyright laws. *Shimbun shūsei Meiji hennen-shi*, VI, 409.

† This high school text contains many statements that must have startled its Japanese readers: e.g., "Viewing history as confined to the series of leading civilized nations, we observe that it has to do with but one grand division of the human family, namely, with the Caucasian, or white race . . . for though the great bulk of the population of the globe has, during the whole recorded period, belonged, and does still belong, to other types of mankind, yet the Caucasians form the only true historical race." William Swinton, *Outlines of the World's History* (New York, 1874), p. 2.

"Let me add one more joy to your store of pleasures. I was promoted one grade today," said Noboru.

Omasa turned to him, startled for the moment. "That's wonderful. Congratulations." She bowed politely and then raised her head. "That's really wonderful."

Osei was also surprised. She reddened a little when she heard that Noboru was promoted. It seemed so strange.

"You say you advanced one grade. Your salary?"

"Just 5 yen difference."

"There's nothing wrong with 5 yen. You've been getting 30, so an increase of 5 yen will. . . ."

"Really, Mother. Someone else's salary."

"An increase of 5 yen means he'll be making 35. That's very good. Isn't that fine, Osei? It's not easy to make that much these days, even by lending money. So, 35 yen. It makes all the difference if you're clever, doesn't it? Osei and I are always saying how different you are from someone like Bunzō. You're still just a young man but you're bright, ingenious and so very clever."

"I'm afraid you exaggerate."

"It's no exaggeration. You're clever and you know how to get around people and you're handsome. Your only fault is that you eat too much," she ended, laughing.

Noboru laughed too. "Oh my, how critical you are."

"Anyway, I trust you will treat us to an outing to celebrate your promotion. Shall we make it at the Shintomiza or the Ichimuraza?"

"Anywhere you say. But as your guest."

"Thank you for nothing." Again she opened her mouth wide and laughed.

"That was just a joke. We can go to the theater some other time. How about seeing the chrysanthemum displays at Dangozaka* the day after tomorrow?"

---

* Each florist in the area had a display of life-size figures made of chrysanthemums, twigs, branches, and leaves. The figures were arranged in tableaux, often depicting a scene from a popular kabuki play. They had

"Chrysanthemum displays? Well, that depends. I don't know, though, just walking around and looking at them. I'd rather not, if you don't mind."

"We might manage to get in a little something extra besides."

"Promise?"

"Certainly."

"Well, all right then, let's go."

"Good."

"Osei, will you come too?"

"To Dangozaka?" Osei was very fond of such outings and she was sure it would be amusing. She was very much inclined to say yes at once, but, convinced it was undignified to agree too readily, she declined weakly at first and immediately afterward consented. A few minutes later Noboru left.

"Noboru is really a fine fellow," Omasa said quietly, as if she were thinking aloud. "He's just a young man and yet he's making so much money. Isn't our Bunzō a weakling compared to him? Here he is twenty-three and he still doesn't know how to behave himself, let alone how to support his mother. I'm completely disgusted with him."

"But Noboru wasn't very good at school."

"You keep talking about education, but what good is it if it doesn't help you to get ahead? There's nothing so wonderful about being able to read a few things if you can't live from day to day.

"Bunzō's just had a lot of bad luck lately. There's nothing he can do about it."

Omasa studied her daughter's face. "Osei, are you sure

ordinary dolls' heads, and when scenes from plays were used, the faces were made to resemble contemporary actors. The tableaux included suitable furnishings and animals and birds made of the flowers. The first literary evidence of the flower figures dates from the beginning of the nineteenth century. In early Meiji the figures were displayed annually all over Tokyo, but by 1882 Dangozaka (in modern Bunkyōku) had become the main place to see them. Today they are displayed only in a few special exhibition halls and parks.

you haven't got some kind of understanding with Bunzō? If you have, you'd better tell me. You shouldn't keep any secrets from me, for your own sake."

"Oh, no. Not again. I told you I didn't yesterday. Can't you understand?"

"There you go again. If the answer is no, it's no. You don't have to get so excited."

"But you're always so suspicious."

Mother and daughter were lost in their own thoughts for a moment.

"Mother, what shall I wear the day after tomorrow?"

"Anything at all."

"If I wear my usual underrobe, I wonder what would look nice over it. Maybe I should wear my yellow silk."

"Wear that other striped crepe again. That one suits you best."

"But it's rather cheap."

"Don't be so difficult."

"It would be nice to have Western clothes at a time like this."

"Why not get yourself a successful husband and have him buy you Western clothes or anything else you want?"

Osei looked at her mother quizzically.

UKIGUMO, PART TWO

S U N D A Y was an unusually fine day. The wind was still; no dust rose in the streets. The almanac gave the date as the second of November, the beginning of what we used to call the month of chrysanthemums. It was a wonderful day for an outing.

The members of the Sonoda household had been bustling about preparing for their excursion since morning. Osei's fretful fussing with her holiday finery angered Omasa. The hairdresser was late and naturally Onabe was blamed. A valuable teapot developed a broken lip and a mortar ran off the shelf all by itself. To make matters worse a woman notorious for making protracted visits came to call. Although they made it quite clear that they were just on the point of leaving for Dangozaka, it did very little good. Their visitor settled down for a nice leisurely talk, much to the ladies' despair. But things turned out better than had been expected. As the guest went home, the hairdresser arrived, and they managed to get ready by eleven o'clock. The household became still except for an occasional laugh.

Bunzō was completely miserable and certainly not in the mood for looking at flower displays. He was so bitter about all the terrible things that had happened to him, he felt he could not possibly compete with Noboru. At the moment, he would have described Noboru as a cherry blossom in full bloom while he himself felt like withered grass. He could not go with the Sonodas to Dangozaka and be further humiliated. Two days before he had firmly refused to join the party when Noboru had invited him, and yet that morning he was far from indifferent to all the confusion in the household. Watching their excitement, he was reminded over and over of his own predicament. He was utterly despondent.

It was all very depressing. It was depressing to see how casually Osei had accepted his decision not to go with them. If she really wanted him to go, she should have insisted on it. Then, if he had continued to refuse, he wanted her to say she would not make the excursion without him. "Aren't you just jealous?" he asked himself, trying to be reasonable. But her reaction continued to bother him.

Sulky and displeased at the world in general, he did not want to go and he did not want to stay home. He kept getting to his feet as if he had some pressing matter to attend to and then sitting down again. It was impossible for him to remain settled.

Thinking he might distract himself by reading, he chose a book at random from the bookcase. He tried to read but it failed to hold his attention. He stared at the page as hard as he could and read the first line over and over, but he could not understand what it meant. Much to his annoyance, he clearly heard Osei laughing downstairs despite his attempt to concentrate on the book. The sound dominated his consciousness and would not give him any peace.

With a gesture of annoyance, Bunzō thrust the book aside. He angrily leaned on his desk, rested his chin on his hand, and stared off into space. All at once he straightened up, his face animated once again, and started to speculate on what would happen if they did not go at all. He caught himself almost immediately. Surprise, chagrin, and anger filled him. He threatened himself and cursed his stupidity, but those devilish worms inside him continued to stir.

Unfortunately it seemed that there were no mishaps, and

Noboru arrived at one o'clock. Today he was in Japanese clothes, fashionable as ever. He wore a black twill haori over a brown silk kimono and his obi was also of a fine fabric. He came thumping up the stairs and abruptly sat himself down without bothering with the formalities of greeting his friend. He stared down his nose at Bunzō. "What's the matter? You look like a drowned man," he said.

"I have a slight headache."

"Oh? It's not because her highness scolded you, is it?" Bunzō was offended already but kept his hurt within him and said nothing.

"Well, are you coming?"

"No, I don't think so."

"Be sensible. Won't you be so gracious as to give us the pleasure of your company? Better? No. Well, too bad." He laughed. "No matter what I say, it has no effect on you." He went on with this silly idle chatter for a few minutes until Osei called to him from the foot of the stairs.

"The rickshaws are here, if you're ready."

"Shall we be going then?"

"Please hurry."

"Oh, Osei!" Noboru called.

"Yes."

"There's somebody here who'd come along if he could ride with you alone."

There was no reply, only the patter of scampering feet.

"Isn't it charming the way she runs off without answering?" he said by way of a farewell to Bunzō and went downstairs.

Looking at his departing figure, Bunzō mumbled bitterly, "Fool!" While the sound of his voice still lingered in the air, there arose in his mind a picture of Osei as she looked when they had gone to see the cherry blossoms that spring at Mukōjima. He stood up abruptly and stared about the room, his eyes lighting on the firepan. Then he recovered himself and sat down. "Fool," he repeated bitterly.

In the afternoon the weather remained clear although a

slight breeze began to stir. On such a fine Sunday merry crowds thronged the streets of Dangozaka. The whole range of fashionable ladies' coiffures was represented, from the simple Western upsweep to the elaborate pompadours, loops, swirls, and twists of the traditional Japanese styles. Here stalked a formidable blue-stocking, looking like the legendary old cat who haunted her tormentor's household.* And then a silly young girl tripped and danced by. There were nuresmaids and housemaids and enlightened women of this modern age walking beside those who were living evidence that polygamy, though decried, was still being practiced. In the great crowd were priests with shaven heads and modern laymen with European haircuts. Men with close cropped hair mingled with others retaining the traditional queue tied at the back of shaven scalps. Sprinkled in the great throng were those beloved children of heaven, fortune's favorites, those men among men, those holders of the world's esteem and envy—once called officeholders, today they are "officials," tomorrow they will perhaps be known as the servants of mankind. And there were merchants and pedlars. Present, too, were the bold and defiant antigovernment politicians who would resort to violence to gain their ends and brave imprisonment for their political views. People of every size and description were on hand that day at Dangozaka. It would be impossible to find the time to describe all the types of faces and varieties of hair styles and scents and clothing gathered there; the narrow street was fairly teeming with people, and to add to the confusion some wretches forced their way through the great crowd riding two abreast in rickshaws.

The poor inhabitants of the neighborhood sat pasting matchboxes while they watched the passing parade. How un-

---

* *Nabeshima sōdō,* an old legend associated with Nabeshima fief in modern Saga prefecture. In one version a tom cat belonging to a retainer is badly treated and takes its revenge by biting and killing the beloved mistress of the lord. Assuming the woman's form, the cat returns to wreak havoc in the household, even endangering the young master of the family. Finally several of the bravest retainers exorcise the ghost.

fair the world is: these poor people never did have time to stop their work and look at the displays themselves.

Along the streets, banners advertising the florist shops waved and fluttered in the fall breeze and the cries of the barkers mingled in the general din. Their flushed and excited faces stood out clearly in the crowd. For all the bustle and confusion, there was nothing really remarkably interesting to be seen along the streets or even within the shops themselves. Chrysanthemums are lovely only when they are left growing in their natural state, whether singly or in gay profusion. Their beauty is marred by forcing them into these artificial and distorted forms. Enormous quantities of yellow and white chrysanthemums—those marvelous flowers which bloom after all others have died—had been picked and brought here to make these ugly life-size figures. These cheap costumes fashioned from lovely flowers rustled at the slightest touch as if they had been starched too heavily. The pity of it is that only one man out of a thousand would be offended by these abominations; the other nine hundred and ninety-nine would worry more about the flavor of their refreshments. You must forgive the bitter complaints of a critical observer, my poor reader. On with the story.

Two rickshaws came flying down the street and drew to a sudden halt. Our old friends Noboru, Osei, and her mother got out. Noboru was dressed as described above. Omasa's grey-checked silk kimono was bound with a black satin obi. The black crepe neckband of her underrobe was lightly embroidered with gold. Her attire was adequately tasteful. Osei wore a pale blue, gold-figured satin obi with a yellow silk kimono and under it a full length scarlet crepe robe and a gold-embroidered pink neckband of the same fabric. Tucked in her obi was a thin pink crepe sash. It was quite an elegant outfit. Yet it was the grace and elegance of her whole appearance which made people stop to look rather than her clothing alone. She wore her usual modest upsweep, but this time she had rolled the bun in some special manner and had decorated it with the large rose-shaped hair pin.

She had used only the lightest cosmetics because of her theory that paint was unnatural.

Noboru was delighted to hear envious passersby trying to guess whether he and Osei were lovers or husband and wife. He was never silent for a second as he proudly guided mother and daughter from one florist shop to another. He continued his usual silly chatter, unconcerned with the fact that he could be overheard by the crowd around him.

Osei was also in an extremely good mood, completely vivacious and charming as she tripped merrily along, chattering away like a bird free of its cage. She laughed gaily at Noboru's nonsense, but this was no compliment to his wit; she could not have controlled her joy even if he had been silent.

Omasa showed little interest in the displays they saw. She looked them over casually, remarking occasionally on how nice they were, but actually paid little attention to them. On the other hand, she was very interested in making a careful examination of any girl Osei's age who came by. She would look first at the girl's face, then at her clothes, her obi, and on down to the tips of her toes. After the young lady had passed, Omasa would turn her head and study the back of her obi and her hair. Then she would dart a quick sidelong glance at Osei, make a rapid comparison, and conclude in her daughter's favor. A curious habit.

As their tour was drawing to a close, they stopped in front of a booth at the foot of the embankment and Noboru remarked that one of the figures bore a striking resemblance to Bunzō when he was yawning. Osei leaned over the railing, convulsed with laughter, and buried her face in her long sleeves. A student standing nearby turned their way and stared at her over his glasses in surprise. Omasa reminded her that she was making a spectacle of herself. Osei's laughter finally subsided and she looked up, her face still wreathed in smiles. Noboru was not at her side. Her smile vanished as she glanced about.

There was Noboru eagerly bowing to the back of a gentle-

man in Western clothes. The gentleman seemed unconcerned and went on standing with his back to Noboru. When
the young man had made his sweeping obeisance three or
four times, he finally turned his stern, bewhiskered face
around and looked at him. Without smiling or removing
his hat, he nodded magnanimously, and Noboru prostrated
himself. He bowed down over and over, babbling obsequi-
ously all the while.

The gentleman was accompanied by a woman and a young
girl. The woman wore her hair in the towering pompadour
then in vogue, while the girl had done hers into a youthful
Western style upsweep. They were two sparkling jewels
which matched so well it was obvious they were sisters. First
Noboru greeted the lady with the pompadour. When he
turned to the girl, she looked away, rather flustered, and
reddened as she returned the bow.

They all stood there talking for a few minutes, but they
were a little distance away and their words were lost in the
general confusion. Whatever it was, Noboru chattered away
without a stop, gesturing at times, always with a smile on
his lips. At one point he must have said something quite
amusing, for the gentleman suddenly opened his mouth wide
and burst out laughing, his shoulders shaking. The lips of
the lady curved into a smile as she too laughed. The girl
started to join in, then quickly hid her mouth in her sleeve
and looked demurely at Noboru with laughter in her eyes.
Still deferential, Noboru smiled broadly, proud of his success. He waited for the gentleman to stop laughing and
started to talk again. He obviously had completely forgotten
that Osei and her mother were waiting for him.

Osei did not pay much attention to the gentleman or the
older lady. Instead she stared with the utmost concentration
at the girl until it seemed she would stare a hole right
through her. She never looked away or drew a breath. She
even failed to answer her mother when she spoke to her.

Meanwhile Omasa saw that the gentleman's party was
starting to move in their direction and she quickly stepped

out of their way, pulling her preoccupied daughter along by her sleeve. They waited at the side of the road, and in a minute Noboru came along following in the train of the gentleman. At one of the shop doorways Noboru bowed to them once again and spewed forth a profusion of polite farewells. They parted company. Noboru walked on casually for a moment and then stopped and looked wildly all about the street as if he had suddenly remembered something.

"Over here, Noboru!" Omasa called. He rushed over to them and apologized for keeping them waiting so long.

"Who was that?"

"That was the chief," he said and smiled to himself. "He wasn't supposed to be coming today."

"Was the lady with the pompadour his wife?"

"Yes."

"And the girl?"

"Oh that, that's uh . . . ," he turned and looked around. "That's just his wife's younger sister. She's much better looking than she seemed at the house."

"She certainly is pretty, and those lovely clothes."

"She looks quite decent today, but in the house they treat her like a maid and she dresses very poorly."

"Has she any education?" Osei asked suddenly, taking Noboru quite by surprise.

"I haven't heard that she has," he replied, "but she may very well for all I know. She's only just come to the chief's house. I don't know much about her yet."

A cold glint filled Osei's eyes. She turned and looked at the girl as she entered a stall halfway up the slope. Osei patted her obi complacently and quickly regained her composure.

The three of them got into the rickshaws they had left waiting at the foot of the slope and started on their way to Ueno Park.

After Omasa was settled in the rickshaw next to Osei, she said, "You should have put on makeup like that."

"I hate such heavy makeup."

"Why?"

"It looks awful."

"There's nothing wrong with it for young people. It makes you look much more attractive. It's very flattering."

"If you like it so much, why don't you use it yourself? If I say I hate something, you say you like it. What a peculiar mother!"

"All I said was I thought it was good looking. You don't have to carry on like that. You really are a strange child!"

Osei realized that it was unnecessary to go on with her verbal assault. She fell silent. Her mood became rather pensive and sad. Her mother tried to get their conversation started again, but Osei refused to join in. Apparently something had gone wrong. Osei's mood was short-lived, however, for by the time they got to Ueno Park, she was no longer depressed and was chattering away again.

Fall in Ueno Park. Ancient pine trees stood row upon row, their branches interlaced, their needles thick and luxuriant, of a green so deep as to saturate the heart of an onlooker. The fruit trees were desolate in contrast; old and young alike covered with withered leaves. The lonely camellia bushes, their branches laden with flowers, seemed to yearn for companionship. Several of the delicate maple trees had turned a blazing red. The cries of the few remaining birds mirrored the sadness of the season. All at once, the wind blew sharply. The branches of the cherry trees shivered and trembled, shaking free their dead leaves. Fallen leaves strewn on the ground rose as if moved by a spirit and danced about in happy pursuit of one another. Then as if by unanimous accord they lay down again. This bleak and dreary autumn scene cannot compare with a bright and hopeful spring day, but still it had a special magic of its own.

Merry visitors on their way to Dangozaka walked among the trees. The tinkling laughter of young girls echoed in the quiet air.

Osei announced that she wanted to get out and walk in the park. The three companions alighted in front of the

Museum of Education and strolled over the stone bridge to the front of the zoo. Instructing their drivers to wait for them near the Kannondō, they left their rickshaws and continued their walk, passing through a grove of cryptomerias so tall they seemed to touch the sky, and came to the side of the Tōshōgū.*

Just then a chubby student of about fourteen dashed out from the back gate of the shrine followed by a friend. Both wore blue serge suits and black caps with gold-plated insignia. The brims of the caps were turned up. The first boy called, "Let us go on," in heavily accented English. "But I want to get something to eat first," he added in his own language. His companion agreed.

"I want something to eat but. . . ." Suddenly he caught sight of Omasa and stopped short.

"Isami!" she cried.

The boy ran over and bowed several times to Noboru, obviously disconcerted. He blushed. "Hello, Mother," he said.

"Where are you rushing to?"

"I went home—and—and Onabe said nobody was there except Bunzō, so I uh—I. . . ."

"Are your exams over?"

"Yes."

"How did they go?"

"Mother, I—uh—have a little favor to ask." He looked at her meaningfully.

* The Ueno Park area in Taitōku was in the process of becoming a public cultural center at this time. It had been the religious center of the Tendai Buddhist sect in the Tokyo area from the completion of the main temple in 1627, under shogunal auspices, until Meiji. The Tōshōgū is a Shintō shrine dedicated to the two Tokugawa shoguns, Ieyasu and Yoshimune. It was built in 1623 for the convenience of worshipers of the Edo court. In 1873 supervision of the shrine was turned over to Tokyo prefecture. The Kannondō or Kiyomizudō, a Buddhist temple, was built at the end of the seventeenth century in imitation of the architectural masterpiece of the same name in Kyoto. The museum and zoo are part of the modern tradition of the park. The Museum of Education was established in 1877 on the site of the present day Tokyo University of Art, and the zoo was built in 1882. The latter was kept under Imperial household supervision until 1924 when it was given to the city.

"You can ask it right here."

The boy glanced over at Noboru. "If you could just step over here a minute, Mother."

"I can just about guess what you want. You're out of pocket money again, I suppose."

"Oh, no, it's nothing like that." He looked over at Noboru again and blushed. Laughing awkwardly he dragged his mother off toward the cryptomerias.

Noboru and Osei strolled around the park until they came to the back of the shrine. It was about four o'clock and the rays of the sun were now slanting. The trees cast a striped pattern on the mud walls of the old tombs. The water of the Shinobazu pond glistened like the scales of a huge fish. Below was the great tiled roof of the horse racing stadium. The stadium itself was hidden behind the earthen bank, but they heard the clatter of the carriages and the neighing of the horses.

Osei stopped at the trunk of a huge tree, closed the parasol which had been shielding her from the sun, and glanced about. She turned to study Noboru's face. "That girl's quite lovely, isn't she?"

"Which girl?"

"The one you said was some relation to the chief."

"Oh, I couldn't imagine who you meant. Yes, she is, isn't she?"

"And you felt she was even prettier than she was at home." Osei's eyes twinkled and her lips quivered with laughter. A second later she burst out laughing.

"Damn it, you trapped me. I wouldn't have expected this from you, and look what's happened. I have to be more careful."

"And the way she blushed every time she bowed to you."

"Oh, stop teasing! That's enough now. Behave yourself."

"But it's true."

"She may be pretty, but she's not nearly so beautiful as somebody else I know."

"Oh, that's enough of that."

"But it's true," he retorted.

"You don't waste any time getting even, do you?"

"Really, I'm not joking." Just then a man who looked like a government official came by leading a ten-year-old girl by the hand. He went by staring at the two young people. Noboru went on. "Seriously, no matter how pretty she may be, I'm not interested in her and she's not interested in me."

"Of course you're not. And you didn't pay any attention to her, did you?"

"Now listen to me. I'm not just referring to that girl. I'm not interested in other women, no matter how beautiful they are, because I have only one 'idol.' "

"Well, aren't you lucky."

"Not at all. It's a case of unrequited love. I go to her house every day just for a chance to see her even though I'm terribly embarrassed. But she always seems annoyed and won't even speak to me properly," he said staring impertinently at Osei.

She smiled but gave no indication that she had caught his meaning. "What a disagreeable 'idol.' "

"Still, why should she be nice to me? After all, she has a sweetheart already."

"I wonder what time it is."

"And I know I shouldn't fall in love with her but I can't stop myself. Lately I even see her in my dreams."

"Oh, you're so silly. Why don't we walk a little more?"

"And after I went to so much trouble to arrange this excursion all we do is walk around together. Her mother is with her the whole time and we don't have a chance to talk at all."

"Speaking of Mother, I wonder what she's doing?" Osei turned her head.

Noboru continued in a soulful tone. "When I finally do get a chance to say something, you pretend you don't know what I'm talking about. I'm not getting anywhere at all."

"You mustn't joke like that." Osei laughed, turning to

look at him again. He seemed very sad and forlorn. The smile left her face.

"Please don't take it as a joke. You know how hard it is for me to get myself to say something like that." He ended with a sigh.

Osei fixed her eyes on the ground and did not say a word.

"I don't want to force myself on you against your will. Just tell me I have no chance and I'll make myself forget about you once and for all. That will be the end of it. I won't see you again."

Osei remained silent.

"Osei," he said, raising his lowered head and staring at her.

She blushed and was visibly upset. Finally she spoke in a barely audible voice. "You're always fibbing." She looked down.

Noboru burst out laughing.

Startled, Osei raised her eyes. "How terrible. You are dreadful. You acted so seriously and had me completely fooled." Her tone hovered between anger and reproach. She smiled in embarrassment.

Behind them a voice suddenly called out, "That's enough, you two." Osei wheeled around to see her mother coming toward them, slipping a purse into her obi.

"It must have been a difficult interview," Noboru observed.

Omasa apologized for keeping them waiting and then, noticing Osei's face, asked, "What's wrong? You're all red."

Osei blushed again at the question. "Oh, am I? I guess I got hot while we were walking," she explained lamely.

"Really, Noboru, that boy is such a problem about his pocket money. He came to see me before his exams started and got a yen advance on his allowance. He used that up in less than ten days and wanted more. If we were at home, I wouldn't have given it to him."

"That's not true, Mother. You love giving him money," Osei ended with a forced laugh.

"Be quiet. You don't know anything about this. As I was saying, we weren't in the house, so I gave him 50 sen and he said that wasn't enough. He wanted 1 yen. I decided that there would be no end to it if I gave in this time so I put my foot down. He took the 50 sen grudgingly enough and then said that day after tomorrow there's to be an outing at Asukayama—an ascetic meet or something."

Osei laughed in genuine mirth. Noboru nodded eagerly. "Athletic meet," he said.

"Ascetic or aesthetic or whatever—he wanted 50 sen more. I told him to come tomorrow to get the money, but he wouldn't listen and insisted on taking it right away. Even that wouldn't have been so bad but he said something terrible. When I asked him if he'd come by tomorrow, he said 'I got the money already so I don't have to. I'll come to see you when I run short again.'"

"Mother, even if there is a charge for an athletic meet, it isn't more than 10 or 20 sen."

"Ten or 20 sen? Then he made 30 sen profit!" Noboru and Osei burst out laughing at Omasa's amazement.

BUNZŌ FELT much calmer after the others had left the house. He settled down beside the desk, his arms folded, his chin buried in his collar, lost in his tortured thoughts.

He was terribly upset about his relations with Osei. He knew in his heart that it was not wise to worry about such commonplace problems, but he could not help it.

Bunzō had always believed that two people in love were bound together and could not act separately. When one of them was happy, the other was happy too, and the sadness of one was shared by the other. Joy and sorrow came to each in their turn. They laughed and swore together. Their thoughts and feelings were readily communicated and they were stirred by the same emotions. They could never disagree, never be out of harmony. Believing this, how could Bunzō explain the fact that Osei did not sympathize with him in his present ordeal?

He could not understand it. He could not comprehend why Osei was indifferent to him.

He was certain that she loved him. Nothing else could explain the complete change in her behavior these last few months. She was no longer a callow girl; she had turned into a gentle and gracious young woman. That was why she became so receptive after that memorable summer's night, and why she looked at him in that special way and was awkward when she spoke to him. It was the reason for her thoughtful, pensive moods. What other explanation could there be for her playfully probing into his thoughts when marriage was discussed? And would she have defied her own mother to defend a stranger if she did not love him?

And yet his beloved Osei had failed him, the girl he had vowed to love and cherish, the girl he had chosen to share his every breath, his every thought and feeling. There is no doubt that she had been aware of his suffering—her cousin, dearest friend, her future husband (he almost dared not think the word!). She had witnessed his misery and had accepted his decision to stay home with the utmost indifference. She had gone on the excursion with Noboru even though she claimed to hate him as much as Bunzō did. And at a time like this. It defied comprehension.

Bunzō was certain that her new attitude toward him contained a significance that he was not yet able to grasp, and he was determined to find out what it was. With an enormous effort he concentrated all his energy on analyzing her behavior to isolate this evasive element. He had little success. He became irritated. And then those devilish worms inside him started their tantalizing dance again, teasing him with one hint after another, and finally tricking him into accepting some absolutely absurd solution. Half realizing how ridiculous it was, he accepted it for the moment anyhow and worked on the idea until he had constructed a whole situation from it. He experienced exactly the same hurt and pain from this artificial hypothesis as he would have if it had been a fact. At last he made himself see it for what it was: a ridiculous fantasy. He was simply looking for trouble. In a rage of self-disgust, he mentally smashed the illusion into a million pieces. He sighed with relief.

He began to examine the problem again calmly. The devils within him tricked him into accepting yet another fantasy as the truth. He smashed this one too. The process was repeated with a third idea and a fourth. No believable solu-

tion came to him. He made no progress. He could not understand why Osei had grown cold to him; he could not grasp
the significance of her behavior that day. He felt all his
strength drain from him and found it impossible to study the
problem further. He stretched out on the floor, leaning on
his arm, closed his eyes, and tried to relax. He tried to escape
from his torment for just a moment, to forget all about
obligations, success, his aunt, Osei—everything. He lay perfectly still, not even breathing, like a dead man. Suddenly
he sat up. "What if it's Honda that she . . . ?" He dared not
finish the sentence. His eyes darted frantically about the
room.

Where had this suspicion come from? Had it dropped from
the sky or risen from the center of the earth? Was it a fantasy
born of his own feelings of persecution? Its origins were in-
determinable, it had appeared too quickly. He knew only
that he had accurately hit upon the element in Osei's coldness which he had been struggling to understand. His hair
bristled.

He was not prepared to accept it. He had no evidence that
it was true. How could he be sure he was right? He reviewed
Osei's actions carefully and found no indication that it was
so. He knew perfectly well that Osei was still young enough
to be easily aroused by a man and that he could not rely on
her to be faithful to him. But you can tell what a girl will
be like when she grows up, and Bunzō knew that Osei would
turn into a fine woman one day. She should be loved and
respected for her intelligence, refinement, and gaiety. In her
search for the new and original, she might well be duped by
a hypocrite who appeared virtuous or by some big, brave
fellow, but she could not possibly be taken in by a beast like
Noboru. She was far too intelligent for that. She had always
treated Noboru with the contempt he deserved, while ad-
miring and respecting Bunzō. He was certain that love went
hand in hand with respect and that no woman could love a
man she did not respect.

"I must be wrong," he said, but he was still troubled. The

suspicion lingered. He shook his aching head. It was still there. Just a tiny little doubt, yet it was as blinding as a dazzling light. It was ominous and frightening.

Bunzō was terrified at what the truth might be. What was he about to uncover? He wanted to drive the whole idea from his mind before it was too late, but the harder he tried to dispel the notion, the more obvious it became that he was right. The suspicion grew into a near certainty. Bunzō was deeply disturbed.

A letter had come from home. It would enable him to escape from his thoughts. Like a starved eagle seizing a small bird, he grabbed the letter and broke the seal. He forced himself to read it aloud in a strong voice. Halfway through he stopped. His mind wandered back to his problems. He started to read it again. Once more his voice petered out and he began to brood. He looked up and burst out laughing. "This is ridiculous. Why should I suspect her of such a terrible thing? I'll tell her all about my silly ideas when she comes home and we'll have a good laugh over it. That will be the end of it once and for all." Another good laugh completely dispelled his doubts and fears.

He turned back to his mother's letter. He had to reread it, for he had not been concentrating on it the first time. It was a reply to the one in which he had told her of losing his job. She did not complain or bemoan her fate as some people might. Despite her disappointment, she accepted the turn of events stoically. However, there was a note at the end of the letter which showed how very miserable she was.

This may amuse you, but when your letter came, I went to the temple to pray for you. I promised to give up tea and asked that you get another job quickly. Remember that I'm praying for you.

He put the letter down and folded his arms. Omasa had already lost interest in him; his own mother was entirely different. She did not accuse him of being worthless and stupid, and was willing to sacrifice one of the few pleasures left to her to encourage him. Her extraordinary love and devotion should have brought tears to his eyes, he knew. But he did not cry. Instead he found himself longing for Osei to come home. "Damn it, what's the matter with me?" he exclaimed in anger. "My mother is so terribly worried, yet I sit here thinking about Osei. I ought to be ashamed of myself." He did not want to go out before he saw Osei again. "I'll go and see about some work right now," he exclaimed all at once, taking himself in hand, and then added, "before Osei comes back."

He ate his dinner, mumbling angrily at himself, and left the house. He walked over to Banchō to call on a man named Ishida who had been his English teacher and who had also been responsible for getting him his first job.

Ishida had been to England and had a fair command of the language. He said that he was an expert at economics, which he had studied there, and that he had been in great demand as an economist when he got back to Japan. But, for some reason he did not care to discuss, he was temporarily teaching English instead. (He had been at this 'temporary' job for eight years.) Ishida also said that one of the many intellectuals he had known in England was the famous Herbert Spencer. They had only had a nodding acquaintance and he doubted whether they would recognize each other after all those years if they met again.

Naturally, Ishida was highly conversant with English society. He knew about all the things that make up the everyday life of the people: the splendor of the Parliament buildings, the prosperity of London, the colorful horses and carriages, the menus, the clothing and canes and footgear, the names of various common objects. He could play cards and tell good black tea from bad by the taste and roll cigarettes with his fingertips and wipe his nose with one hand.

On the other hand, he knew absolutely nothing about Japanese life. This did not bother him at all, however. In fact he refused to pay attention to anything preceded by the adjective "Japanese," be it object or idea. Although he was still in his forties, he lived entirely in the past, like an old, old man, eagerly recounting his adventures abroad to anyone he met. It was almost impossible to stop him, and if you did, he would not have anything else to talk about. Those who knew him were apt to be highly critical. Some said he was lazy, others that he was audacious, still others that he was ridiculously conceited. Whatever else they felt, all agreed on one point: he was terribly conceited. Some people said that for all his faults he was harmless enough. This was an astute judgment, for being without any particular ambition, he was free to act just as lazy, brazen, and conceited as he cared to. Of course it was possible that he acted so badly only to make it appear that he was unambitious. In any case, Bunzō considered him harmless enough.

Luckily Bunzō found Ishida in when he got to his house. He told him what had happened at the office and that he was looking for work again. Ishida readily agreed to help, but so casually that Bunzō doubted that he would make any serious effort on his behalf.

"If we were in England I could easily get you a job, but it's a different matter here. Believe it or not, I had all sorts of contacts in England. On the *Times* staff alone there was . . . ," and he went on to list all the names he could remember. Bunzō had heard about his influential friends in England many times before, but he could hardly say so at such a moment. He pretended to be hearing it for the first time. It was difficult to sit through the boring recital and as the hours wore on he began to fidget and squirm. Finally the time came for him to leave and his patience was rewarded. "There are some translations to be done for the newspapers," Ishida said. "If you come by day after tomorrow, I'll have some waiting for you."

Bunzō told him how grateful he was.

"Well, it's just newspaper work. And compared with an English newspaper the ones here are nothing. They're so stupid and unsophisticated." Bunzō said goodbye quickly to keep Ishida from getting started again and left the house.

Once outside the door the young man sighed with relief and cheerfully hurried home. He was very anxious to see Osei and talk over his foolish doubts and fears with her; he wanted to show her how his faith in her had helped him to overcome them. Much to his disappointment, she was not at home. Onabe told him she had been back but had gone out again to the bath. He went up to his room, lit the lamp, and waited impatiently for her return. Each minute seemed like a thousand years until finally the front door opened. He heard her gentle voice in the hallway and her footsteps on the stair.

Osei's glossy black hair was still damp and shone like velvet. Her white skin glowed like a jewel, colored only by the most delicate flush of pink. An air of mischief playing on her features did little to detract from the beauty of her gentle, smiling mouth.

At the sight of her, Bunzō forgot all his worries and welcomed her with a grin. "Did you have a good time at Dango-zaka?"

"It was terribly crowded, being Sunday and such nice weather and all," she answered, sitting down. She covered her face with her hands. "I feel dreadful. Noboru made me drink some sake although I said I didn't want any."

"And your mother?" Bunzō asked, as if he had not caught what she said.

"She went shopping after the bath. And when I told him I couldn't finish it, he said he'd help me, even though he was pretty drunk already by that time. He just kept drinking and drinking until he hardly knew what he was doing."

Bunzō's smile began to disappear.

"He got terribly forward after we came home. And Mother didn't even try to stop him. She said she'd overlook anything tonight and so, of course, he took that as permission to act just as silly and bold as he wanted." She laughed as she remembered what had happened. "He's terribly bold."

Bunzō was furious and commented, with a scowl, "How entertaining that must have been."

Osei apparently missed the implication entirely. After a brief silence, she laughed again. "He really is terribly bold."

Suddenly all Bunzō's plans were frustrated. How could he talk now, with any confidence, of the suspicions he had conquered? How could he expect an avowal of her loyalty? He did not care about her drinking with Noboru. That was nothing. He could forgive her letting the man flirt with her, if it were just this once, because, after all, people act silly when they are drunk. He was no moralist. Actually there was nothing in what she told him to make him so upset, and, yet, all his doubts and fears were set in motion again. Why did she keep talking about that wretch Honda in such a pleasant tone of voice? He knew he did not understand what was in her mind at all. He sat there in silence, his eyes downcast.

"Why are you so depressed?" she asked.

"I'm not depressed."

"Oh, I thought maybe you were worried about that girl Otome." *

He stared at her in disbelief, amazed at the absurdity of her suggestion, and sighed deeply.

"I must be right. That's why you won't answer me."

"I wish it were as simple as that. I had a letter from my mother today. She's quite worried about my having lost my job and she's given up tea for me."

"Really? How dreadfully old-fashioned of her."

He glanced at her sharply. "You may find it amusing but I don't. I feel simply terrible to think that I am causing my mother so much concern just because my future is so uncertain. And then there's your mother."

"Did she say something again?"

"No, not since the first time. But she looks at me in such a terrible way. She won't even talk to me. And now. . . ."

The word "you" welled up within him, but he did not want to show her how jealous he was. "Anyway, I decided that I really must try to get a job right away so I went to see Ishida.

* "This is presumably the name of the girl Bunzō's mother suggested he marry" appears here in brackets in the original text.

But I'm afraid I can't depend on him. I'm terribly discouraged. I wouldn't mind so much for myself, but everything is at loose ends because of me."

At last Osei was moved to sympathy. She grew sad and sat with him silently for a while. Then she yawned. "I'm so tired. I think I'll go right to bed. Good night," she said, getting up. "Oh, by the way, Bunzō, do you know the chief's sister-in-law?"

"No."

"I saw her today at Dangozaka. She's about seventeen and quite pretty, except she had on heavy, old-fashioned makeup with a modern hairdo. A little powder is fine, but she looked very cheap. Now see how silly I am? I'm starting to gossip all over again. Good night."

In the hall she ran into her mother, who had just come home. "Osei! What's the idea of going upstairs?"

Exasperated, the girl went directly to her room and quickly changed into her nightclothes. For a few minutes she glanced over the newspaper, but it soon slipped out of her hands. She lay there quietly without moving, her eyes wide open. Why, she wondered, why did her cousin have to be so stodgy?

Suddenly she stretched and smiled. She leaned forward and blew out the lamp beside her pillow. Resting her head on the pillow, she soon settled into a comfortable position and slipped easily into a deep sleep.

IT WAS THE fourth of November. The weather was still
fine, the sky clear and blue. Only Bunzō's grieving, forlorn
heart was cloudy. Since morning he had closeted himself in
his room brooding about the way his aunt had reacted to
his news. At breakfast the day before he had told her of his
visit to Ishida in some detail. Her lack of interest had been
painfully obvious; he might have been a complete stranger.

About one o'clock Isami arrived and came up to Bunzō's
room. He began to gossip in his boyish, awkward way about
anything that came into his mind, not paying any attention
to whether Bunzō answered him or not, totally unconcerned
that his thoughts were foolish and immature. His subject
shifted from one thing to another: different kinds of wres-
tling, gymnastics, music, discussions he had had with the
prefect—everything from how bravely the boys had protested
the dreadful food at the school to the questions on his exams
and why he had failed.

At first Bunzō made an effort to concentrate on what the
boy was saying, but his interest was soon exhausted. He let
his thoughts wander back to his own troubles, back to his
doubts about Osei and their future. From time to time a sigh
escaped his lips.

Osei poked her head over the landing and called her brother.

The boy paid no attention. "So I answered him right back. Don't you think it's positively reprehensible to arrange the seating in the boat according to our place in regular class?"

"Isami, I called you. What's wrong with your ears?"

"All right, all right. What is it?"

"Mother wants to sew up that rip in your shirt. Take it off."

Isami began to unbutton the shirt slowly. "He said it had to be by the marks. I thought that was pretty funny. In fact, I thought it was reprehensible."

"Can't you hurry a little?" Osei asked. "I'm waiting, you know."

"You don't have to be in such a rush. It's just reprehensible."

" 'Reprehensible'? What's all this about 'reprehensible'?" Osei snapped. "I ask you to hurry and you take your time anyway. You're so aggravating. I won't wait, so be quick about it."

"I bet you don't even know the English word 'bridle path.' Or 'I was at our uncle's' or 'I will keep you. . . .' "

"Shush!" Osei listened to something downstairs. "That must be Noboru," she said, smiling broadly. She rushed down the stairs.

"Hey, Osei, don't you want my shirt? For heaven sakes. She's gone. She's so snobbish lately. We had quite a fight the other day. She said she was going to have a calling card made with 'Sonoda Seiko' on it because it sounds so dignified. I told her plain 'Oseikko' was good enough for her,* and she got so angry. Imagine a woman wanting a calling card anyhow!"

* It is likely that Osei's legal name was "Sonoda Sei," the most common form for girls' names at the time. It was fashionable for educated women to add the suffix *ko* to their names themselves. By the 1910s, however, the suffix was used by almost every family for their daughters. "Oseikko" is probably Isami's nickname for his sister. It is a word used for calling animals in hunting.

Bunzō burst out laughing, more out of chagrin than anything, but the young dialectician assumed he was being rewarded for his keen wit and went proudly down the stairs
repeating, "Oseikko is good enough for her. Imagine a woman
having a calling card made. She's so snobbish."

For a few minutes Bunzō continued to sit in the same position, his arms folded. Suddenly struck with an idea, he rose,
changed his haori, and went down holding his hat in his
hand.

He slid open the door of the sitting room. There was
Noboru, sitting cross-legged beside the hibachi. Osei was
sprawled beside him, chattering foolishly away. Our young
dialectician was concentrating on peeling the skin from a
steamed sweet potato, his head cocked to one side. He wore
a coat with nothing underneath. Omasa was awkwardly
stitching the torn shirt, the sewing box before her.

Noboru winked at Bunzō. Osei turned around to look at
him, but her expression was cold and disinterested, as if she
were only vaguely curious about who had come in. She turned
away quickly. "Really?" she asked, looking coyly into Noboru's eyes.

"It's true."

"You'll be sorry if it's not."

It is not at all pleasant to listen to someone else's conversation and not know what they are talking about. "I'm just
going over to Banchō," Bunzō explained to his aunt and
started to leave.

Noboru stopped him. "There's something I'd like to tell
you, Utsumi."

"I'm in rather a hurry."

"I am too."

With an effort, Bunzō lowered his eyes to meet Noboru's.
They glared at each other for a moment, and he reluctantly
entered the room and sat down.

Omasa stopped sewing and stared peculiarly at Noboru.
"From what I hear at the office, they're going to take back
a couple of the clerks they let go. At least I think so from

something the chief said. You can't afford to be out of work for long and your aunt and, of course, Osei . . . ," he glanced slyly at her and grinned. The girl pouted and pretended to be angry. ". . . are so worried about you, I thought you might like to try to get your old job back. If you agree, you should let the chief know before they decide who they're going to choose. I'd be glad to put in a good word for you if you find it hard to see him yourself. What do you think?"

"That's awfully kind of you," Bunzō began. His voice trailed off. He tried to hide his annoyance, but his reaction showed plainly on his face.

Noboru was quick to understand his hesitation. "You don't like the idea? I won't say anything if you don't want me to. It's all up to you. But wouldn't it be a good idea to swallow your pride just this once?"

Bunzō changed color.

"It's no use your saying that," Omasa interrupted. "Our Bunzō is very proud. He couldn't possibly do anything as crude as that."

"Oh? That's a very noble attitude indeed. Then I've been just excruciatingly rude to you," Noboru said, laughing.

Bunzō turned pale at his words. He began to shake with fury. He clenched his fist and gnashed his teeth, looking at Noboru's profile with hatred. It seemed as if he were about to pounce on him, but he recovered himself in time and relaxed.

Everyone felt uncomfortable. Not a word was said. Isami stared at Bunzō, his cheek swollen with the potato he was gorging on. Osei was also puzzled and watched him carefully.

"Osei is looking at me," Bunzō thought. "I really should fight back somehow. I wish I could think of something to say, some very dignified curse. I'd like to beat him down with one word and twist his nose and get his ugly face all red." Despite his rage, he was unable to think of the right word. He looked at Osei again. She was still watching him. "Is that all?" he asked hoarsely. The words slipped out, startling him.

"All what?" Noboru asked, knowing perfectly well what he meant.

"Is that all you wanted of me?" Bunzō reddened, horrified at his inability to gain the upper hand.

"Yes, I'm through. That's all I wanted to say."

The atmosphere was intolerable. With a slight bow Bunzō sprang to his feet and left the room. He had only gone a few steps when a loud chorus of laughter burst out behind him. Again he trembled with rage and turned ashen. He stared at the door of the room, rooted to the spot. Finally he recovered sufficiently to drag himself from the house.

He was mortified. With enormous effort he held his burning fury within him until he felt his very heart would burst. How horribly he had been insulted—and by a dog like Noboru. Until three days ago they had worked in the same office and in almost the same kind of job, and yet now Noboru had hurt him terribly. What had brought on this exhibition of pure malice? What was behind this attack?

Bunzō could not remember ever having insulted Noboru, although he had been offended by him often enough. Without the slightest justification Noboru had treated him like dirt, as if he had special license to insult anybody he wanted to. And to make matters worse he had done it in front of Osei and her mother.

He doubted Noboru's story about the rumor at the office. Even if it were true, why should such a man put himself out and risk his own position to help him? Had he acted out of friendship and concern, there would have been no need to do it that way, looking down on Bunzō as if he were a shabby orphan, cut off from the benevolence of the bureaucracy, saying it would be best for him if he could possibly go back to work there.

He might have been able to stand such condescension, but that was not the worst of it. The chief was, after all, Bunzō's boss as well as Noboru's. Yet Noboru had repeatedly spoken of the "chief" as if he owned him and had gratuitously of-

fered to put in a good word for Bunzō. How he boasted of
having the man's piddling good will. He was actually proud
of being treated like a loyal slave. Surely he did not have
the influence he claimed. If no one were hurt by his stupid,
idle boasting and bragging, it would not matter. Let him
advertise his own fawning position all he wanted. But Bunzō
could not tolerate being confronted with it and having it
used to insult and shame him.

Noboru had arrogantly told him to swallow his false pride.
What had he said that showed false pride? Bunzō could
never act like Noboru did: making short shrift of his own
work to do what the chief wanted, smiling and flattering,
crawling around on his hands and knees, and acting like a
beggar for a dole of 35 yen. And Noboru was proud of it.
Proud enough to use the admiration of a silly, ignorant
woman like Omasa to bolster his ego until he believed himself the cleverest man in the world. And when Bunzō had
refused his offer out of the purest motives, he had the nerve
to imply that he had some other reason—false pride and,
back of that, jealousy of Noboru's great influence in the
office.

The worst of it was that it had happened in front of Osei.
"You didn't fight back even though he insulted you," a little
voice chirped. "No, I didn't have a chance. I couldn't possibly start a row there," Bunzō angrily told himself. "I'm a
man. I have courage. I know Noboru is just a weakling but
what could I do there? I had to be patient because of the
women. I would have played right into his hands if I had
argued with him. I would have looked even more ridiculous."

But Osei did not know his reasons. She was just a young,
impressionable girl, for all her intelligence, and she had seen
him made a fool of by a miserable, crawling worm like
Noboru who thought it virtuous to lick someone's boots for
personal gain. She had watched him retreat shamefully without striking back. She must have thought him a terrible
coward. Even if she did not, he was ashamed of himself for

her sake. "It's all your fault, Noboru. I'll get even with you,"
he vowed to himself, gnashing his teeth and clenching his
fists. He glared wildly about.

His angry stare fell on a passing policeman who stopped
and looked at him in surprise. After watching him for a moment, the policeman continued his rounds.

Bunzō awoke from his trance and found himself standing
at the entrance to Yasukuni shrine.* He had only the vaguest
recollection of crossing Manaita bridge and coming up the
incline. He entered the shrine and turned left into a grove of
cherry trees whose leaves were withered. He wandered about,
his hands locked behind him, his face twisted and distorted.
Ishida's lodgings were directly outside the rear gate of the
shrine, but he was seething with rage and he thought it best
to walk awhile.

"And Osei behaved terribly too," he mumbled to himself. "The girl I. . . . She didn't even seem upset when she
saw me being tortured by that bastard Honda. She watched
so calmly." He was haunted by the memory of how they had
laughed when he left, afraid that it proved she had lost interest in him completely. He collapsed on a bench set beneath the cherry trees as if all his strength had been sapped
from him.

For a few minutes he sat there without moving, lost in
thought, his arms folded, his chin buried in his collar. Suddenly his head shot up. "Did he act like that to make Osei
stop loving me? To get her to take up with him instead? That
must be why he chose that moment to deliberately insult me.
That's what he meant by the look he gave her. I must do
something about it." He sprang to his feet, pale and determined.

But what could he do?

By some extreme act, by showing extraordinary courage,

---

* A Shintō shrine dedicated to those who have given their lives for the
country. The souls of victims of every modern war are enshrined there,
starting with those who displayed loyalty to the Emperor at the time of
the Restoration.

he would prove what a brave, strong man he really was. He must demonstrate that his restraint stemmed from generosity and consideration, not from weakness. He must do something so remarkable that he would shock Noboru and bring Omasa to her senses. And Osei—if he had indeed forfeited her love—he would restore her faith in him and, most important, regain his own self-confidence. But how?

Should he tell Noboru just what he thought of him and put an end to their relationship? But Noboru was so glib. A verbal duel would not be the best idea. A physical fight was also impossible. Bunzō sat down again. For an hour he sat there without moving, pondering the question.

Someone called his name and tapped him on the shoulder. Startled, he looked up. A man wearing a filthy, patched suit stood before him. He seemed quite drunk and reeked of alcohol. It was Bunzō's former colleague Yamaguchi, about whom we heard in the first chapter. He too had been fired.

"You startled me. How has it been going?"

"How indeed."

"You seem to be keeping yourself amused."

"What else can I do? It's been five days and I've been drunk every day." His stomach rumbled to prove it.

"Why are you letting yourself go like this?"

"Oh, I'll be all right. But the whole thing is so disgusting. What's wrong with us? Why did we get fired? What's so good about those fellows they didn't fire? Why are they still there instead of us?" He grew red with anger. A gardener in a black uniform who was passing by saw his face and sneered. Bunzō began to feel uncomfortable.

Yamaguchi ranted on. "I don't want. . . ."

Bunzō interrupted him. "Lower your voice a little. People can hear you."

"I don't want to sound conceited," he continued in a quieter voice, "but we were just as good at our jobs as the others, weren't we?"

"Yes, we certainly were."

Yamaguchi warmed to his subject. "But we didn't indulge

in outside activities and so we got fired. Isn't it disgusting?"

"What's the good of talking about it?"

"It's enough to drive you crazy."

"By the way, Honda says a couple of people might be taken back, but I can't trust his word. Did you hear anything?"

"No. Really?"

"So he says."

Yamaguchi thought for a minute. "Even if they do, I won't be one of them." His voice reflected his misery and torment. "The chief hates me. I'll never get my job back." He paused. "Did Honda get a raise?"

"That's what I hear."

"You see. It's quite a different story if you're good at those outside activities. A simple-minded fool like me can't pull it off."

"Who can?"

"He must be quite proud of himself, that louse."

"I don't mind if he's pleased with himself, but something he said got me furious." Bunzō sensed at once that he should not have mentioned it.

"What was it? What was it?"

"Oh, nothing important."

"Come on, tell me."

"He told me I should go to see somebody and try to win him over. It was terrible of him to suggest it and I flatly refused. Then he accused me of being too proud to do it."

"And you let him get away with it?" Yamaguchi was livid.

"I thought about fighting with him, but it would be childish to take him seriously. I decided to ignore it."

"That's no way to go about it. You're too easygoing," he said contemptuously. He grew even more indignant and, looking straight into Bunzō's face, said, "If it had been me I would've punched him right there on the spot."

"I could have easily, but I don't like violence."

"Violent or not, you have to punch a louse like that every once in a while. I wouldn't hesitate for a minute."

After a silence, Bunzō changed the subject. "How do you happen to be over this way?"

"Oh, I forgot all about it. I have some relatives living in Ichibanchō. I'm going over there to borrow some money, now that I've had enough alcohol to build up my nerve. I'd better be going. Drop by some time. So long." He left without waiting for Bunzō's farewell, hurrying off toward the back gate of the shrine. "Even he thinks I'm a coward," Bunzō said to himself as he watched him go.

B U N Z Ō went to Ishida's house and received some items for translation which had been left for him. He started back along the route he had come. The evening lamps were being lit in all the shops along the way by the time he reached Manaita bridge. He did not want to go home without eating because he was afraid they would say he could not afford to eat out, so he stopped in at a small restaurant.

The shop had apparently only just opened for business. It looked attractive enough from the outside but inside confusion reigned. There were a great many customers and the inexperienced waitresses were quite incapable of handling them. Things were mixed up at the counter too and the orders were late. Bunzō had to wait a long time for the meat and sake he had ordered. He asked the waitress for his dinner several times but still she did not bring it. Whenever she appeared with something, it turned out to be for customers who had arrived after him. Bunzō finally lost patience and furiously demanded to be served at once. He felt very vexed and irritated while he was eating and paid the check quickly, paying no attention to the proffered thanks. He considered himself lucky to escape from the bedlam.

He wandered through Jimbōchō, looking idly at the open stalls which lined the streets. Calmed by the sake, the turmoil within him gradually subsided, and thoughts of Noboru's insults, Osei's laughter, and the disturbing conversation with Yamaguchi were forgotten. Even the unpleasantness at the restaurant disappeared from his mind. He was aware only of the cool evening breezes which fanned his face. His peace, however, was not fated to last long.

He returned home. He casually opened the gate and went in. Laughter and voices came from the sitting room. He strained his ears and heard Noboru's voice among them; obviously he had not gone home yet. Bunzō hesitated. "If he's rude to me again," he thought angrily, "I won't be able to control myself." Steeling himself like a soldier before battle, Bunzo went around to the sitting room.

Inside he saw Noboru tottering unsteadily among the rubble of dirty dishes. On his back was pasted a round piece of paper. Beside him were Osei and Onabe, convulsed with laughter. Omasa was not in the room. They looked right at Bunzō but did not deign to speak to him. Even when he asked for his aunt, no one answered him. Trembling with rage, he walked away. From behind him he heard this:

"Now which of you did it?"

"It wasn't me. It was Onabe."

"It was the young lady."

"Well, it doesn't matter. I'll get even with both of you. I'll start with the chubby one."

"Not me, not me. Stop it! Help! Save me!"

The sound of scampering feet and riotous laughter mingled with the screaming voices as Osei wildly encouraged the maid to scratch Noboru.

Bunzō's attention was arrested by the uproar within the room and he stopped in the hall to listen. He was on the point of turning back when suddenly someone came along and ran into him before he could step aside.

"Watch out! What a place to be standing. Who is it anyway?" Omasa asked in an irritated voice.

"It's me. I'm terribly sorry. I hope you didn't hurt yourself."

Without answering him she went into the room and slammed the door behind her. The young man looked after her, rather hurt and, after a minute, went upstairs. He groped for the lamp, lit it, and crouched down near his desk.

"How disgusting," he thought to himself. "I don't give a damn about my aunt and Honda, but imagine Osei taking part in such a vulgar display. After all her talk about 'nobility.' Carrying on with him like that. What's she done with all her fine philosophy? Why did she bother studying to begin with? If you don't respect yourself, no one else will respect you, as the saying goes.* She ought to know that much at least. Imagine acting like that. It's disgusting. I just won't stand for such goings on when my uncle is away. I'll talk to my aunt very sternly about it tomorrow." He stopped short, remembering with a feeling of utmost despair his present ignoble position in the household.

Finally he recovered sufficiently to take out the copy he was to translate from English into Japanese and began to read it. "The ever-difficult task of defining the distinctive characters and aims of English political parties threatens to become more formidable with the increasing influence of what has hitherto been called the Radical party. For over fifty years the party. . . ."

His recital was interrupted by laughter from below. "How rude they are," he thought. "They know I'm home, yet they're so busy entertaining Honda that not one of them has come to ask me if I've eaten. More laughter. That was Osei. She can take up with anybody she likes for all I care. I'm through with her. Damn it. I'm a man. I'm not interested in a fickle girl like that." He began to read again with determination. "The ever-difficult task of defining the distinctive characters and aims of English political. . . ."

The front gate opened and the laughter ceased. Bunzō tried to make out what was going on. Someone rushed along the hall and he heard Onabe at the foot of the stairs asking

---

* *Mencius*, Book IV, Part I. James Legge, *The Chinese Classics* (London, 1861), II, 175.

about a lamp. Then it became completely quiet. Apparently another guest had come.

Bunzō had been able to guess what Osei and Noboru were doing downstairs as long as they were laughing and carrying on, but now that they were so quiet he became very uneasy. "Omasa must be in the front room entertaining the new guest," he calculated, "and if Onabe is with Osei it's all right. But if she is working in the kitchen instead, the two of them are alone." Bunzō jumped up and then sat down again. He remembered that he had been thirsty since dinner and he decided that just a sip of water would make him feel much better. Unfortunately water came only from the kitchen and there was no kitchen on the second floor. So if he wanted a drink he would absolutely have to go downstairs. "It may seem like an odd time to go to the kitchen," he reasoned with himself, "but it's ridiculous not to get some water when I'm this thirsty." He went down.

A small lamp was burning in the kitchen, but Onabe was not there. She had started to wash the dishes and then left them in the middle, indicating she had been sent out on an errand. He heard soft voices whispering in the sitting room but he could not make out what they were saying, although he tried very hard to. He stealthily drank some water and started to creep out of the kitchen when the door to the other room slid open. He wheeled around. Osei was standing with her back to him, grasping hold of the door, half in and half out of the room.

"Oh, come on back," said Noboru.

Osei shook her head coquettishly. "No, you're too naughty."

"I'll be good. Come on back."

"No."

"All right, if it's no, it's no."

"Promise you'll behave? Shall I come?" A coy tilt of the head.

"Oh, come on."

"No. You come here."

"You little devil." It sounded as if he were getting up.

Brimming with laughter, Osei turned and started to run away. She almost ran into Bunzō. "Bunzō! When did you get back?"

He said nothing and went stolidly upstairs.

Osei followed him and without further comment flopped down beside him. Her manner was more intimate and informal than usual. She scowled and swayed peculiarly as she said, "Honda is terribly bold."

Bunzō stared sternly at her, but love, alas, is a tricky thing. Even while he was trying to be firm he could not help but notice how lovely she was. He was very much in danger of weakening, but he caught himself in time and turned away, sneering icily.

Just then Noboru came thumping up the stairs. When he saw them he thrust out his chest and said in an affected manner, "So here's where you are. You just go off and desert such an important guest."

"Certainly, when you act like that."

"Like what?" he asked, sitting down.

"You know perfectly well. Like you did."

"This is getting us nowhere. Explain yourself, young lady."

"Shall I go ahead and say it?"

"Of course."

"All right, then. Here goes. Bunzō, he. . . ." She looked at Noboru and checked herself. "Maybe I'll forgive you."

"Can't get it out?" asked Noboru. "Then I'll say it for you. 'Just now Noboru. . . .'"

"Stop it!"

" 'Noboru tried to. . . .' "

"I didn't give you permission to tell him. Stop it."

"Are you afraid to have your lover hear it from me?"

"That has nothing to do with it. I'll get a bad reputation."

"Why?"

"Because I was insulted by you."

"That's ridiculous. I was just having a little fun."

"A little fun. May I be so bold as to ask you a question?

Just what do you believe in? You always pretend you want equal rights for women but you don't really."

"What do I want then?"

"Just the opposite."

"And if I do?"

"Then I don't want to have anything to do with you."

"That's a very harsh decision, isn't it? I'm just as conscientious about defending women's rights as anybody."

"No, you're not. You're just the kind of defender I hate. Conscientious or not."

"Then what more can I say? I think it's terrible of you to say you hate me. What kind of defender do you like?"

"Well, someone like. . . ." Her voice trailed off as she gazed up at the ceiling.

"Someone like Bunzō," Noboru suggested in a low voice.

"Yes," she whispered playfully in English, with a gesture of exaggerated coyness. Then she covered her face and burst out laughing.

Bunzō looked at her in surprise. The color drained from his face as he realized he was being made a fool of.

"I'm terribly, terribly jealous," countered Noboru. "What do you think of that piece of news, Utsumi? 'I like a man like Bunzō,' she said. However shall I bear it? I won't be able to sleep tonight."

"Say what you will, all I meant was that I like a man who defends women's rights the way Bunzō does. I didn't say I like Bunzō, so stop it."

"What kind of excuse is that? If you like a man like Bunzō, you must like him."

"All right, then, I do like Bunzō, but he hates me, so you can forget all about it. Isn't that so, Bunzō?"

"He hates you? Oh no, on the contrary. He's head over heels in love with you."

Bunzō was enraged. Osei caught a glimpse of his expression. "You've been joking too much. Bunzō is angry."

"He just looks that way because he can't tell you how

happy he is. Anyone can see what a handsome fellow he is, so strong and silent. If his chin were just a little shorter, he'd be perfect." Noboru ended with a laugh. Giggling, Osei glanced at her cousin again from the corner of her eye. "Utsumi is such a lucky fellow to have a beautiful girl like you taking care of him," Noboru continued, slapping Osei's knee. "And the way you protect him when his aunt picks on him. In fact, you protect him all the time. I'm so envious. He's the Tanji of the Meiji era,* a veritable Don Juan. What I wouldn't do to be like him." He and Osei laughed again. "Hey, you handsome fellow. Stop frowning and tell me about your romance. Come on, Tanji. Why don't you answer?"

Osei gave a forced laugh, glancing at Bunzō again. "I'm thirsty from laughing so much," she said. "Shall I go down and make some tea?"

"Why don't you stay with your lover for a few minutes so he can look at you?"

"That's enough nonsense. Shall I bring the tea up here?"

"I'd rather have some cold water."

"With sugar?"

"No, thanks."

"Lemon?"

"If you put in lemon, you'd better put in some sugar too."

"You're being so difficult," she exclaimed as she stood up. She left the room.

The two men sat in embarrassed silence for a few minutes

* "Tanji" or "Tanjirō" was widely used as a nickname for a man notorious for his powers with women and also implied that the man was weak and cowardly. The origin of the name was the popular love story by Tamenaga Shunsui (1790–1843) entitled *Shunshoku umegoyomi,* published in 1833–34. The hero, Tanjirō, is tricked out of his family fortune by the villain and, through the intercession of two geisha, is taken into one of the licensed quarters in Edo to live. All ends happily after a long series of romantic entanglements. Tanjirō recovers his fortune, marries the girl he was originally supposed to, and takes one of the geisha as his mistress. *Nihon bungaku daijiten,* IV, 18–19. For the text, see *Umegoyomi harutsuge-dori* ("Teikoku Bunkō," Tokyo, 1909), X, 76–224.

until Bunzō spoke in a subdued voice. "Honda, are you drunk?"

"No."

"Then I want to ask you something. Wouldn't you say that friends have to respect each other?"

"What? What on earth are you talking about? Yes, I suppose they have to."

Bunzō started to go on but fell silent again. Then he continued, his voice trembling. "We've been friends for some time but tonight is the end. I don't want to have anything more to do with you."

"What brought this on all of a sudden?"

"Ask yourself the reason."

"Don't say such crazy things. I can't think of any reason."

"You can't? After insulting someone like that?"

"Insulting someone? Who? When? What are you talking about?"

"Oh, what's the use." Bunzō stared hard at Noboru. His voice grew louder. "Why are you pretending that you don't know what I'm talking about? I'm trying to end our friendship in a decent, dignified way—even somebody like you ought to be treated like a human being. But you go on acting so innocent after you insulted me, not once, but twice."

"I wish you'd speak plainly when you're talking to me. I'm not sorry to lose you for a friend, so you can just go ahead and stop seeing me for all I care. But how do you expect me to understand what you're talking about when you just keep babbling that I've insulted you?"

"Why did you tell me to swallow my pride in front of my aunt and cousin?"

"Is that what's bothering you?"

"It most certainly is. And why did you call me the Tanji of the Meiji period? That's tantamount to saying I'm a coward."

"You are a strange one. What else?"

"It doesn't make any difference what kind of insults they

were. You have embarrassed me by saying that I was a Tanji and that I was too proud. It all amounts to the same thing. It is a product of your scorn. Friendship is impossible with such scorn. I suggest we stop seeing each other. Have I made myself clear?"

"Anything else?"

"I'm not in any position to forbid you to see the Sono-das so it's none of my business if you come here every day and play cards with my aunt and," he sneered, "and treat my cousin as if she were a geisha. I'm not going to criticize your behavior so you don't have to struggle to invent excuses."

"How your jealousy shows. Anything else?"

"I have nothing further to say. And what's more there's no need for you to say anything more. I just wish you'd get out of here."

"On the contrary, I have been unjustly accused and I have to explain myself. I won't go until I have. Why was it an insult to advise you to swallow your pride? I could under-stand a stranger being insulted if I spoke too frankly, but I thought we were friends."

"There are rules of behavior even between friends. It's not right for you to tell me such a thing."

"Why not? I just said you should swallow your pride. Or did I say 'It would be better' if you did? I forget which, but either way I only meant it as advice. I'm not trying to imi-tate you and pretend I'm a philosopher, but generally you give somebody advice when you see him make a mistake. You wouldn't have to say anything if what he did was wise and correct. If it's insulting to call a mistake a mistake, then all advice is an insult. If my advice makes you angry, I won't say another word. I apologize. Was that what was wrong?"

"I'm always happy to get advice. But what you said was not intended as advice. You meant it as an insult."

"What makes you so sure?"

"Why else would you have said it with other people around?"

"Weren't they members of your own family?"

Bunzō was reluctantly forced to agree with him. Noboru laughed at his confusion. "They are part of my family," Bunzō finally conceded, "but oughtn't you to have been less offensive?"

"You keep changing your train of thought and I find it hard to follow you. Do you mean you were offended by the way I spoke to you?"

"Yes, by your tone and attitude as much as by what you said."

"Then I can only ask to be excused again. You may have taken it as an insult but I only meant to give you some good advice. Shall we forget it? There's no need to put an end to our friendship after all, is there?"

Bunzō could not think of a good way to answer him and his frustration made him even more furious. Under different circumstances Noboru's superficial cleverness would not have bothered him, but as things were he grew more and more enraged with each passing minute. Noboru began to laugh in a loud, theatrical manner. Perspiration stood out on the tip of Bunzō's nose. He bit his lower lip and yet he could only stare in angry silence at his enemy.

Osei came back carrying a glass of water filled to the brim on the tray. "Here you are," she said.

"Sorry to have kept you waiting," he countered.

"What's that?"

"What?"

"Such an innocent expression?"

Noboru laughed. "What took you so long?"

"I had something else to do."

"You weren't busy with somebody else, were you?"

"I'm not you," she retorted.

"And I'm not as fickle as all that, young lady. You're going to bring up the chief's sister-in-law, I can tell. I have Bunzō to use against you so I can get even, I warn you."

"What a funny person you are. You're suspicious before I've even said anything."

Turning to Bunzō, he said, "Speaking of suspicions, how are we doing, Captain? Are you still angry?"

"Everything you said was just an excuse," Bunzō said.

"What do you mean?"

"I don't need to explain. It's a 'self-evident truth.'"

"Have we progressed to the exalted level of a 'self-evident truth'?"

"What's the matter?" Osei asked.

"Listen to this. We are having a most interesting discussion." He turned to Bunzō again. "We've disposed of one problem. Let's go on to the other. What was that about now? Oh yes, Tanji. How did I insult you by calling you Tanji? Is that a 'self-evident truth' too?"

"What's wrong?" Osei asked.

"He said I offended him by calling him Tanji. He's obviously furious about it. I'm afraid your boyfriend is still just a country boy at heart."

"Honda," Bunzō said.

Noboru put down the glass from which he had started to drink. "Uhm?"

"There's no point in arguing with you. First you insult me and then say I have misjudged your motives. And to make matters worse, you have the effrontery to try to get out of it by inventing excuses. I have nothing else to say except that I will not change my mind. I don't want to have anything more to do with you. Get out."

"You really are a poor sport, aren't you?"

"What did you say?"

"You just can't take it, can you? Surely you must be able to see how badly you're behaving."

"Don't be so rude. Wouldn't it be better to go after I've asked you to?"

"Please stop it," cried Osei.

"Now Osei is worried too," Noboru said with a laugh. "She's right. We'd better stop. Come on, Utsumi, smile. This is really ridiculous. You say you don't want to see me any more because you were hurt by the way I spoke to you. Aren't you being childish? Think how foolish it makes you look. Let's have a smile."

Bunzō was silent.

"Still no good? What can I do? All right then, I'll take the blame for the whole thing. I really didn't mean it the way it sounded, and if I hurt your feelings, I most humbly apologize. Will that do?"

Bunzō spoked with ill-suppressed rage. "I asked you to leave."

"You still won't forgive me? In that case I'll go. You won't listen to anything I have to say now anyway. You're too excited."

"What did you say?"

"I was talking to myself," Noboru answered, getting up.

"Fool."

At last it was Noboru's turn to be offended. He stopped and looked hard at Bunzō. Then he grinned. "You don't know what you're saying." He went downstairs.

Osei got up and followed Noboru, looking back at Bunzō over her shoulder. Bunzō gnashed his teeth and banged on the desk with a clenched fist. "Damn it," he cried. He heard Osei and Noboru laughing together at the foot of the stairs.

THE FAMILY gathered at breakfast the next morning. Both Bunzō and Omasa scowled throughout the meal and barely said a word. Osei, by contrast, was restless and fidgety, chirping away and tittering foolishly. Silenced by a sudden thought, she would become serious for a moment and then stare at Bunzō, hovering on the brink of laughter. Her face reflected a great range of emotions. When the meal ended, she got up and left the room. They heard her joking with Onabe in the hall and then softly reciting Chinese poems in her room.

His frown deepening, Bunzō started to rise, but Omasa indicated that he should stay. He glanced at her face and concluded unhappily that it looked particularly long and sharp that morning.

Omasa blew several smoke rings, slowly and deliberately, and watched Onabe clear away the dishes before she said anything. "I'm sure you'd rather I kept out of it, but I gather from the way you turned down Noboru's kind suggestion yesterday that you must have found some other job. Otherwise you couldn't possibly have rejected his generous offer so abruptly."

"I had other reasons. I don't have another job."

"And yet you foolishly refused his help?"

"I know it seems ridiculous when I haven't been able to think of any alternative. But that was just a rumor anyway."

Osei passed the room on her way to her English lesson. She generally went on her daily round without saying goodbye to her mother.

"It's obviously just a rumor," he went on.

"Well, what of it? Will they announce it officially?"

"I shouldn't think so."

"Then you have to depend on rumors, don't you?"

"Of course, but when Honda says something. . . ."

"You can't rely on it," she said, finishing his sentence.

"I didn't mean to imply that. But no matter how desperate I am, I couldn't go to the chief for—for that."

"Are you going to tell me you couldn't ask him for a favor, no matter what? Such arrogance!"

Bunzō became very upset at this new outburst. "That wasn't my only reason. I couldn't possibly manage to stay on there very long even if they did take me back. It would be much better if I didn't try to go back in government service. I'm not suited for it."

"You're going to give up the government? I can't understand what you mean. Just the other day when I asked you what you'd do, you said you'd look for another government job. Now you've changed your mind. It doesn't matter if your mother starves. Go ahead and forget about a government job."

"That's not what I meant at all. There are other places where I can work, you know. I could even support my mother by teaching."

"Nobody said you couldn't. It's all up to you. You can become a teacher or a rickshaw man or anything else you please for all I care."

"But you're so angry."

"Who said anything about being angry? It's no business of mine what you do. Nobody's getting upset or angry over it one way or the other. My only point is that Noboru spoke to you very considerately. If you let him help you, the chief might very well take an interest in you and do something for you later on, even if he can't take you back now. I was thinking about your mother as well as you. I just want to see— well, I just want to see everyone and everything settled once and for all. (Bunzō's head shot up at this hint and he stared at her.) That's why I brought the matter up. But there's nothing more to be said if you won't accept his help." She was silent for a minute and then called the maid, who thrust her face in at the door. The girl was chewing on something. "Haven't you finished eating?"

"No, not yet."

"Well, when you're done, order a rickshaw for me. I'll need it to go to Hamachō and back."

"Right away."

Bunzō waited impatiently for the maid to leave and then turned again to his aunt. "I'm sure you're quite right in what you say. My stubbornness has caused both you and my mother all kinds of trouble. I'll think the matter over again carefully."

"It won't make any difference, will it? You've already made up your mind not to work for the government."

"Yes, but—if it will do any good—well, maybe I should reconsider."

Omasa smiled icily. "Then think it over. It's all the same to us if you don't go back. Do as you please." Bunzō nodded meekly. "There's something else I'd like to mention while I have you here. I understand that you quarreled with Noboru last night. That puts me in a very embarrassing position. He's a friend of yours and you are free to say what you like to him, but he is also a guest in our house." Bunzō's thoughts lingered on her earlier hint and he nodded at the appropriate time without actually understanding what she said. "He's so good-natured that he probably won't let that stop him from helping you if you'll let him, and maybe. . . ." Omasa stopped herself from dropping further hints. "At any rate, there's no point in going into any other considerations now. Let's wait until you've made your decision."

Bunzō looked up, returning suddenly from his reverie.
"Yes?"

"I suggested we wait."

Mumbling politely, he returned to his room. He stood stiffly in the center of the floor for some time, lost in thought. "What should I do?" he groaned at last and sank to the floor, dissolving like a snowman in the sun.

What was his dilemma?

Bunzō's first reaction to his aunt's attack on him over losing his job had been hurt and rage. He was certain at the time that she was a cold, insincere woman. When his initial anger had died down, he began to suspect that he might be mistaken in passing such a severe judgment. Certainly she was not particularly wise or strong-willed and she obviously could not understand what her nephew thought and felt, but she was by no means a total fool. She had her own opinions about things and at times was quite logical. She also understood how people should act. Then why was she so angry about his job? She knew how irrational it was and yet she succumbed to wave after wave of fury. Why had she forced poor, innocent Bunzō to beg her forgiveness on his hands and knees?

He had believed that the answer lay in the fact that she did not want Osei to marry him. This was obviously not the case. How could she possibly have been planning to let them marry all along and then have changed her mind the minute she heard the bad news? Would she have decided so quickly to infuriate him and alienate him from Osei? It was hardly likely.

Torn by these contradictions, Bunzō set out to reexamine the events of the past few days: his aunt's complaints, the angry tone of her voice, the expression on her face, everything that might explain her attitude. After careful deliberation he finally realized how he had hurt her by refusing Noboru's offer.

There was no doubt, he reasoned, that Omasa had long been looking forward to seeing Osei happily married. She had been awaiting the coming spring eagerly and had been secretly planning the wedding trousseau. His disastrous failure had completely shattered her hopes, and she had grown despondent. It was the sort of despair that often leads to nagging and complaining. "I may have been altogether wrong in thinking she hates me. Perhaps she spoke as she did only out of her disappointment," he said to himself.

Bunzō's rancor began to seep away. He felt, instead, terribly sorry for his aunt. They had both altered so much so quickly.

In the five short days since their argument her manner and appearance had undergone a complete transformation. Bunzō had never been a great favorite of hers and she had never treated him especially courteously, but she had always been casual and pleasant. Now her eyes were stormy and a sardonic smile twisted her lips. Her words had been direct and without maliciousness; now they were biting and cruel. Her intimate manner was replaced by an unnatural coldness. Everything about her was belligerent. When Bunzō spoke to her, she either pretended not to hear him or narrowed her eyes and glowered disapprovingly. All of this strange, bitter reaction on her part was a direct result of his losing his job.

Bunzō was loyal and faithful to his family. No matter how badly Omasa treated him, she was his aunt, and he felt deeply grateful for all she had done for him in the past. He wanted to give her his love and respect and to get along well with her. Above all, he wanted to avoid any misunderstanding between them. But we cannot help reacting to what happens around us. Whenever Omasa hurt him, he suffered and, for an instant, longed to show her how deeply she was tormenting him, but his fine inclinations usually forced him to hold back his anger. Deep in his heart he knew, as he had always known, that he must close his eyes to her cruelty and accept it in silence.

Bunzō understood how painful it must have been to her to realize that this uncertainty in his life had put Osei's future in doubt. Very few people can suffer in silence and manage to get by when faced with a problem. Most cannot. They will find the cause of their suffering in someone else rather than themselves. If that proves impossible, they will blame fate instead. But if there is someone they can accuse, they will hate that person. Otherwise they would never find consolation. Bunzō realized that this is what had happened to his aunt. He decided he would shut his eyes and remain silent no matter what she said.

Believing that "sincerity moves even heaven," * as the ancients said, Bunzō had been trying to win his aunt's affection whenever he had the chance. Unfortunately his efforts made little impression. He was convinced that he would be the happiest man on earth if she could only care more for him and sympathize with his problems as his mother did, but she rejected his every overture and remained aloof and adamant, causing him the greatest unhappiness.

He might have borne even the pain of this rejection were it not for his one great, overwhelming worry. It now appeared that Omasa was trying to come between Osei and him. So far she contented herself with warning Osei not to be as friendly with him as she had been in the past. She had not yet taken any steps that would keep them apart, but his mind recoiled with horror at the thought of what she might do if she continued in her present state of mind. Doubts and suspicions rose in his mind; ghosts and phantoms loomed up before him. He created a living hell for himself out of these fantasies, and the more he pursued them, the further he sank into an abyss of pain.

Since Omasa's first hint that morning, he had been wondering whether he should do as she suggested. She was used to having her own way. He understood now what an effort it must have cost her to suggest so gently that "everyone and everything would be settled" if he relented a little. His aunt would undoubtedly be furious if he refused to give in and he

* *The Book of Documents,* The Counsels of the Great Yu, Legge, Vol. III, Part 1, p. 66.

did not want to sow the seeds of further discord. On the other hand, if he agreed to do as she suggested, she would be mollified, and he might be able to marry Osei. He would make his mother happy and find some rest for his troubled mind.

"Should I forget about conscience and honor and go to see the chief as she wants me to?" he asked himself. "She would be satisfied if I made a casual inquiry, and things might work out, assuming Osei still wants me. Besides, no one could accuse me of being a coward for doing it. My own mother has been terribly upset and I should be prepared to make whatever sacrifice is necessary for her sake anyway."

But as a consequence he would have to become friendly with Noboru again, much as he hated to. Were he to bypass Noboru and try to win over the chief on his own, Noboru, the sneak, would be sure to interfere. He would have to apologize to him. Bunzō might compromise his honor, crush his self-respect, and cajole the chief for his mother and Osei, but no matter how destitute he was, no matter how great his suffering, he could not bow to Noboru—Noboru who had arrogantly told him to swallow his pride, who had toyed with him like a child and pretended to accept defeat while actually winning a great victory. Noboru was his sworn and hated enemy. He despised him intensely. He could never under any circumstances ask him for a favor. Bunzō did not worry whether cajoling the chief was the same as asking Noboru for something. He only knew that, right or wrong, whatever the results, he could not kowtow to him.

The alternatives as he saw them were terrible: he must either defy his aunt or kowtow to Noboru. For two hours Bunzō sat in his room, lost in thought, trying to work out a solution to the problem.

Even the most hopeless suffering must end sometime.* Bunzō reached a decision: he would talk to Osei.

* Literally, "Everything must end; the oldest mat becomes a soaring bird," a quotation from the story of a hostess at a wayside inn by Naoe Mokudō (1666–1723), a haiku poet of Bashō's school. It was included in the *Fūzoku*

To a degree, he felt that Omasa was right in what she said. He also hated to see her when she was angry. But the real reason he did not want to defy her was that he was afraid of having to break with Osei. When he had definitely determined that Osei loved him, he would be able to endure any amount of suffering. It would be possible to refuse his aunt's request and then he would not have to lower himself to Noboru. With the power of Osei's love, he would stand firm were the heavens to storm and the earth to decay; the seas to dry up and the rocks to crumble. Omasa's disapproval, indeed even the most dire poverty, would mean nothing. "A brave man is ashamed to succumb to want." *

Yes. His need for Osei's love was at the very root of his dilemma. With her assurance, his confusion would vanish. He would know what to do. Why had he not realized that from the very beginning? He would talk to Osei. That was the best possible solution; he would not find a better alternative.

If Osei accepted their current problems as merely a temporary setback on the path of their unchanging love and shared his thoughts and feelings, anything which was hateful to Bunzō would be hateful to her. She would not want him to degrade himself. She would say, "It doesn't matter what Mother tells you to do. Don't ask Noboru for any favors." And when he asked her for assurance of her future loyalty, she would say, in a sad voice, "Do you think me such a fickle girl?" With such words, he would fear no man. He would walk through fire or plunge into the sea. And merely defying his aunt would become an insignificant challenge, something to be finished off before breakfast.

Happy with his decision, he rose. But again he hesitated. "Judging by the way things have looked lately, maybe she finds Honda . . . what if she . . . well, it doesn't matter. If she does, I'll let it go at that. I'm a man, after all. I won't

monzen compiled by Morikawa Kyoroku (1656–1715) and first published in 1706. Kijitsu-an Kinkō, *Fūzoku monzen tsūshaku*, pp. 373–74.

* A reference to the *Analects,* Book XV, 1. Legge, I, 294.

shed any tears over a fickle woman. I'll break off with her for good. This time I'll do something and show them how brave I am. I'll get the best of Honda yet. She'll be sorry." He went down the stairs, mumbling defiant words to himself.

Isn't this strange? He managed to forget that Osei had not sympathized with him about the excursion to Dangozaka and how she had acted after she came home. The way she had laughed behind his back and her behavior when he was quarreling with Noboru were put out of his mind. In his heart of hearts Bunzō still believed that Osei loved him and had always loved him. He was certain that when he talked to her she would agree with him and encourage him in his plans. He had no reason to feel this way. He felt this way because he wanted to.

B u n z ō came down the stairs. Osei was sitting in her room, chin in hand, lost in thought. She stirred a little as he slowly opened the door. She must have been in the same position a long time for her hand had left a red mark on her cheek.

"May I come in?"

"Of course."

He sat down. "I must apologize for last night."

"Oh, that's all right."

"No, I mean it. I'm awfully sorry. I shouldn't have done anything like that in front of you. Your mother scolded me this morning about it."

Osei's laugh was forced and cold. Her manner was markedly different from what it had been that morning.

"There's something I'd like to talk over with you. Your mother was saying—perhaps she's told you about it?"

"No."

"Of course, she hasn't been home. Well, she suggested I see the chief and let Honda do what he can for me because he'd been so kind about offering to help. As your mother says, if I agreed I could get started on my career again and make my mother happy. Everybody and everything (he stressed these words) would be settled once and for all. I'd do it if I could, but it would mean sacrificing my sense of honor and decency. I'd have to go crawling to the chief. That would be impossible for people like us, wouldn't it?"

"If you feel you can't, that's all there is to it."

"But I'm afraid that if I don't, your mother will be furious."

"I don't see how that matters."

"You don't care?" he asked, smiling happily.

"It's not that I don't care. I shouldn't think it would matter what anybody said as long as you do what you think is right without making any compromises."

He stopped smiling. "I'm not so worried about her being angry but I'm very frightened of what might happen as a result. It could bring about something which would be terribly painful to me, although I'm not sure whether it matters so much to you. That's why I'm so uncertain about what to do. It all depends on. . . ." There was a long pause. He finished in a barely audible whisper, ". . . depends on you." He lowered his eyes.

It was hard to tell if Osei realized what he meant. She was perfectly casual as she said, "I still don't understand what you're talking about. What's so terrible about going to see the chief? Isn't it the same as asking Mr. Ishida for a favor?"

"It is not," he answered, looking up. "It's entirely different. Ishida understands me. The chief doesn't."

"How can you be so sure? You haven't tried asking him yet."

"I can tell from past experience. It's perfectly obvious that he doesn't. And anyway, if I did go to see him, it would mean making up with Honda first, although the chief is my chief too."

"Well, what if you did have to make up with Noboru?"

"Do you want me to?" Bunzō's expression began to change.

"I don't say you must, but shouldn't you anyway?"

"Make up with Honda?" he said, as if he could not believe his own ears.

"Yes."

"That loathsome insect? That lackey?"

"What a terrible thing to say."

"Lackey is too good a word for him. You want me to go groveling to a skunk like that?" He glared at her.

"You're just angry because of what happened last night. He's not such a bad person."

"Oh no?" Bunzō turned away, a pained smile on his face. He turned back quickly. "But when he was bold with you the other day you felt differently, didn't you?"

"I was angry at the time but since then I've seen more of him and I'm sure he's not as bad as you say."

He stared at her in silence. It was a bad sign.

"When we went down last night after your quarrel he told me not to say anything about it because Mother would get angry. He didn't want to get you in trouble. I didn't tell her. Onabe did."

"What a sneak he is! He said not to tell?"

"There you go again. You're terrible, Bunzō. He asked me to be quiet for your sake even though you were so insulting, and you call him a sneak." Her face grew red and her words came more quickly. "The reason you can't get along with him is that your personalities are so different. You're so quiet and he's so lively. But you can't dislike someone just because he's different. You mustn't go around insulting people and using such terrible language."

Bunzō was furious. "Are you trying to tell me you've taken a liking to Honda?"

"That has nothing to do with it. He's not what you say he is. You have no right to insult somebody for no reason at all and call him such dreadful names."

His tone became more belligerent. "Just answer my question. Do you mean you've taken a liking to him?"

Now Osei was angry. She glanced sharply at him. "Why do you ask? What business is it of yours?"

"It is my business."

"In what way?"

"It doesn't matter in what way. I don't have to explain myself."

"Then I don't have to answer your question."

"All right. Forget it." He averted his eyes. He went on speaking, sadly, as if he were talking to himself. "Avoiding an answer—what a sneaky way to act."

"What did you say? Sneaky? All right then. If that's the way it's going to be, there's no point in my hiding it. I'll give you your answer." She paused and then went on defiantly. "Yes, I've become quite fond of Noboru. What of it?"

Bunzō trembled and turned ashen. He could not speak. He stared at her with hatred and his eyes became damp. He recovered himself quickly. "So that's the way it is, is it?" His voice trembled. "Everything that's happened up till now. . . ." He could not go on; his heart was too full. After a moment he steadied himself. ". . . is so much water over the dam."

"What do you mean by everything that's happened?"

"Oh, stop pretending. If we're going to break off, can't we do it nicely?"

"Who's pretending? Who's doing the breaking off?"

"Come now, you can do better than that." His voice was shrill with anger. "Who indeed? All this time you've been toying with my affections and now you take up with Honda, and all you can do is try to twist my words around."

"Who's been toying with your affections? Tell me who?" There were tears in her eyes. He stared without saying a word. "Stop insulting me. You're so conceited. Heaven knows what you've been dreaming up in your own mind."

Bunzō jumped up while she was still talking. "I have nothing more to say. I won't listen to another word. I'll never speak to you again. Don't forget that."

"I certainly won't."

"And I hope you have many, many love affairs!"

"What?" But Bunzō had already left the room. "Damn.

The idiot. What do I care if he never speaks to me again. The idiot."

Osei was still angrily cursing to herself when her mother came in. She had just returned home. "What's the matter?" she asked.

"Damn it."

"I asked you what was wrong."

"I had a fight with Bunzō, damn him."

"Why?"

"He came bursting in here to talk over what you'd said to him this morning. I tried to reason with him the way you told me to last night but. . . ." Omasa cautioned her to lower her voice. ". . . but he got angry and said all kinds of things to me." She told her mother briefly what had happened, leaving out anything that might put her in an unfavorable light. "It was simply terrible," she concluded, wiping her tears on her sleeve.

"Is that the way he spoke to you? Well, then that really is the end. I didn't want to interfere with your father's plans since Bunzō is his nephew. I've tried to help that young man by making a few suggestions, hoping he'd come around, but if he's going to be so arrogant and selfish, I just can't forgive him." She stopped to think for a moment and then turned to her daughter and said, in a lower voice, "I've kept this a secret from you till now. Your father intends to have you marry Bunzō some day. I don't think you like the idea now."

"No! Never!"

"Are you sure?"

"I'd rather starve!"

"Then don't forget what you've said now, because if you're absolutely certain, I have a plan in mind."

"Mother, let me move to a boardinghouse."

"Now what—out of the blue?"

"I don't want to see Bunzō again."

"Well, you'll have to anyway. Have a little patience. I'll straighten everything out soon enough."

Osei was silent and thoughtful.

"From now on, you should pay attention to my advice. Don't talk to Bunzō so much."

"I'll never speak to him again."

"That applies to Noboru too. Don't carry on so freely with him the way you did last night. I'm sure you wouldn't do anything wrong, but this is the most important time in your life, right before you're married."

"You sound like somebody else. Don't worry. From now on I won't even speak to him when he comes."

"I didn't mean that. Just don't act the way you did last night."

"I won't even talk to him any more."

"But I said you could."

"I won't, I won't." She shook her head back and forth violently.

"You're crazy. All I have to do is say a word and you get angry. You're impossible." Omasa rose and left the room.

UKIGUMO, PART THREE

Chapter 13*

THERE is a great deal to be learned from studying the psychology of any man, be he wise or foolish. An examination of the mental processes of Utsumi Bunzō will prove this.

When Bunzō was rebuked by Osei, he returned to his room where he gave himself over to a fit of blind rage. Osei's declaration of love for Honda alone did not enrage him; she may have said it in the heat of the moment without really meaning it. Rather he felt he had been thoroughly deceived by her in another matter as well.

Soon after, he left the house, determined to rent a room somewhere. Not that he was fully resigned to giving up Osei. It was the growing certainty that he would eventually have to that unsettled him. This time there was no debate about whether he should move or not. He tried to rush ahead and do it although his every instinct was against it. Bring on the poison. He would drink it and ruin his life.

If he was to move, he should take rooms far away. He looked for a place in Hongō but found nothing. Then, finally, after he had been wandering about Koishikawa for some time, he located a vacancy in a house in Suidōchō. The room was quite adequate and the price was fair. When he realized

* The chapters in Part Three do not have titles; no explanation has been offered for this.

he should take this room, if any, he found himself hesitating again. "I'll have to think it over," he mumbled as he left.

As he walked along, he became more and more timid about moving. "My uncle will be very upset when he hears I left because I quarreled with Osei. But I can't stay there any more. Why don't I just take that room and get it over with?" The best course of action still eluded him. Irresolute and disturbed, he looked at his watch and saw that it was only three thirty. He did not want to go home that early. He walked on to the Ushigome gate, talking to himself about his troubles and startling passersby. In Banchō he stopped at Ishida's house.

Fortunately the man was back from school and saw Bunzō at once, but the interview was far from satisfactory. He went on and on about classroom problems and his former students, his travels abroad, London, the *Times,* and Herbert Spencer.

"I may have to move to a boardinghouse," Bunzō ventured.

"How lucky you are. I wish I were free to live like that again," Ishida answered enviously, not realizing how unhappy Bunzō was. The young man left soon after.

He had been full of energy when he started out that afternoon. Now he could barely drag himself back home. It was about eight o'clock. He looked about for Osei but did not see her. Why should he want to see a girl he had broken with? "Human nature," Bunzō would say, "is a strange thing."

When Onabe came up with the charcoal, he made casual inquiries. Osei had not felt well, the maid said, and had gone to bed with hardly anything to eat.

"She didn't eat?"

"Hardly anything," the girl confirmed.

His first reaction was regret and concern. His mood changed quickly. "She'll probably be wanting some nice hot noodles soon," he said with a malicious laugh.

Onabe thought this response rather peculiar, but she had been away earlier in the day and knew nothing of their quarrel. She went downstairs.

Alone, he laughed derisively once more. But this was no time to be thinking about stupid, mundane things. He must concentrate on finding an adequate excuse to offer his uncle. Still his mind kept wandering and he could not concentrate. He tried to return to the problem of what to tell his uncle, but he could not. He kept thinking of something totally unrelated. No matter how he tried to extricate himself from this distraction he could not. Despite his irritation, he thought of Osei and began to worry about her. He tried over and over to stifle thoughts of her, but it was impossible. "What if she too is suffering now as I am?" All at once Bunzō regretted what he had done that day, and he grew flustered and ashamed of himself.

Bunzō had a reputation for being more likely to apologize than rebuke. Surely there is something in that.

Chapter 14

B UNZŌ awoke early the next morning after a troubled night's sleep. He heard the crows calling, the squeak of the shutters being opened, and the creaking of the bucket as it was drawn from the well. Although he was still tired, he got up and went downstairs. A sleepy-faced Onabe was lighting a fire under the kettle. No one else was up yet. There was no reason to expect to see Osei at that hour; she always slept late. He was certain she would not be nice to him and yet he longed desperately to find out how she was.

A half hour passed, then an hour. Soon she would be getting up, he thought expectantly, and she would come in, beautiful, her hair tousled, her face still pale with sleep, her eyes ever so slightly puffy. And only yesterday this same young man was determined to move to a boardinghouse!

He finished breakfast and was on his way out of the sitting room when Osei finally emerged. They met in the hall. Bunzō was visibly ruffled despite all the preparations he had made in his mind. The girl merely glanced at him indifferently and went on into the room. That was all there was to it.

That was quite enough, however, for her look burned deeply, unforgettably into him. His heart contracted and he became terribly depressed. Shortly before noon the clouds of the morning turned to rain, and as the drops fell he grew utterly disconsolate.

Saying she was ill, Osei did not go for her English lesson. She stayed quietly in her room. He saw her again at lunch where she carefully avoided looking directly at him and assumed a most indifferent expression whenever their eyes chanced to meet. The nastiest look would have been less painful. Between her cold glances, the general depression in the household, and the ceaseless beating of the rain, Bunzō felt he wanted to weep.

It stopped raining as the wretched day finally drew to a close. Noboru stopped by for a visit. His cheerful voice called out from the gate and Onabe welcomed him with a boisterous laugh. Osei was in the sitting room at the time and tried to get up and leave, but Noboru caught sight of her and she sat down again, unable to escape. He knew nothing of what had been happening and began to joke with her suggestively as usual. She refused to smile and merely bowed stiffly as duty required. He was puzzled and on the point of asking what was wrong when Omasa diverted his attention with a great stream of chatter. One would have thought she had not spoken to anyone for days. This gave Osei the opportunity she had been waiting for and she tried to slip out again. Noboru saw her and asked where she was going. She left the room, pretending she had not heard him.

Her room was pitch black. Groping about, she found matches but could not locate the lamp. Onabe must have forgotten to bring it. She called the maid, waited a minute, and called again. There was no reply. She shouted over and over and was about to give up when the foolish girl finally responded. "I've been calling and calling you. Why didn't you answer?"

"I was busy in the back."

"What has that got to do with it?"

"I'm sorry. What did you want?"

"Oh, nothing, nothing at all. Don't you realize I'm in the dark?"

It took several more tries before Onabe finally got the point and brought the lamp. The inconsiderate girl left without shutting the door behind her.

Swearing at the maid in a most unbecoming way, Osei got up and pushed the door closed. She had just settled down beside her desk when the door was opened again. Cursing to herself, Osei wheeled around. To her surprise, it was her mother. She turned away.

Omasa called to her urgently. Osei was obviously irritated at being bothered. "Why are you acting so peculiarly? Noboru will wonder what's the matter with you. Come back." Omasa waited a moment. Her daughter gave no indication that she would go. Omasa raised her voice. "When I say come, come."

"You have no right to talk to me like that," she answered, lifting her head.

Omasa saw tears in her eyes and for a moment was at a loss what to say. "All right, do what you like," she began, but her tone softened as she went on trying to coax the girl to join them.

Osei did not answer.

"Oh, for heaven's sake. Then stay here by yourself," she said in disgust and returned to the sitting room.

It was her own fault that she was being left out this way, but still Osei felt very annoyed as she sat there waiting for someone to come back for her. No one came. Even if they had, her pride would not have let her join them. Meanwhile she could hear them laughing and gossiping merrily together. In a fury, she picked up a colored pencil and began to mark up the cover of her brand new textbook. Poor Swinton!

She had just finished making the cover a lurid shade of green when someone came down the hall. Quickly she opened the book and pretended to study the contents carefully, not noticing that it was upside down. It looked for all the world as if she had been lost in her studies for hours.

The door slid open. Osei trembled, her eyes still on the book. Noboru came in casually. She knew who it was before he spoke. "You ran away," he said cheerfully. "Am I too handsome for you?"

Osei raised her head slowly and spoke in a cold, calm voice. "I'm sorry, but I haven't finished my lessons for tomorrow."

Noboru was not one to be put off so easily. "I don't mind," he said, settling down beside her.

"Really, I'm not finished yet."

"What's the matter? Did your mother scold you? No? Well then, what can it be?" He tilted his head and thought a moment, then slapped his side. "Oh, I see. Now I understand. You should have told me sooner. You're fascinated with me, aren't you? And you couldn't say anything in front of your mother. That must be it. So you lured me in here. How marvelous. Let me hear you say you love me. You'd make me so happy. If I'm right, everything will be fine, don't worry, because I've liked you for a long time. We'd go together hand in glove. No problems. Let's have a little hug before anything gets in the way." He held out his arms and drew closer to her.

"I'm trying to work," she cried as she pulled away from him.

"No good? Sorry, sorry," he said, realizing his timing was a bit off. Just then, Onabe called to him from the hallway. Seeing that he was not getting anywhere with Osei and that she would probably burst out crying if he touched her, he was happy enough to escape.

Meanwhile upstairs Bunzō moved restlessly about his room. He had been very uneasy ever since Noboru came. He heard their voices, but only dimly. Finally he could restrain himself no longer and he invented an excuse to go down. He walked past Osei's room, listened for a moment, and then stole up to the door and looked inside through a crack. Osei was bent over her desk, crying. "I've got to talk to her," he suddenly decided.

Chapter 15

B u n z ō was delighted with his decision. It had come upon him spontaneously, without any inward struggle. If he were patient just a little while longer, everything would work out all right. Poor Bunzō—he was living in a dream.

He waited two days for his opportunity. That morning Omasa left the house with a moneylender she knew and Bunzō felt his hour was at hand. He listened anxiously for some sign that Osei had returned from her morning lesson. At last he heard her gently speaking to the maid and asking for her mother.

At the sound of her voice, Bunzō stood up. His heart began to flutter and with faltering steps he went downstairs. He assumed Osei was in her room, but as he circled the house he came upon her leaning against a pillar in the doorway, looking contemplatively at the sky. He stopped and she turned around and saw him. Obviously annoyed, she went into her room, pushing the sliding door shut with such force that it rebounded several inches from the pillar.

Bunzō peeked through the opening, a pained expression on his face. He hesitantly moved forward, put a trembling hand to the door, and shakily slid it open. Osei was sitting before her desk, staring fixedly at the wall. He called to her tentatively. She did not answer. His timid heart grew a trifle bolder and he called again. Still no answer. Thinking this a good sign, he felt brave enough to go in and sit down. "There's something I'd like to talk to you about," he began.

Osei slowly turned her head, moving as if the veins in her neck had grown taut. Her lovely eyes looked at him scornfully, mockingly.

Bunzō shuddered and shrank back. Carefully he examined her face. She turned away without saying anything and he felt somewhat relieved. He smiled awkwardly and began to apologize for what he had said at their last meeting. As he struggled to get out the words, Osei suddenly stood up. He was caught completely off guard and the printed pattern of her obi dancing before his eyes awakened an impulse within him. He seized her sleeve.

"What are you doing?" Her voice was harsh.

"I just want to talk to you."

"I have no time now." She pulled her sleeve free and quickly left the room.

Bunzō realized that he had missed the opportunity he had been waiting for. He tried to go after her but his courage failed him. Slowly he dragged himself back upstairs.

He cursed himself and blushed with embarrassment and remorse. "She'll tell her mother when she gets home, damn it. Damn, damn," he cried as a thousand regrets filled him. At that moment the signal marking noonday sounded in the distance. Onabe announced lunch but he could not bring himself to leave his room. He had to be called several times before he started down tremulously.

Omasa had returned and she and her daughter were eating together at a small table. Bunzō bowed without speaking and took his place. Fearful that Osei had told her mother what had happened, he looked at them timidly. Osei seemed unperturbed and he could not tell from Omasa's expression whether she knew or not. He began to eat uneasily.

Suddenly Omasa's voice roared, "Why don't you watch what you're doing? You're not a baby." Terrified, Bunzō looked up from his plate, but it was nothing serious. Osei had just spilled some tea on her lap. Vexed at being scolded, she paid no attention to her mother. "Hurry and wipe it up," Omasa directed. "Why on earth are you sitting there like an idiot. You're not a three-year-old. There must be some limit to your foolishness." Still Osei would not obey.

It was a ludicrous scene. Onabe could not bear to watch in silence. With a gulp she choked down her food and began to giggle. Bunzō laughed, too, finding release for the tension within him. Osei wheeled around and glared angrily at him. The maid stopped laughing and stared. Bunzō himself turned very pale.

"So I'm a fool," Osei declared bitterly. "Go ahead and laugh all you like. How rude you are. What's so funny about my being scolded?"

"What's all this fuss about? Just wipe up that tea and stop making such as issue out of it." Omasa tossed her daughter the cloth from the hibachi.

Osei refused to touch it. "I may not be so bright, but I don't forget what I say like you do, Bunzō. Just keep out of it, hear? You ought to think about yourself instead of laughing at me. What kind of man are you? You swore you'd never talk to me again."

"Osei!" her mother cried, trying to silence her.

She paid no attention. She grated her teeth and darted a fierce look at Bunzō from the corner of her eye. "Less than three days later you come to my room and. . . ."

"What's the matter with you?"

"I'm furious, that's what. First he insults me and calls me a harlot and then a few days later he walks right into my room and grabs my sleeve and starts saying he wants to talk to me. How much more can I stand? If you have something to say, go ahead and say it in front of my mother."

Omasa tried to stop her, but Osei went on raving. Omasa let her go on for a time, and when she felt she had heard enough she signaled to Onabe. The maid roused herself from her own thoughts, hurriedly put down her chopsticks, and rushed to Osei's side. She tried to coax the girl into leaving the room with her, but Osei refused to go. "No, leave me alone," she cried. "He said he wanted to talk to me. I haven't heard what it is yet. No, leave me alone. I won't go until he tells me. I've been too deeply insulted now. Leave me alone, leave me alone." But she was no match for the maid's strength and was dragged to her feet and taken away screaming.

It took Bunzō some time to recover. He had expected Osei to be somewhat angry, but he had never dreamed she would attack him so violently. He was speechless with shock and his confused mind could not fully understand what had happened, let alone register anger. He longed to disappear from the spot. Omasa smiled wanly at him when he looked her way. He had to say something. "I—I behaved very badly the other day. I haven't told you yet but I said something to Osei that. . . ." He could not go on.

"I've heard a little about it," she admitted. "She must have said something to upset you, she's such a selfish girl."

"Oh no, it wasn't her fault."

"I'm certain that it was," she cried, cutting him off abruptly. Her voice resumed its normal tone as she went on. "I'm sure you said what you did for her own good, but we must be very careful what we say about a young girl before she's married. I know she deserves to be scolded but I should be very sorry to see any rumors get started about her."

"I've never said anything to damage her reputation."

"I'm not suggesting that you did. Only things like that do happen after all. Please see that they don't. I hope you won't misunderstand."

Bunzō was completely crushed. There was nothing he could say. He looked at her miserably.

"You can't understand this if you don't have a child of your own. A girl is always a worry until she's married. Outsiders may imagine that it doesn't matter what becomes of such a naughty girl, but a child is a child, as any doting parent will tell you. Even the slightest hint could do a lot of damage to her chances for a good marriage. Besides, Bunzō, nobody likes to be insulted, do they?"

He could no longer restrain himself. "Do you mean to imply that I've insulted Osei?"

"What a horrible thing to say!" Omasa answered, turning vicious. "Who said you insulted her? I was only trying to explain how miserable it is to feel insulted, as I ought to know very well myself since I've had some experience in that direction." Her tone became sharper. "Are you trying to start a quarrel with me? Do you think just because I'm a woman you can get me all upset?"

Bunzō apologized. Tears of hurt and anger filled his eyes. He could not lift his head. He continued to apologize.

"You make me sound so unfair. Don't try to get out of it by apologizing. You must have had something in mind. You owe me an explanation."

He went on apologizing, his head bowed. "I didn't mean it the way it sounded. I'm terribly sorry."

Omasa watched him silently for a time. There was no more to be gained from this. "She's the cause of all my trouble," she said, scowling. "I'm going to put her in her place once and for all." She left the room.

At last the tears began to fall. He sat there for some time without moving. When Onabe came back, Bunzō had to drag himself to his feet. On the way up to his room, he heard Osei screaming, "I hate being in this house! I hate being in this house!"

Chapter 16

EVEN AFTER being so thoroughly humiliated, Bunzō could not make up his mind to leave the house. Night and day he remained in his room, silent and withdrawn, not going downstairs unless he had to. He rarely spoke and often did not answer when he was called. Some nights he was so quiet that Onabe forgot to bring his lamp. He would make no effort to remind her of it and sat disconsolately in his pitch black room, thinking.

His outer calm contrasted sharply with the activity within him. Jolted into awareness by the cruel treatment he had received, he suddenly saw things in an entirely new light. The veil of passion which had been distorting his reason was torn away and his mind grew clear. With his dormant intellect finally awakened, he was able to evaluate the world around him sensibly and objectively. In some intangible way, Bunzō was reborn, although not completely, of course. And when he reviewed the events of the past few days with the benefit of this new insight, he was amazed at how foolish he had been.

Omasa's personality required little thought; he had always known that she was superficial. But he had made a serious error in evaluating Osei. She was not a nice girl at all. She was actually capricious, impulsive, and meretricious. He had mistaken superficial beauty for true virtue. She had robbed him of his powers of judgment.

The first mistake had been to think she cared for him. Love requires mutual understanding, and Osei did not have the faintest idea of what Bunzō was really like. She had never loved him; she had flirted with him because he interested her for the moment.

Like all highly impressionable people, Osei was quick to perceive uniqueness and originality in something and equally quick to become enamored of it. Unfortunately her evaluation of the object was formed spontaneously from her first impression. She rarely sought to uncover any more profound meaning that might be hidden beneath the surface. Seeing her wild enthusiasm for something new, anyone would have thought her earnest and sincere, but her interest was so superficial that she would forget about it before she had even fully savored it. She became disenchanted with things as quickly as she became fascinated with them. In the same way, her enthusiasm for obtaining something new was coupled with indifference once she had it. She would hardly look at books she had eagerly bought. The English lessons she had fought so hard for were attended with little preparation. She behaved this way about everything. Now she had lost interest in Bunzō, not because of anything that had happened between them, but because of her own volatile temperament.

Then, too, their personalities were in conflict. Osei was gay and superficial while Bunzō was withdrawn and reserved. It is only natural that they would not get along forever. Even if he had not lost his job and been threatened with poverty and disgrace, Osei would have stopped caring for him sooner or later.

She was certainly rash and impulsive, but this was her nature and she could not be blamed for it. The most mature, intelligent person cannot overcome his basic personality; certainly such an innocent young girl should not be expected to. She did not have the slightest degree of self-awareness and behaved as her instincts dictated. If you condemn Osei for her foolishness, what might you say of a more educated and knowledgeable person who loses control of himself? What might you say of Bunzō—yes, indeed, Bunzō himself?

He realized that there was no point in blaming anyone else, it was all his own fault. Osei had behaved very badly but so had he. He finally knew what it meant to have to accept the burden of responsibility for his actions.

But while he was reaching this new level of self-awareness, he felt certain that Osei did not understand the consequences of her foolhardy behavior. All that was pleasant and attractive in her was being destroyed by her rashness and the ugliness of her outbursts, and she was incapable of seeing the tragedy involved. Night after night Bunzō lay awake thinking of her, wondering what would become of her.

Poor Bunzō—apparently he has not yet suffered enough.

Chapter 17

ON THAT fateful day when her daughter behaved so badly, Omasa had spent two full hours sternly chastizing her, and from that time on relations between the two improved considerably. Their mutual dislike of Bunzō naturally drew them together; yet there perhaps was more to it than that. Osei grew extremely considerate of her mother, almost as if she were trying to flatter her.

Deprived of their accustomed bickering, they found they actually had little to talk about after they had exhausted the subject of Bunzō. Noboru had abruptly stopped coming to see them and the household became dull and lifeless.

"I'm so bored," Osei exclaimed tearfully one evening, yawning and stretching.

Omasa, who was scanning the newspaper, looked up over her glasses. "Don't just sit there doing nothing. Why don't you get out your book and go over your lessons at least."

The girl frowned at the suggestion. "I've already done my work for tomorrow."

"Oh?" Omasa took up her paper again.

"Mother," Osei said musingly. "Why do you suppose Noboru doesn't come any more?"

"I wonder."

"Maybe he's angry."

"Perhaps."

Omasa was obviously not interested in talking to her. Osei bit her lip and stared pensively into the lamp. A few minutes later she stirred uneasily again. "Mother."

"What is it?" Omasa sat up, annoyed at the interruption.

"Do you think maybe he doesn't come because he's offended?"

"At what?"

"Well, because I wasn't nice to him the last time he was here." She looked searchingly at her mother.

"Oh, for heaven's sake," Omasa said with a smile, realizing what a little girl her daughter still was. "He doesn't come here just to see you, you know."

"No, of course not," Osei faltered, smiling in embarrassment.

It was just at that moment that Noboru stopped in at the house, jocular and unceremonious as ever, unaware, of course, that he was being discussed.

"Well, speak of the devil," Omasa called out happily. "We were just talking about you. What? Well, naturally. How could we speak well of you in all conscience." She laughed. "I'm just joking, but it has been a while since we've seen you. Did you find yourself another hole? Oh, you did? What a slippery eel. Better an eel than a worm, of course. Speaking of eels, there's quite a nice new restaurant for broiled eel around the corner. Not that I expect you to treat us or anything—but you have been neglecting us lately." She laughed again.

Osei ordinarily found such double meaning banter repulsive, but that night she tolerated it for reasons of her own. She made a wry face and looked at Noboru out of the corner of her eye, laughing merrily all the while. Was she trying to hide her embarrassment or was she just extremely happy? It would be impossible to know without asking the young lady herself.

Noboru began to tease her. "What was wrong the other day? You wouldn't say anything except that you had to do your homework. That seemed very curious."

"I didn't feel very well," she answered, giggling coyly.

"I still can't understand what it was all about." There was an awkward silence, and Noboru attempted to fill the gap by explaining why he had not been to see them. He had been asked to go to the chief's house every other evening and help his wife and her sister practice their English. He added that it was a very tiresome obligation.

Strangely enough, Omasa took him at his word and strongly advised him to make the best of this opportunity to further his position. But, she laughed, she was a little worried about what he might teach them, since they were such lovely students.

Osei became quiet and sober. "What is the girl's name?" she asked with a wan smile.

"Hana or Mimi or something."

"Is she good at it?"

"At English? No, not very. She's only just started."

"Oh, well then," she said with a deprecating smile. That very morning her own teacher had corrected her for saying "I will ask to you," but that was beside the point.

"What has happened with Utsumi?" Noboru asked Omasa.

She frowned. "He's still here," she answered with a hopeless expression. "I can't believe the impudence he has. But that's not the worst of it. He has said something to Osei."

"He did? Tell me about it."

Omasa eagerly related all that had happened from the time Bunzō had stolen into Osei's room, adding a few touches of her own. Noboru listened, stroking his chin. He burst out laughing when he heard how Osei had attacked him. "That must have hurt," he roared.

"He seemed rather crushed at the time, but he was his old self a few hours later. There's no end to his impudence."

"And he accused me of flirting."

"So I hear. There's no point in his living here when he's

so angry at everybody. If I were he, I'd move to a lodging-house once and for all. It's so strange to have him hanging about, dragging himself through his meals, despite all that's happened. I can't imagine how long he intends to keep this up."

Noboru smiled bitterly. After a moment he said, "I don't see any easy way out of it."

"Neither do I," Omasa replied.

While they were talking, a messenger from a neighborhood restaurant announced himself at the kitchen door. For a moment Omasa was puzzled, but then she smiled as she realized that Noboru had arranged to have something brought in. She gushed and cooed over him, and when she lifted the lid of the box went into further raptures over its contents. Had there been time one would have wondered why Osei sat back calmly and listened to this gibberish. Omasa hurriedly added charcoal to the hibachi, blew on the coals, put a sake bottle in a pot of water, and set the kettle over the fire. In no time they were all drinking.

Rather than bothering with the formalities of drinking usually practiced with guests, they made jokes and merrily played tricks on one another, told tall tales and laughed uproariously. As they drank more, they fell to humming amorous tunes and parodying popular songs. But we shall pass over the details to get on with the story.

When all the food had been consumed, Omasa got up and left the room. Alone, Osei and Noboru glanced coyly at each other. The girl giggled and then quickly assumed a solemn, sedate manner.

"I wonder what on earth you're giggling about."

"Nothing special."

"Are you happy to see your handsome hero again?"

"I'm revolted. What an ugly face!"

"What?"

"I said, 'What a handsome face.'"

He watched her in silence.

She repeated her words, cautiously, teasing and laughing.

Noboru drew closer and she tried to move back, but their arms became entangled and she found her hand held securely.

"What are you doing?" she asked, rather calmly.

"Nothing. I've just made you my prisoner, that's all."

She tried to get free. "Ouch," she cried, frowning. "You're hurting me."

"Hurt a little?"

"Turn me loose. Come on. If you don't, I'll bite your hand."

" 'I love you enough to eat you . . . ,' " Noboru hummed, indifferent to her protests.

Osei tried to look fierce. "I asked you to let me go. I'll scream," she said in a sugary voice.

"Go ahead and scream."

"Noboru is holding my hand," Osei informed the world in a whisper, choking with laughter.

"You poor little thing."

"Really, let me go."

"Why? Would it be so terrible if Utsumi found out?"

"What do I care about that beast?"

"Then let me hold your hand a minute. It's all right, I won't do anything wicked. But how about a little . . . ," he whispered something in her ear.

Osei became very serious. "Oh, no. How can you possibly suggest such a thing?"

Noboru watched her sober expression with interest. "Why not? Just a little?" he bantered, smiling.

"No. What an idea. I asked you to let me go." She tried to shake herself free, and as they struggled they heard footsteps in the hall. Noboru dropped her hand and burst out laughing. Omasa came in.

"You mustn't leave Osei unattended," he said. "She took my hand and tried to seduce me. It was terrible."

"Oh, you liar. You are the limit, really."

Noboru looked up at the ceiling and laughed.

Chapter 18

A WEEK passed, then two. Noboru continued to call on them regularly, and he and Osei became very friendly. It was easy for them to relax with each other, for they were both gay, frivolous people. Osei could be as carefree as she liked with him. There was no clash of personalities as there had been with Bunzō, and whenever they met, they joked and teased each other merrily. If Osei did try to introduce a serious tone, Noboru pretended not to notice, countering instead with some light or amusing remark which drew her into his mood. Poor Osei tried as hard as she could not to laugh. She bit her lip, puckered her eyebrows, and grew quite red, but his mirth was terribly infectious, and she had to sacrifice her coveted dignity and give in. It reached the point where the mere sight of his face made her laugh. Osei criticized Noboru constantly. "He really is dreadful. All he does is make people laugh," she would say.

While he was always joking with Osei, Noboru was more restrained with Omasa, although of course there was no formality between them. They joked and bantered too, but they also talked of more serious things which they were both interested in. Naturally their "serious" subjects were all rather mundane; they spoke of interest rates and government bonds, rumors of property sales, or the misfortunes of having a tenant who did not pay his rent.

Although these subjects were totally uninteresting to Osei, as she listened to them she gradually became aware of the sympathy which existed between them, animating their conversation and infusing it with a special vitality and warmth. Transformed by this sympathy, their banal subjects became more important, more interesting than women's rights and the temperance movement ever were.

Their conversations were so interesting, in fact, that once they started talking about the renewal of government bonds, the internal affairs of some bank, or the extravagant habits of the chief, they completely forgot about Osei. Even Noboru neglected to be charming to her. She was left to sit and listen to them, utterly bored, yawning and aching to escape to her own room, but somehow she always missed her chance. As she sat there, lost to the conversation, she would become very drowsy and their faces would grow dim, their voices recede far into the distance. As she drifted off, she would be jolted back to consciousness when Noboru roared suddenly, "Oh, just 10 yen!" Embarrassed, she looked at them stealthily, but they had obviously not noticed. She relaxed. Soon her eyelids grew heavy again and she was carried peacefully off to sleep. A few seconds later someone shook her, and, as she opened her eyes, she heard them laughing. She smiled and explained that she was tired.

After gamely trying to relieve her boredom and discomfort by shifting and squirming, she would decide to join in their endless talk of money and business at any cost to avoid falling asleep again. It was terribly difficult to get a word in, for as soon as one of them stopped speaking, the other started. When she finally found an opening, the gap was filled while she wasted time groping for something to say. Experience breeds wisdom; she would plan a statement beforehand. Angrily jabbing at her hair with a hairpin, she thought of something, saw her moment, and cut in with "How much are government bonds now?" Even Osei realized that her question sounded odd.

Omasa and Noboru burst out laughing, tremendously amused to hear something like that come from her. They said surely she must have meant collars for her kimono or something for her dolls instead. This made Osei sulky, but if they tried to coax her out of her mood, she would resent it, for it meant that they were treating her like a little girl. Whichever way, she obviously did not fit in.

Osei was unhappy with her situation and threatened to stop seeing Noboru altogether if he did not change his attitude. Her threats made little impression. She accused him of being self-centered and tyrannical but she still continued to be friendly with him. As the days passed, he went on treating her like a silly child, playing and joking with her, and she seemed to enjoy it for all her protests. In fact, when Noboru did occasionally try to carry on a serious conversation with her, that also failed to please her, and she coyly coaxed him into teasing her again. If he did not respond, she was quite displeased. To make her feel better, he would try to take her hand, but she shrieked with laughter, made funny faces, and ran away. One would wonder what would really please her, since she was not happy when he joked with her and was not happy when he ignored her either.

Omasa saw everything that was going on, although she pretended not to, and was very angry. In Omasa's knowledgeable eye, what her daughter was doing was all wrong. Osei's behavior was extremely ineffective. She gravely lectured her daughter on proper behavior and gave her rules for dealing with men, rules learned through long years of experience. She told her what to do when men flirted or teased or flattered her. Unfortunately children never learn to take advice from their parents. Foolish, immature Osei, who knew nothing of the world, did not listen to what her mother said and brazenly replied that women in the Meiji period were no longer supposed to act like professional entertainers. Such artifice had no place in the modern world. Her mother tried to explain that she was merely talking about the proper way for a young lady to behave, but such profound ideas were wasted on the immature Osei. She retorted that such things were not mentioned even in the old-fashioned *Onna Daigaku.** In the end, Omasa gave up in disgust. Osei was hopeless.

As it turned out, Osei changed her habits of her own free will before her mother had any real reason to worry. This is how it came about.

Omasa's friend Ohama has been mentioned in Chapter Four. One day she and her daughter came to see Omasa to tell her all about the girl's impending marriage to a businessman. Ohama's daughter was a year younger than Osei, and although she was not as pretty, she had a subdued, charming manner and was fairly accomplished in the traditional Japanese arts. Omasa liked the girl very much and considered her quite clever; Osei thought her old-fashioned. In fact, she hated her. Omasa habitually enraged Osei by comparing her unfavorably to the girl.

Omasa could scarcely conceal her envy of the girl's engagement and congratulated them effusively. Ohama triumphantly proceeded to describe the bridegroom's financial assets. She carefully calculated the cost of the wedding preparations, enumerating each item separately. Her recital was accompanied by repeated exclamations of surprise and envy from Omasa. Certainly their good fortune was due to the girl's gracious manner and impeccable behavior, Omasa declared.

"I can't imagine what they find so wonderful about getting married," Osei thought to herself. "It's harder for a cat to

---

* A short treatise stressing the importance of educating young girls to be intelligent, obedient wives. It states that the girl's parents are responsible for seeing that she knows her role in relation to her mother-in-law, her husband, and her husband's relatives. It is the girl's duty to be calm, considerate, and diligent. *Onna daigaku, Nihon kyōiku bunko,* comp. Dōbunkan (Tokyo, 1910–11), IX, 153–58. The work is generally attributed to Kaibara Ekiken (1630–1714), a philosopher of the Chu Hsi school, but was actually written shortly after his death from material appearing in one of his essays.

catch a mouse. She keeps her eyes down—so shy and demure
—but you can tell she's awfully pleased. Her pride is stick-
ing out all over her face. It's disgusting to look at her." Although she couldn't possibly be envious or jealous, Osei was
apparently not satisfied to keep her thoughts to herself. She
smiled sarcastically several times, hoping to show them what
she thought of this foolishness, but no one paid any attention
to her.

Envy of her friend's good fortune drove Omasa to voice her
own worries. "Somebody I could name," she said archly,
"ignores her mother. She won't listen to anything she's told.
She doesn't even think of settling down."

"A pretty girl like that will get a fine government man for
a husband someday, I'm sure. Then she'll make her mother
happy, won't she?" Ohama said with a complacent laugh,
glancing at Osei. Her daughter followed suit.

Osei blushed and lowered her eyes. A few minutes later
she retreated to her own room, where she allowed herself to
give vent to her anger. "I don't care, I'll never get married,"
she cried in protest.

Omasa and her guests talked all that day, and even when
they left she continued to speak enviously of the engagement.
Osei could stand it no longer. She angrily let out the resentment that had been building up within her, hoping to make
her mother stop. But Omasa was making some sense and the
girl was forced to temper her statements. She realized that
there was some truth in what her mother said, but she kept
on arguing, out of sheer stubbornness.

Beguiled by a sudden thought, Omasa hinted casually.
"Suppose I were to mention Noboru. Would you still consider marriage such a bad idea?"

"I don't want to get married," Osei said. All emotion was
wiped from her face.

"I wonder why. He seems to be very nice. He's quite
clever and has a decent income. Most important, he's good-
looking."

"I don't want to get married."

"But what if he asks for your hand? What should I tell him?"

Osei hesitated a moment. "N—n—no, I don't want to get married."

Omasa glanced at her and laughed aloud. She let it go at that.

Osei tried to resume an indifferent expression, but somehow her mind kept wandering, and she was soon deep in her daydreams. She sat silently lost in thought. When Omasa reminded her of the time at eleven, she was brought abruptly back to reality and sighed deeply.

Back in her own room, Osei changed her clothes and sank weakly onto the bedding spread on the floor. For some time she sat there, her face expressionless. What was she thinking? Was she groping for an answer to her mother's question? Did she regret wasting her time with Bunzō when she should have been finding herself a husband? Or had her hazy confusion been destroyed by the sharp light of her mother's words? Did she realize for the first time that she had come to the brink of her former, carefree life, and that this was the moment at which her fate would be decided? Or was she being led to wild dreams, flying toward a joyful, happy future which she could not know of? Was she making her hopes into facts, seeing dreams as reality, at once happy and fearful? Her thoughts were not reflected in her vacant expression, and so we cannot tell. For a time she did not move. Some ten minutes passed.

Suddenly her eyes sparkled brightly. Her face became radiantly beautiful as a smile floated to her lips and her cheeks grew flushed. To see her was like watching a flower unfold, so pure and innocent was her happiness.

She sprang joyfully from the floor, flew to the mirror hanging on the pillar, and peeked at the dim reflection of her own smiling face. Hugging herself tightly, she hopped around the bedding and danced and skipped about the room. Again she collapsed on the bedding, seizing the pillow and thrusting it beneath her head. With a strangled cry, she burst out laughing, rocking her body back and forth.

For some days after this Osei was restless and uncomfortable in Noboru's presence, for she was trying to hide her feelings. She hoped to keep him from guessing that anything had changed between them by acting as childishly as she always had. Despite her best efforts, she gave herself away. A barely perceptible thickness crept into the tone of her voice when she spoke to him, she laughed at inappropriate moments, and kept bobbing in and out of the room. She carried on casual conversations with her mother, vainly pretending not to notice that Noboru was watching her. When their eyes met, she became flustered and turned quickly away. Omasa indiscreetly teased her about the way she was acting, hoping to call Noboru's attention to Osei's interest in him; she thereby caused her daughter even further embarrassment.

But as the days passed and Noboru remained his old joking, playful self, Osei's behavior changed. Gone was her bashfulness; her awkwardness before him vanished. She no longer cared whether he appeared or not, and his presence failed to cheer her. On the contrary, the mere sight of him made her sad and pensive. She was cold and distant, treating him like an estranged relative. Had they quarreled or had she just grown tired of him? Perhaps the novelty of her infatuation had worn off. It is impossible to tell.

Noboru continued his attempts at bantering with her from time to time, but he got no response—in fact, Osei merely ignored him. The edge went off his jokes; they fell absolutely flat.

When he was not in the house, Osei affected great cheerfulness, playing and joking merrily with whomever happened to be present. She made a great show of reciting poems and singing songs and dancing about with Onabe, who could not imagine what was happening. Running, cavorting, laughing —Osei created a gay clatter about the house. But the moment

Noboru came, her mood changed and she grew quiet and forlorn.

However, she grew quite gentle with her mother. She did not quiet down when Omasa scolded her for making such a clamor around the house, but she did not answer back as she used to. She grew sweet and affectionate to Omasa. At first her mother was rather vexed by her childishness but in the end she was charmed by it and, instead of scolding her, she smiled. Osei was slightly cranky when she first got up in the morning, but outside of that she flitted happily about the house, bright and congenial.

One day Osei announced that she wanted to take evening knitting classes. Omasa suggested she might go instead to study Japanese needlework with a nice woman she knew in the afternoons. No, Osei insisted it be knitting. Had she been a young lady of the West, she would have clung to her mother and kissed her cheek, but she had no such weapons at her disposal. As it was, she looked at her with such a pathetic, pleading expression on her face that Omasa could not help but give in.

Knitting proved more interesting than English. Every other evening Osei tripped happily off to her lessons, her face heavily painted, wearing her prettiest kimono. She had, of course, always decried the use of makeup and now felt compelled to explain that she had to wear it since all the other girls did. She was obviously displeased when her mother suggested a less glamorous costume might do for the evening, although she did not argue about it. Watching her restless daughter leaving the house, Omasa inevitably felt uneasy.

Noboru had been spending his time elsewhere of late.

Chapter 19

OSEI DID not openly insult Bunzō again after her one violent outburst. She may even have felt she had gone too far,
for in the weeks that followed she was cold and distant but
never malicious. Omasa, by contrast, obviously grew to dislike him more and more as time went on and was quite anxious to have him leave her house. The most cheerful conversations stopped instantly when he came downstairs, and
Omasa above all displayed her irritation openly. She would
criticize him for being late, or glare at him, or audibly fret
and fume at the sight of him.

So obvious a demonstration of displeasure was unnecessary.
Bunzō was not stupid or insensitive. He was painfully aware
of how happy they would be to see him move out. But he
decided not to go. Why? Was he too irresolute to do anything so definite, so final, in spite of the way they had
treated him? Or did he still retain some fondness for Osei?
Perhaps it was hard for him to admit that his love had ended
in such a fiasco; many men would have found it so. Weakness, love, shame—all were holding him there. But more
important was his sense of obligation. Bunzō remained tied
to the Sonoda house by a profound sense of obligation.

Bunzō could not help but compare the household in those
first weeks after Osei's attack with their past life. What had

become of the gentle, tranquil spirit that once filled their home? How happy they had been; how harmoniously their lives had blended. Beneath the surface of their joy was the awareness that greater happiness awaited them in the future. They had only to be patient and it would come. When Bunzō, his aunt, and Osei met, they smiled naturally, pleasantly. No artifice was necessary. Nothing inopportune or disturbing was said, so close were they in mind and spirit. Each was somehow elevated by this unity of purpose—a girl who would one day be a wife, a man who would be her husband, a mother who would gain a son. Omasa, too, contributed in no small way to the happiness of the family. If she had not been there to keep them apart, the two young people would surely have become too intimate, and the tranquillity thereby been destroyed. Then all at once the warm affection, the joy, the gentle harmony, the happy smiling eyes had all faded. Bunzō lost his job. Noboru took his place in the family.

Today all was chaos. The gay, noisy, carefree atmosphere was only superficial. Underneath lay a loathsome, greedy, self-indulgent, immoral, cruel mass. Gone was the spirit of communion which once bound them and the love which cleansed their selfish hearts. They thought only of themselves. They spoke only in self-interest and acted to satisfy their greed. They deceived each other and were deceived. Calculation, deception, lies, tricks—every despicable human practice was at work.

Omasa was trying to arrange a match between Osei and Noboru. She had been worried about her daughter's future for years and wanted to see her settled. She was also afraid the girl might become interested in Bunzō again. But Osei was tactless. She was not helping her mother's plans along at all and Omasa was very upset. Noboru knew perfectly well what Omasa had in mind, but he did not want to get too deeply involved with her daughter, fearing the problems it might bring. Vacillating, he hovered about, watching Osei from the corner of his eye, licking his lips, like an old fox resisting the bait. (Bunzō had somehow always imagined

Noboru would marry an ugly, stupid woman with well-placed and influential parents.) Omasa realized what Noboru was thinking, and he, in turn, was perfectly aware of her every scheme. Each knew the other understood and assumed an innocent, naïve pose in an attempt to gain the upper hand. One was as much a rogue as the other; neither won or lost. Now they had grown weary of the game and were furtively watching each other before making the next move.

Bunzō realized that he could not sit by calmly. Osei was in the gravest danger and did not know it. She was being swept blindly along by the life in this greedy, contaminated household, and she was thoroughly enjoying it. She was a very confused girl, living in this ugly situation without seeing its sordidness. Like a drunken woman, she was alert to only a few select impressions. Her mind was so dazzled that she was unable to comprehend the true meaning of what she saw and heard and ideas did not filter through. Not only did the outer world become more distant; she was no longer able to experience her own emotions. It was as if she had become separated from herself, and her every word and action were impelled by some mysterious force within her. Everything sparkled. The world was beautiful. Everyone loved her and lived for her sake alone. Was it possible that anyone could be unhappy in this marvelous world? Forgetting that people age and love fades, she felt that youth and beauty would last forever. The future? How could it be anything but bright and gay.

In growing close to Noboru she was unknowingly destroying herself. To a large degree, she was responsible for what was happening. She did not really love Noboru. Basically she was seeking the love of any man, preferably someone young and handsome. With Bunzō her desires had been kept down, but now she was very excited. Her excitement silenced the voice of reason, dulled her perceptions, and, with overwhelming power, forced her to do terrible things.

This was the turning point of her life and it was imperative that she be made to realize it. A great deal could be learned from this experience; a new level of self-understanding could be achieved. An accurate appraisal of her feelings would open her mind to more mature thoughts. She would become a mature human being. The opportunity would never come again.

Someone had to save her. But who?

Magobei was not at home. Even if he were, he would be of no use. Omasa's love was so misguided that she was unwittingly twisting her daughter's moral values. She would certainly obstruct any effort to help Osei. Only Bunzō remained. He was, at least, slightly more perceptive and experienced than Osei. Inadequate though his assistance might be, he knew the responsibility rested with him.

And so he stayed on, impervious to Omasa's hints. He could not leave Osei now. It was his duty to help her through this crucial time. Night and day he remained in his tiny room, staring at the walls, hoping to find a way to save her.

He was lost in grief. He wanted desperately to find some way to save Osei, but he could not discover any. Each day he asked himself over and over what he should do, but he was unable to think of an answer. He was left only with a deep sense of frustration. In trying to escape from his suffering, he lost his judgment and his imagination got away from him. He was unable to control his fantasies, and although he had not yet discovered any way to save Osei, he started dreaming of the wonderful day when she would be saved.

But he was not given to dreaming all the time. He thought of many plans, among which were two that might possibly work. The best idea seemed to be to tell Magobei in great detail what had been going on and let him talk to Osei directly. She would be likely to take her father's advice seriously. But Osei was not a stranger; Bunzō himself was deeply involved with her. He felt unhappy at the idea of informing against her to her father, although he would be doing it for her own sake. He might ignore his own misgivings and talk to Magobei about the problem, but even if Magobei succeeded in making Osei understand that what she had been doing was wrong, he would be unable to prevail upon the willful Omasa. Magobei might very well be persuaded that there was nothing wrong. Bunzō decided against talking to Magobei.

Well, then, should he explain the danger to Osei himself? It was not very likely that she would even listen to him. He would place himself in an extremely vulnerable position if he interfered so openly in her affairs. Bunzō was frightened of the consequences of either plan.

His thoughts churned round and round as he tried to reach a satisfactory solution. No single plan seemed to be practical. Should he tell his uncle? Should he approach her himself? Exhausted with worry, a series of fantasies again played in his mind. He even toyed with the idea that everything that had happened was merely a joke and that Osei was only testing him. Any moment now she would come up the stairs, laughing merrily, and drive away his hurt and confusion. But then he remembered how she had looked that terrible afternoon, and the fantasies dissolved. It was ridiculous for him to be spending his days like this. Still when he tried to forget her, he felt as if he had dropped some important work halfway, and his agonized thoughts returned inevitably to Osei.

Continuous concentration on a single problem exhausts the brain. It loses its power to discriminate. Bunzō could not keep totally unrelated scraps of ideas from darting into his mind.

Once when he was lying on his back staring up at the ceiling, his arms folded behind his head, the grain of the wood above him caught his eye. "It looks like a track made by running water," he thought in surprise, becoming fascinated with it and forgetting all about Osei for the moment. "Depending on how you look at it, one part seems higher than the other. Could that be what they call an optical illusion?" He remembered the bearded face of the foreigner who had taught him physics, and then several of the students who had been to school with him appeared in his mind's eye. One had a pencil behind his ear; another carried books under his arm; a third was reading. Bunzō himself stood among them. The lecture on electricity had just ended and all the students were gathered around some machine in the laboratory. They were making a great row. What could it be about? Suddenly machine and students vanished into thin air. Bunzō saw the grain in the wood again. "Is that an optical illusion?" he asked with a smile. "I think Sully's *Illusions** is the most interesting book I've ever read. I finished it in two days. What a remarkable mind he has. How can anyone be so clever?"

There is no apparent relation between Sully's mind and Osei, but at that very moment she burst into his thoughts again. He cried out as if he had been struck on a tender wound and sat up. Even as he did so he forgot about her. Why had he gotten up? In a moment he remembered. But now her problem seemed like something removed from the real world. It no longer interested or amused him and, for the moment, he emptied his mind of it.

In the end, Bunzō was forced to admit that he lacked the strength to carry out his resolutions. Weeks of worry had left him nearly mad, but he had done nothing to help the situation. Nature was taking its course; Osei was sinking deeper and deeper.

Suddenly something utterly delightful and completely unexpected happened. Osei became estranged from Noboru. Bunzō had been able to follow the dizzying path of her emotions up to this point, by carefully watching and listening, but now he lost his way. What had happened? It was hard to believe that something had come between them. Understand it or not, he could not help but be encouraged by the change in Osei's attitude toward him which followed. Gone were the glowers and sneers; she stopped treating him like an

---

* A long and careful scientific analysis of various types of errors made by the senses and the intellect. Subtitled "A Psychological Study," *Illusions* was written in 1881. The English philosopher James Sully (1842–1923) was the author of many books describing the mental processes involved in recognition, learning, and understanding.

enemy. If he happened along when she was clowning with Onabe, she would look at him and laugh. Bunzō toyed with the notion of speaking to her. She might answer pleasantly. Should he try to talk everything over with her in private? His bitter memories held him back. Feeling extremely foolish for hesitating, he waited.

It was a few days after Osei had started knitting lessons. Bunzō was on his way to the sitting room when he saw her standing in the hall with her back to him. She was engrossed in doing something, presumably knitting, since that was the latest novelty in her life. She obviously mistook him for Onabe, for, without turning, she said, "Aren't you ready yet?" How startling to be spoken to so gently after all these weeks! Curious at receiving no answer, Osei turned and saw him. She gave a little cry of surprise but did not appear particularly upset. She smiled and turned back to her knitting.

He was drunk with joy. What should he do? He nearly swooned with excitement. He remembered that Omasa was not at home. This seemed a unique opportunity. He was debating whether to speak to her when the door of the maid's room slid open, and he disappeared instantly into the sitting room, even before he consciously realized that he did not want to be seen there.

He heard Onabe apologize for keeping Osei waiting. Osei whispered something to her and both girls giggled. "Really, Mr. Utsumi?" Onabe asked in her rough voice.

"Shush. He's still in there," Osei cautioned in a whisper.

"Is he?" Onabe lowered her voice.

"Yes, really."

Embarrassed at spying on them, he left his hiding place, pretending not to have heard anything. Onabe stared at him and, with a slight bow, announced that they were going to the bath. She suddenly remembered something. "If the mistress should come home and want dinner, I've put it in the cupboard, so please go ahead," she said. "Are you ready? Then we'll be going now."

Osei glanced at Bunzō, laughter sparkling in her eyes, and, quickly tossing her knitting into the sitting room, left with the maid. They chattered merrily as they walked away. The two girls were nearly the same age and had recently become good friends. Before this Osei had been too snobbish to speak freely to a servant.

Bunzō smiled as he watched them go, accepting his happiness without question for the moment. His favorite fantasies came to the fore again. Perhaps there was nothing to worry about after all. Perhaps it had all been a product of his suspicious mind. But no, something certainly was wrong. He could not overlook her vicious, senseless attack; her initial defiance of her mother followed by her new submissiveness; her gradual estrangement from Noboru, with whom she had been on such intimate terms. These were tangible contradictions to his fantasy. Something was wrong, and he did not know how to reach a greater understanding of the problem. He did not even know if he should feel happy or sad.

Restlessly he wandered about the house. Eventually he reached a decision. He would try to talk to her when she came back. He would gamble everything on her response. If she would not listen, he would leave that house once and for all.

He went back upstairs to wait.

Bibliography

THE BIBLIOGRAPHY includes only works cited in this study. For additional bibliographic information pertinent to the study of Futabatei Shimei's life and works, and to the study of the development of gembun itchi, the reader is referred to:

Kindai bungaku kenkyū sōsho. Edited by Shōwa Joshi Daigaku Kindai Bungaku Kenkyū Shitsu. Tokyo, 1958.
    A chronological list of all books, articles, interviews, and other items written by Fubabatei, X, 213–38.
    A chronological list of over 4,000 books, articles, and interviews wholly or in part concerned with Futabatei, X, 260–344.
Kōno Toshiō. "Futabatei Shimei kenkyū bunken nempyō nōto," *Bungaku,* XXII, No. 10 (October 1954), 65–78.
    A chronological list of works by and about Futabatei, with some annotation. Now largely superceded by the bibliography in *Kindai bungaku kenkyū sōsho.*
Nakayama Shōzaburō. "Futabatei Shimei bunken shō," *Bungaku,* V, No. 9 (1937), 113–17.
    A chronological list of works by Futabatei followed by a brief list of works about him. Both lists have brief annotations. A pioneer study now superceded by the bibliography in *Kindai bungaku kenkyū sōsho.*
Okano Takeo. *Meiji bungaku kenkyū bunken sōran.* Tokyo, 1944.
    The standard bibliography of secondary sources for the study of the period. Now largely outdated.

Yagū Shirō. "Kindai bungaku to kotoba kankei bunken moku-roku," *Bungaku*, XXVI, No. 7 (1958), 72–90.
A chronological, annotated bibliography of primary and secondary works relating to the gembun itchi movement covering the years 1879–1957.

Works by Futabatei Shimei

Aibiki. Futabatei Shimei zenshū. Vol. I. Tokyo, 1953–54.
"Bijutsu no hongi," *Futabatei Shimei zenshū.* Vol. IX. Tokyo, 1953–54.
"Bundan gosoku," *Futabatei Shimei zenshū.* Vol. IX. Tokyo, 1953–54.
"Bungaku no honshoku oyobi heimin to bungaku to no kankei," *Futabatei Shimei zenshū.* Vol. IX. Tokyo, 1953–54.
"Denki no bunji," *Futabatei Shimei zenshū.* Vol. IX. Tokyo, 1953–54.
Futabatei Shimei shū. Gendai Nihon bungaku zenshū. Vol. X. Tokyo, 1928.
Futabatei Shimei zenshū. Edited by Ikebe Kichitarō. Tokyo, 1910–13.
Futabatei Shimei zenshū. Tokyo, 1953–54.
"Gakujutsu to bijutsu to no sabetsu," *Futabatei Shimei zenshū.* Vol. IX. Tokyo, 1953–54.
"Kātokofu shi bijutsu zokkai," *Futabatei Shimei zenshū.* Vol. X. Tokyo, 1953–54.
Kuchiba shū: hitokagome. Futabatei Shimei zenshū. Vol. XI. Tokyo, 1953–54.
Ochiba no hakiyose: futakagome. Futabatei Shimei zenshū. Vol. XI. Tokyo, 1953–54.
"Sakka kushin dan," *Futabatei Shimei zenshū.* Vol. IX. Tokyo, 1953–54.
"Shōsetsu sōron," *Futabatei Shimei zenshū.* Vol. IX. Tokyo, 1953–54.
"Shuyo sakan," *Futabatei Shimei zenshū.* Vol. X. Tokyo, 1953–54.
"Sōbetsu kai sekijō no tōji," *Futabatei Shimei zenshū.* Vol. X. Tokyo, 1953–54.

"Tsurugeenefu *Chichi to ko (Kyomu-tō katagi),*" *Futabatei Shimei zenshū.* Vol. XV. Tokyo, 1953–54.
Ukigumo. Tokyo, 1887.
Ukigumo. Futabatei Shimei zenshū. Vol. I. Tokyo, 1953–54.
Ukigumo. Shinchō bunko. Tokyo, 1960.
"Yo ga gembun itchi no yurai," *Futabatei Shimei zenshū.* Vol. IX. Tokyo, 1953–54.
"Yo ga hansei no zange," *Futabatei Shimei zenshū.* Tokyo, 1953–54.
"Yo ga hon'yaku no hyōjun," *Futabatei Shimei zenshū.* Vol. IX. Tokyo, 1953–54.
"Yo no aidoku sho," *Futabatei Shimei zenshū.* Vol. XV. Tokyo, 1953–54.
An Adopted Husband. Translated by Buhachirō Mitsui and Gregg M. Sinclair. New York, 1919.
Mediocrity. Translated by Glenn W. Shaw. Tokyo, 1927.

Works in Japanese

Chūgoku gakugei dai jiten. Edited by Kondō Moku. Tokyo, 1959.
Engeki hyakka dai jiten. Edited by Kawatake Shigetoshi. Tokyo, 1960–63.
Fenollosa, Ernest. "Bijutsu shinsetsu," *Meiji bunka zenshū.* Vol. XII. Tokyo, 1928.
Fukuda Kiyoto. *Ken'yūsha no bungaku undō.* Tokyo, 1950.
Fukuzawa Yukichi. *Danjo kōsai ron. Fukuzawa Yukichi zenshū.* Tokyo, 1959.
Hasegawa Ryūko. "Arishi hi o shinobu," *Futabatei Shimei kenkyū,* I, No. 1 (October 1937), 4–6.
Homma Hisao. *Meiji bungaku shi.* Tokyo, 1937.
———. *Tsubouchi Shōyō.* Tokyo, 1959.
Inagaki Tatsurō. "Futabatei no hyōron," *Futabatei annai.* Tokyo, 1954.
Ishibashi Ningetsu. "Futabatei shi no *Meguriai,*" *Futabatei Shimei zenshū.* Vol. II. Tokyo, 1953–54.
———. "*Ukigumo* no homeotoshi," *Gendai bungakuron taikei.* Edited by Nakashima Kenzō and Yoshida Seiichi. Vol. I. Tokyo, 1955.

Ishibashi Shian. *"Aibiki o* yonde," *Futabatei Shimei zenshū.* Vol. II. Tokyo, 1953–54.

Itō Sei. *Nihon bundan shi.* Tokyo, 1960.

Jōruri meisaku shū. Edited by Hakubunkan Hensan Kyoku. *Teikoku bunko.* Vol. LXVII. Tokyo, 1897.

Kambara Ariake. "Aibiki ni tsuite," *Futabatei Shimei zenshū.* Vol. II. Tokyo, 1953–54.

Kamei Masaji. *"Ukigumo* to sono hyōgen," *Kokugo kokubun,* XXXI, No. 2 (February 1962), 23–39.

Kataoka Ryōichi. *Kindai Nihon no shōsetsu.* Tokyo, 1956.

Kawatake Shigetoshi and Yanagida Izumi. *Tsubouchi Shōyō.* Tokyo, 1939.

Kijitsu-an Kinkō. *Fūzoku monzen tsūshaku.* Kyoto, 1929.

Kokin waka shū. Edited by Saeki Umetomo. *Nihon koten bungaku taikei.* Vol. VIII. Tokyo, 1959.

Kokumin no tomo. Tokyo, 1887, 1889.

Kuroita Katsumi. *Kokushi no kenkyū: sōsetsu.* Tokyo, 1931.

Kuwabara Kenzō. "Hasegawa kun no ryakureki," *Futabatei annai.* Tokyo. 1954.

Maeda Akira. "Futabatei shujin no koto," *Futabatei Shimei kenkyū,* I, No. 6 (May 1938), 1–8.

Maruoka Kyūka. "Ken'yūsha to *Garakuta bunko* no yurai," boxed with facsimile reprint of *Garakuta bunko.* Tokyo, 1927.

Matsushita Teizō. "Gembun itchi ron to sono hantai ron," *Kokugo kokubun,* XXIX, No. 11 (October 1960), 39–56.

———. "Yamada Bimyō no gembun itchi shisō," *Kokugo kokubun,* XXIX, No. 1. (January 1960), 16–29.

Meiji bunka kankei Ōbei jimmei roku. Edited by Shigehisa Tokutarō and Amano Keitarō. Tokyo, 1937.

Meiji bunka shi. Compiled by Kaikoku Hyakunen Kinen Bunka Jigyō Kai. Tokyo, 1953–57.

Meiji bunka zenshū. Edited by Yoshino Sakuzō. Tokyo, 1928.

Motoori Norinaga. *Motoori Norinaga zenshū.* Tokyo, 1927.

Mozume Takami. *Gembun itchi. Meiji bunka zenshū.* Vol. XII. Tokyo, 1928.

Nakamura Mitsuo. *Futabatei Shimei.* Tokyo, 1956.

———. *Futabatei Shimei den.* Tokyo, 1958.

———. "Gaikokugo Gakkō to Futabatei," *Tembō,* No. 5 (May 1946), pp. 74–88.

——. "Shōgai to sakuhin," *Futabatei annai*. Tokyo, 1954.
Nakamura Tatsutarō. "Chikuba no tomo tarishi Hasegawa kun," *Futabatei annai*. Tokyo, 1954.
Nihon bungaku dai jiten. Edited by Fujimura Tsukuru. Tokyo, 1951–52.
Nihon kyōiku shi shiryō. Compiled by Mombu Daijin Kambō Hōkoku Ka. Tokyo, 1892.
Okuno Shintarō. "Kaisetsu," in San'yūtei Enchō, *Botan dōrō*. Tokyo, 1955.
Onna daigaku. Nihon kyōiku bunko. Compiled by Dōbun Kan. Vol. V. Tokyo, 1910–11.
Ōtaguro Jūgorō. "Shuju naru omoide," *Futabatei annai*. Tokyo, 1954.
Sakamoto Hiroshi. *Futabatei Shimei*. Tokyo, 1941.
Sasaki Nobutsuna. *Meiji bungaku no hen'ei*. Tokyo, 1934.
Seki Ryōichi. "Futabatei to Shōyō," *Kaishaku to kanshō*, XXVIII, No. 5 (May 1963), 15–24.
Shimbun shūsei Meiji hennen shi. Compiled Shimbun Shūsei Meiji Hennen Shi Hensan Kai. Tokyo, 1935–40.
Shintaishi sen. Edited by Yamada Bimyō. *Meiji bunka zenshū*. Vol. XII. Tokyo, 1928.
Shūji oyobi kabun. Translated by Kikuchi Dairoku. *Meiji bunka zenshū*. Vol. XII. Tokyo, 1928.
Tamenaga Shunsui. *Umegoyomi harutsuge dori. Teikoku bunko*. Vol. X. Tokyo, 1909.
Tamai Kansuke and Kurita Hiroyuki. "Futabatei Shimei shiryō nōto," *Bungaku*, XXII, No. 10 (October 1954), 79–87.
Tayama Katai. "Futabatei Shimei kun," *Futabatei Shimei zenshū*. Vol. II. Tokyo, 1953–54.
——. *Tōkyō no sanjūnen. Bungakuteki kaisō shū*. Edited by Masamune Hakuchō. Tokyo, 1958.
Tōkyō Teikoku Daigaku gojūnen shi. Compiled by Tōkyō Teikoku Daigaku. Tokyo, 1932.
Tokutomi Sohō. "Ukigumo no mampyō," *Futabatei Shimei zenshū*. Vol. I. Tokyo, 1953–54.
Tsubouchi Shōyō. "Futabatei no koto," *Kaki no heta*. Tokyo, 1933.
——. "Futabatei Shimei," *Shōyō senshū*. Vol. XII. Tokyo, 1926–27.

——. "Jo," in San'yūtei Enchō, *Botan dōrō*. Tokyo, 1955.
——. *Mirai no yume. Shōyō senshū*. Vol. II of *Bessatsu*. Tokyo, 1926–27.
——. *Shōsetsu shinzui*. Edited by Yanagida Izumi. Tokyo, 1957.
——. *Shōyō senshū*. Tokyo, 1926–27.
——. *Tōsei shosei katagi. Shōyō senshū*. Vol. I of *Bessatsu*, Tokyo, 1926–27.
Tsubouchi Shōyō, trans. *Gaiseishi den. Shōyō senshū*. Vol. II of *Bessatsu*. Tokyo, 1926–27.
——. *Jiyū no tachi nagori no kireaji. Shōyō senshū*. Vol. II of *Bessatsu*. Tokyo, 1926–27.
——. *Shumpū jōwa. Shōyō senshū*. Vol. II of *Bessatsu*. Tokyo, 1926–27.
——. *Shunsō kiwa. Shōyō senshū*. Vol. II of *Bessatsu*. Tokyo, 1926–27.
Tsuchiya Daimu. "Sanjūnen mae no Hasegawa kun," *Futabatei annai*. Tokyo, 1954.
Uchida Roan. "Futabatei Shimei no isshō," *Kinō kyō*. Tokyo, 1916.
——. "Futabatei yodan," *Kinō kyō*. Tokyo, 1916.
——. *Roan zuihitsu: shien no hitobito*. Tokyo, 1935.
Yamada Bimyō. "Kojin to boku," *Futabatei annai*. Tokyo, 1954.
Yamashita Yoshitarō. "Shippai shitaru keiseika to shite no Hasegawa kun," *Futabatei Shimei kenkyū*, No. 5 (March 1938), pp. 5–8.
Yanagida Izumi. "*Ukigumo* o chūshin ni shite," *Bungaku*, V, No. 9 (1937), 21–37.
Yazaki Saganoya. "*Ukigumo* no kushin to shisō," *Futabatei annai*. Tokyo, 1954.
Yōkyoku taikan. Compiled by Sanari Kentarō. Tokyo, 1930–31.
Yoshitake Yoshinori. *Meiji Taishō no hon'yaku shi*. Tokyo, 1959.

Works in Western Languages

Aston, W. G. *Nihongi*. London, 1956.
Belinsky, V. G. *Selected Philosophical Works. Translated* by M. Yovchuk. Moscow, 1948.
——. *Sobranie Sochinenii*. St. Petersburg, 1911.

Berlin, Isaiah. "A Marvellous Decade (1)," *Encounter,* IV, No. 6 (June 1955), 27–39.

Berton, Peter, Paul Langer, and Rodger Swearingen. *Japanese Training and Research in the Russian Field.* Los Angeles, 1956.

Blacker, Carmen. *The Japanese Enlightenment.* Cambridge, England, 1963.

Bonneau, Georges. *Histoire de la Littérature Japonaise Contemporaine.* Paris, 1940.

Borton, Hugh. *Japan's Modern Century.* New York, 1955.

Bowman, Herbert E. *Vissarion Belinski.* Cambridge, Mass., 1954.

Craig, Albert M. *Chōshu in the Meiji Restoration.* Cambridge, Mass., 1961.

Dobrolyubov, N. A. *Selected Philosophical Works.* Translated by J. Fineberg. Moscow, 1948.

——. *Sochinenia.* St. Petersburg, 1911.

Feldman, Horace. *The Growth of the Meiji Novel.* Ph.D. dissertation, Columbia University, 1952.

——. "The Meiji Political Novel: A Brief Survey," *Far Eastern Quarterly,* IX, No. 3 (May 1950), 245–55.

Giles, Herbert. *Gems of Chinese Literature.* Shanghai, 1922.

——. *A History of Chinese Literature.* New York, 1923.

Goncharov, Ivan. *The Precipice.* Translated by M. Bryant. New York, 1916.

Hall, John Whitney. *Tanuma Okitsugu.* Cambridge, Mass., 1955.

Harootunian, Harry. *The Samurai Class During the Early Years of the Meiji Period in Japan.* Ph.D. dissertation, University of Michigan, 1956.

Herzen, Alexander. *Selected Philosophical Works.* Translated by L. Navrozov. Moscow, 1956.

Hibbett, Howard. *The Floating World in Japanese Fiction.* New York, 1959.

Japan Weekly Mail, 1884, 1886.

Jippensha Ikku. *Shank's Mare.* Translated by Thomas Satchell. Tokyo, 1960.

Karlina, R. "Belinsky and Japanese Literature," *Literaturnee Nasledstvo,* LVI (1950), 501–12. Also in Japanese in *Bungaku,* XXII, No. 10 (October 1953), 992–1005.

Keene, Donald. *The Japanese Discovery of Europe.* London, 1952.

———. *Major Plays of Chikamatsu.* New York, 1961.

———. *Modern Japanese Literature.* New York, 1956.

———. *Modern Japanese Poetry.* Ann Arbor, 1964.

Koyré. Alexandre. "La philosophie et le problème national en Russie au début du XIX siecle," *Bibliothèque de L'Institut Français de Léningrad,* Vol. X (1929).

Legge, James. *The Chinese Classics.* London, 1861.

Lewin, Bruno. *Futabatei Shimei in seinen Beziehungen zur russischen Literatur.* Hamburg, 1955.

Malm, William P. *Japanese Music and Musical Instruments.* Tokyo, 1959.

———. *Nagauta.* Tokyo, 1963.

Masaryk, Thomas G. *The Spirit of Russia.* Translated by Eden and Cedar Paul. New York, 1919.

Mathewson, Rufus W., Jr. *The Positive Hero in Russian Literature.* New York, 1958.

Matlaw, Ralph E., ed. *Belinsky, Chernyshevsky, and Dobrolyubov: Selected Criticism.* New York, 1962.

Margoulles, George. *Le Kou-Wen Chinois.* Paris, 1926.

Mori Arinori. *Education in Japan: A Series of Letters.* New York, 1873.

Nagai Michio. "Herbert Spencer in Early Meiji Japan," *Far Eastern Quarterly,* XIV, No. 1 (November 1954), 55–64.

Okazaki Yoshie. *Japanese Literature in the Meiji Era.* Translated by V. H. Viglielmo. Tokyo, 1955.

Passin, Herbert. *Education and Society in Japan.* New York, 1965.

Ryan, Marleigh. "A Study of Futabatei Shimei," *Researches in the Social Sciences on Japan: Volume Two.* New York, 1959.

Sansom, G. B., *The Western World and Japan.* New York, 1951.

Seki Keigo, ed. *Folktales of Japan.* Translated by Robert J. Adams. Chicago, 1963.

Shibusawa Keizō. *Japanese Life and Culture in the Meiji Era.* Translated by Charles Terry. Tokyo, 1958.

Sully, James. *Illusions.* New York, 1888.

Tsunoda Ryusaku, Wm. Theodore de Bary, and Donald Keene. *Sources of Japanese Tradition.* New York, 1958.

Turgenev, Ivan. *The Borzoi Turgenev.* Translated by Harry Stevens. New York, 1955.

Wilson, Edmund. "Turgenev and the Life-Giving Drop," *New Yorker,* XXXIII, No. 35 (October 19, 1957), 163–216.

Zenkovsky, V. V. *A History of Russian Philosophy.* Translated by George L. Kline. New York, 1953.

Zolbrod, Leon M. *Takizawa Bakin: Major Edo Author.* Ph.D. dissertation, Columbia University, 1963.

Index

Index

STUDIES OF THE EAST ASIAN INSTITUTE

The Ladder of Success in Imperial China, by Ping-ti Ho.
New York, Columbia University Press, 1962; reprint, John
Wiley, 1964.
The Chinese Inflation, 1937–1949, by Shun-hsin Chou.
New York, Columbia University Press, 1963.
Reformer in Modern China: Chang Chien, 1853–1926, by Samuel
Chu.
New York, Columbia University Press, 1965.
Research in Japanese Sources: A Guide, by Herschel Webb with
the assistance of Marleigh Ryan.
New York, Columbia University Press, 1965.
Society and Education in Japan, by Herbert Passin.
New York, Bureau of Publications, Teachers College, Co-
lumbia University, 1965.
*Agricultural Production and Economic Development in Japan,
1873–1922,* by James I. Nakamura.
Princeton, Princeton University Press, 1966.
The Korean Communist Movement and Kim Il-Song, by Dae-
Sook Suh.
Princeton, Princeton University Press, 1967.
The First Vietnam Crisis, by Melvin Gurtov.
New York, Columbia University Press, 1967.
Japan's First Modern Novel: Ukigumo of Futabatei Shimei, by
Marleigh Grayer Ryan.
New York, Columbia University Press, 1967.
Cadres, Bureaucracy, and Political Power in Communist China,
by A. Doak Barnett with a contribution by Ezra Vogel.
New York, Columbia University Press, 1967.